CONTESTATIONS

CORNELL STUDIES IN POLITICAL THEORY
A series edited by
WILLIAM E. CONNOLLY

Also by Fred Dallmayr:

The Other Heidegger

Fred Dallmayr

Cornell University Press

Ithaca and London

International Standard Book Number 0-8014-2909-9
Library of Congress Catalog Card Number 93-13757
Printed in the United States of America
Librarians: Library of Congress cataloging information
appears on the last page of the book.

For Dominique and Philip

Behüte dein Herz mit allem Fleiss,
denn daraus gehet das Leben.
—Proverbs 4:23

(Inscription over the door of Heidegger's
house in Freiburg-Zähringen)

Contents

Preface

This book has been in gestation for some time. Several years ago, I mentioned to some colleagues and friends that I was contemplating writing a book on Heidegger. Since then, I have been asked repeatedly about the state of my planned undertaking; but my answer has tended to be evasive. Although my intent was firm, my self-confidence and sense of capability were not on the same level. To put it simply, I was daunted by the monumental character of Heidegger's work, wondering how I could possibly measure up to it or contribute anything worthwhile to the topic. My hesitations were reinforced by the publication, in the late 1980s, of a series of books dealing with Heidegger's political past, books that became the catalyst of intense debates both inside and outside academia. With tempers and emotions running high, little room seemed to be left in that situation for quiet judgment and a balanced assessment of issues. In fact, even attempts at such assessment were liable to add fuel to the controversy.

Still, the controversy has hardly been fruitless. In my own case, the twists and turns of the debate finally encouraged me to bracket my self-doubts and to venture forth again on the path I had contemplated several years earlier. If the debate convinced me of one thing it was the inadequacy of a univocal or monolithic image of Heidegger—whether the image is that of the inveterate fascist, the liberal antifascist, or the pure philosopher completely above the political fray. What my own reading of Heidegger's work suggested to me was a more complex picture, akin to a multilayered tapestry—a tapestry in which his fascist involvement is *one* (easily the most deplorable) strand, but not the only and not even the dominant one. Exploration of this fabric steadily led me in the direction of a Heidegger somewhat shielded from view, a Heidegger estranged from his contexts and exposed to otherness—what in this volume I call the "other Heidegger." The effort of my book is not to deny Heidegger's Nazi involvement or to excuse this grievous mistake but simply to be alert to this other dimension of Heidegger's thought and its political implications. Instead of absconding from politics into the sphere of pure contemplation, I have sought to delineate precisely the contours of an alternative political perspective in Heidegger's thought, one at odds with traditional metaphysics and the prevalent ideologies of his time. As I try to show, this perspective surfaces initially in attempts to chart an alternative future for Germany and later in the vision of an alternative future for world politics.

In exploring this other Heidegger (or the element of otherness in his thought), I necessarily take issue with prevalent readings of his work, especially ideological or abstractly contemplative readings. To this extent, my book properly belongs in a series with the overall title "Contestations." As the reader will note, however, my mode of contesting is on the whole nonbelligerent and nonaggressive, deviating from counterpositions more by way of implication than direct assertion. This approach has to do perhaps with a personal distaste for polemics, but more so with the topic under discussion. My effort is not to champion a solution or to have the last word in the "*affaire* Heidegger" but only to indicate the possibility and legitimacy of an "other" reading. To accomplish this, I rely on close textual exegesis, letting the reader judge to what extent my interpretation is appropriate and fair-minded. Generally speaking, I follow an old rule of hermeneutics: the rule of exegetic generosity, which requires the interpreter to make a text as strong as possible rather than to indulge in the demolition of a straw man.

This volume contains a series of philosophical-political essays in which the boundary between philosophy and politics remains hazy and the discussion shifts readily across this disciplinary divide (as well as across the margins of literary criticism). My aim is not to present a systematic account of Heidegger's political philosophy—something I consider ill conceived. The essays are not randomly assembled. In the Introduction I elaborate on the common themes and interconnections of the essays, in addition to explicating the overall perspective of the book. To go beyond this is in my view hazardous and largely misguided. Heidegger never wrote a systematic work on political philosophy; in fact, he explicitly disavowed any ambitions as a political philosopher. Thus, anyone working on Heidegger's relevance for political thought has to cull this relevance from his writings on a great diversity of topics. What Heidegger offers are suggestive clues, never a systematic theory. I felt it imperative to respect the suggestive and tentative character of Heidegger's thoughts and not to impose on him an argumentative structure he would have found thoroughly uncongenial. A book on Heidegger's political thinking must honor the dispersed and fragmentary quality of his many "paths" (*Wege nicht Werke*), which accounts for my preference for essays over a formal treatise.

As indicated, the volume is an exercise in hermeneutics, not in ideological partisanship. I offer an interpretation based on my reading of some Heideggerian texts—a reading that, of course, remains contestable. My ambition is modest. I am satisfied if the volume succeeds in loosening up some of the hardened positions surrounding *l'affaire* Heidegger; I disclaim any ability to change someone's parti pris. Dictated by political sensibilities of the case, interpretive modesty is also desirable in view of the vast array of available Heidegger studies—a field populated by many impressive scholars and experts. The present volume offers me the welcome opportunity to express my indebtedness to some of those experts as well as to other mentors. My major debt of gratitude, of course, goes to Heidegger himself—whom I never had the good fortune to meet but who, over the years, has provided me with so much intellectual nourishment and guidance. Among his immediate students, I am particularly and lastingly indebted to Walter Biemel and Hans-Georg Gadamer; and among the broader circle of his followers to Manfred Riedel, John Sallis, and Calvin Schrag. Many other colleagues and friends, more distant from Heidegger, have nonetheless supported my endeavor over the years; among these are William Connolly, Drucilla Cornell, James Glass, William McBride, and Stephen White.

I want to express my appreciation for the editorial assistance I received in preparing the manuscript for publication; my special thanks go to Roger Haydon, Elizabeth Holmes, and John Thomas. I am also grateful to the original publishers of some parts of this book for permission to use material that has been previously published. Chapter 1 first appeared in *The Heidegger Case: On Philosophy and Politics*, edited by Tom Rockmore and Joseph Margolis, © 1992 by Temple University; reprinted by permission of Temple University Press. Chapter 2 appeared as "Rethinking the Political: Some Heideggerian Contributions," *Review of Politics* 52, no. 4 (1990): 524–552; it is reprinted by permission of the *Review of Politics*. Sage Publications has granted permission for the inclusion of Chapter 3, which appeared in somewhat different form as "Postmetaphysics and Democracy," *Political Theory* 21 (Spring 1993). Chapter 5 is a revised version of an essay published in my book *Margins of Political Discourse* (SUNY Press, 1989); it appears by permission of the publisher.

A still more direct debt of gratitude needs to be acknowledged: that to my wife and children, who often had to put up with my own "estrangement" or peregrinations into otherness while I was preparing and completing the book. Their support always provided these peregrinations with the welcome relief of homecoming. Given its concern with alternative political visions of the future, the book is dedicated to our children, Dominique and Philip, in the hope that their future may be marked less by warfare and struggle for planetary domination than by global cooperation and a "gentler entwinement" of humankind.

FRED DALLMAYR

South Bend, Indiana

The Other Heidegger

Introduction

Martin Heidegger is widely hailed as one of the greatest thinkers of our age; he is also one of the most controversial. His work exudes the aura of quiet meditation and speculative depth; but it is also the center of a stormy debate. This debate has acquired cyclone strength in the past several years due to a series of publications centering on Heidegger's political past, particularly on his involvement in the Nazi movement around 1933 and perhaps beyond.[1] Although he never claimed to be a political theorist, politics nonetheless has come to overshadow a work ostensibly of a purely philosophical character.

The shadow, one must recognize, is dark and disturbing. For many students of Heidegger's thought, especially in America, the effect of these publications has been profoundly disorienting if not shattering: reared in the framework of existential phenomenology, they suddenly feel betrayed by their mentor and perhaps abandoned by a whole tradition of inquiry. How could a thinker of this stature, they rightly ask, commit a sinister mistake of this magnitude? In raising this question, these students implicitly reject a modus vivendi that has been accepted

[1] The most important such publications are Victor Farias, *Heidegger and Nazism*, trans. Paul Burrell and Gabriel R. Ricci (Philadelphia: Temple University Press, 1989); and Hugo Ott, *Martin Heidegger: Unterwegs zu seiner Biographie* (Frankfurt-Main: Campus, 1988). See also Tom Rockmore and Joseph Margolis, eds., *The Heidegger Case: On Philosophy and Politics* (Philadelphia: Temple University Press, 1992); Richard Wolin, ed., *The Heidegger Controversy: A Critical Reader* (New York: Columbia University Press, 1991); Philippe Lacoue-Labarthe, *Heidegger, Art, and Politics: The Fiction of the Political*, trans. Chris Turner (Oxford: Blackwell, 1990); Luc Ferry and Alain Renaut, *Heidegger and Modernity*, trans. Franklin Philip (Chicago: University of Chicago Press, 1990); Jürg Altwegg, ed., *Die Heidegger Kontroverse* (Frankfurt-Main: Athenäum, 1988).

by many older colleagues friendly to Continental thought: namely, to treat Heidegger's politics as irrelevant to his philosophical opus, and vice versa. This theory of the "two Heideggers"—the good philosopher and the bad politician—no longer seems tenable or adequate in light of a contemporary sense of the entwinement of thinking and action and of knowledge and power.

In presenting a volume on the "other" Heidegger, it cannot possibly be my intent to revive or legitimate the older two-Heidegger formula. In my view, this formula never made much sense, given Heidegger's strong emphasis on human "being-in-the-world" and on the worldly finitude of experience—an emphasis that militates against a rigid bifurcation between abstract theorizing and everyday life. I deeply respect and appreciate the agony of those students who, feeling betrayed by the politics of their mentor, are ready to turn away from his work as a whole. Although I respect their attitude, however, I do not share it, for several reasons.

One reason, not a negligible one, has to do with biography and the different path that led me to Heidegger. In contrast to most of these students, I have not been trained as a professional philosopher and thus have not been tutored either by Heidegger himself or by any of his disciples (in Europe or America). I received my early training in law and later studied political science, with a focus on political theory. Given this background, I have always been drawn to the political dimensions of human experience, particularly as they are reflected in philosophical and literary texts. The notion of a purely nonpolitical philosophy never had great appeal for me; as a corollary, a strictly philosophical Heidegger abstracted from his politics did not hold much interest. Actually, the reverse happened: it was precisely Heidegger's politics, more accurately his politics around 1933, that prevented my access to his entire work for a great number of years.[2] If these were the consequences, I reasoned, his entire work could not be of much benefit. What attracted me during these (my formative) years in recent Continental thought was primarily the perspective of "critical theory" as articulated by the Frankfurt School and also the works of French phenomenologists, most notably Maurice Merleau-Ponty and (to a lesser extent) Jean-Paul Sartre. Although philosophical or reflective in character, the writings of both critical theorists and French phenomenologists carried strong political overtones—over-

---

[2] Despite the sensational character of the newer publications, much of the information and many of the charges were previously available in such books as Paul Hühnerfeld, *In Sachen Heidegger* (Hamburg: Hoffman & Campe, 1961); and Guido Schneeberger, *Nachlese zu Heidegger* (Bern: Suhr, 1962).

tones incompatible with fascism. By comparison, Heidegger throughout these years was a hazy figure on the horizon who remained politically suspect.

There is a further reason for this distance which is even more closely tied to biography. As a native of Germany, I experienced during my early childhood the horror of the war years and the devastation brought upon the country by the Nazi regime. After the war, I (like many others) first learned about the holocaust and about the full extent of Nazi atrocities. These childhood experiences, like all traumatic events, are deeply lodged in my memory. Fortunately for me, these experiences were not entirely colored by the Nazi regime. As it happens, in secondary school I was introduced by some upright and caring teachers to a different legacy of German thought and life: the legacy of Klopstock, Lessing, Herder, Goethe, Schiller, Kant, Hegel, Marx, and Nietzsche—a legacy that has been worthily continued in our century by Max Weber, Rainer Maria Rilke, and members of the Frankfurt School (to mention only a few). Thus, when I moved to America, I brought with me not only the memory of horror but also a fondness for what has been termed the "other Germany," a Germany that has been badly tarnished but not completely destroyed by the cataclysms of our century. As one may notice, although focused on philosophical thought and culture, that other Germany was never simply nonpolitical in outlook: it held up an alternative, more elevated vision of politics in opposition to chauvinistic arrogance.

Although somewhat sketchy, the preceding observations should help to explain the motives and depth of my reservations regarding Heidegger's work. Like ingrained habits, these reservations persisted tenaciously and only hesitantly gave way to rapprochement. Several factors were at work in this change; one was the role of accident or serendipity. One day I picked up one of Heidegger's later writings—it was his *Letter on Humanism* in which he responds partly to Sartre—and was intrigued almost against my wishes; the argument seemed lucid and coherent and untainted by any of the sinister pronouncements I had expected. As I continued reading, my interest grew. Little by little my defenses were lowered; clinging stubbornly to them, I felt, would have been counter to basic standards of fairness and open-mindedness. Although, as Gadamer has taught us, we are bound to approach texts with our prejudices and assumptions, we can also modify the latter (as he has likewise insisted) in the course of a closer reading.

Yet, accident was hardly the decisive element. Heidegger's text, I came to realize later, would not have touched me if it did not address or resonate with a certain state of my intellectual development. In those days I was greatly troubled by an eclipse of self-assurance or, more broadly, by the elusiveness of selfhood—what I subsequently came to term the "twilight of subjectivity." From Husserl I had learned that consciousness is the constitutive source of all knowledge and experience of phenomena, a source that at the same time transcends these phenomena. Through my study of modern Western thought I also knew that consciousness, or subjectivity, is the linchpin of modern philosophy and modes of life, a linchpin that undergirds and warrants the promise of noumenal human freedom and autonomy. Although fascinated by these assertions, I was troubled by the status of this consciousness and freedom. Given the radical transcendence of consciousness vis-à-vis phenomena and worldly beings, how and in what sense was it still possible to claim that consciousness exists? Likewise, given its noumenal-intangible quality, how could freedom hope to have an impact in the world? If, together with Sartre, one assumes that consciousness or freedom is a kind of nothingness in contrast with worldly beings, how could this nothingness be a nihilating force or simply *be* anything at all? Differently put, what is the being status of nihilating or transcending consciousness?[3]

In looking for answers to these questions, I was initially stymied; in fact, most of the writers I consulted either did not address the questions or treated them philosophically as inappropriate. I disclosed my worries about the "question of being" to a leading spokesman of critical theory— only to be told that this was a nonquestion or else a false question that had been laid to rest by Kant and more recently by Ernst Tugendhat (who showed that being cannot be a predicate of anything). This response left me stranded or, worse, up in the air—for, together with all other beings, my own being seemed to dissipate. In a more serious vein, the response seemed to run counter to a long line of philosophical inquiry that wondered how there can be anything rather than nothing. On closer reading I discovered that Heidegger's text as well as his other writings not only addressed the question but were sustained and animated by it throughout. His *Letter on Humanism* in particular, I found, took seriously the elusiveness of modern selfhood, the "twilight of subjectivity," that

[3] See in this context especially Jean-Paul Sartre, *Being and Nothingness*, trans. Hazel E. Barnes (New York: Philosophical Library, 1956); also Martin Heidegger, *Letter on Humanism*, in *Martin Heidegger: Basic Writings*, ed. David F. Krell (New York: Harper & Row, 1977), pp. 189–242. See also Fred Dallmayr, *Twilight of Subjectivity* (Amherst: University of Massachusetts Press, 1981).

troubled me—without in any way endorsing a frivolous antihumanism (which became fashionable much later).

Continuing my study of Heidegger's writings, I came to realize that he dealt with numerous important corollaries of the question of being which, at that time, I only sensed vaguely and would not have been able to articulate either for myself or for others. In short, the study proved for me a learning experience, just when some of my previous mentors seemed to abandon me at a crucial crossroads of my inquiries. This was the occasion for a sustained reading of *Being and Time*, which earlier I had only skimmed and which had remained a book with seven seals. Again, I was struck by the lucidity and cogency of the presentation—and the complete absence of any sinister fascist overtones; above all, I was impressed by the treatment of human *Dasein* not in terms of ego or subjectivity but as "being-in-the-world," by the discussion of the crucial characteristics and modalities of *Dasein* and especially the modality of "being-toward-death," and finally by the analysis of the temporal dimensions of existence. In their combined effect, the arguments of the book indicated a route beyond traditional metaphysics in both its idealist (mind-centered) and empiricist (matter-centered) forms. As I came to see, this exit route was pursued more intensively in Heidegger's later writings, especially those after his so-called turning (*Kehre*)—a turning that, without relinquishing the importance of *Dasein*, endeavored to insert human experience more emphatically in the context of history, of language, and of the "happening of being" (*Ereignis*). Taken a step at a time, these later writings did not seek to entice me into a nebulous mysticism (as is sometimes charged) but rather offered reflective guidance at the boundaries of contemporary thought (provided that reflection is not identified with arid calculation).[4]

In my reading of Heidegger's texts, I should state again, my attention was drawn not so much to abstract theoretical formulations as rather to possible political implications, although the latter were perhaps not always spelled out by the philosopher himself. Intuitively, these implications seemed to me both profound and far-reaching in several domains—

---

[4] See especially Heidegger, *Being and Time*, trans. John Macquarrie and Edward Robinson (London: SCM Press, 1962). I am aware that efforts have been made to find fascist elements in *Being and Time*, for example, by Mark Blitz in *Heidegger's Being and Time and the Possibility of Political Philosophy* (Ithaca: Cornell University Press, 1981); this project, however, seems a sheer ex post facto construction. Although some passages may be bent into a fascist direction, the entire book can be (and has been) read from a liberal, conservative, and even Marxist angle—which means that it is ideologically nonspecific.

including the conception of social action, the status and meaning of freedom, and the relation of individual and political community.[5] Still, in pursuing this path, I was bound to run headlong into a major dilemma: I could not (and did not intend to) bypass the stark fact of Heidegger's involvement with the Nazis in 1933 and beyond, an involvement that had been the initial obstacle to my rapprochement. Faced with this fact, how could I take Heidegger's work seriously without transforming it into a purely philosophical opus? If the focus on politics is maintained, what can possibly be learned from Heidegger beyond the strictly negative injunction *not* to imitate his 1933 example (a lesson, to be sure, that remains important even in our own time)?

As it happens, my reading of Heidegger's texts suggested to me the possibility of a different approach, one that takes account of the Nazi debacle without erecting it into an expression of Heidegger's genuine worldview or else into a necessary consequence of all his writings. As previously indicated, my study of *Being and Time* had shown to me the feasibility of a nonfascist reading of that text; the same seemed true of the *Letter on Humanism* and still later texts on language, poetry, and technology. Was there, I came to wonder, perhaps an alternative political agenda, or a host of alternative agendas, operative in Heidegger's work? Although not clearly specified or developed, were these alternatives perhaps part and parcel of the intrinsic multivocity and open-ended character of Heideggerian thought? In following that road, might one not reclaim Heidegger as part of the legacy of the "other Germany" mentioned above? Or, given the undeniable reality of the 1933 engagement, might one not detect in his multiple personae at least the outlines of an "other" Heidegger linking up with that legacy?

The difficult test for this hypothesis is Heidegger's thinking during the Nazi period, especially those works composed after his resignation from the rectorship of Freiburg University in early 1934. These writings quickly became a focus of my concerns. As it happens, many of these works have only recently been published or made available, including several of his lecture courses in Freiburg and, above all, the so-called *Beiträge zur Philosophie* of 1936–38 (which has been hailed as his second magnum opus after *Being and Time*). It is no surprise that the evidence of these years is not entirely unambiguous. Occasionally, as in the *Introduction to Metaphysics* of 1935, one finds statements explicitly harking back to

[5] I explore some of these themes in Fred Dallmayr, *Polis and Praxis: Exercises in Contemporary Political Theory* (Cambridge: MIT Press, 1984).

the earlier involvement. Strewn through many of the writings, one also encounters passages emphatically supportive of Germany and German "culture" with a distinct edge against the emerging superpowers (America and the Soviet Union). Still, one also detects in these works a strong countercurrent pulling in a very different direction.

An example is the lecture course Heidegger offered in 1934 shortly after resigning from the rectorship. In the midst of German chauvinistic euphoria—it was the year of the mammoth party congress in Nuremberg—the lecture course was pervaded by profound disenchantment, in fact, by a sense of mourning and indeed of "sacred mourning" (over the flight of gods). A similar sense of loss is present in the *Beiträge zur Philosophie;* a clear manifestation of Heidegger's own "turning," the dominant theme or mood of the text is captured in such terms as "reticence," "reserve," and "renunciation." Later in the same period, during the war years, several lecture courses devoted to Hölderlin's poetry made prominent the topic of estrangement or journeying abroad, together with the notion of a homecoming from afar. Drawing on Hölderlin, these lecture courses articulated an alternative vision for the future of Germany in opposition to the prevailing chauvinistic militancy, and in doing so also testified to Heidegger's own estrangement or "inner emigration." In a separate lecture held in 1943 on one of Hölderlin's hymns, Heidegger explicitly praised emigration as a way of salvaging a better vision or hope:

> Supposing that the inhabitants of the native soil are not yet those who have properly returned home; supposing also that the poetic quality of homecoming implies an openness to joyfulness beyond the mere accidental possession of native goods and sheer survival needs: assuming both these things, are then not those compatriots who—far from the native soil but with their eyes turned toward the joyfully dawning home—live and perhaps sacrifice their lives for a reserved promise, are they not the closest kin of the poet? Their sacrifice harbors the poetic appeal to the loved ones at home that the reserved promise may be preserved.[6]

Again, the evidence available from the period is not entirely conclusive. Perhaps Heidegger never troubled or managed to sort out neatly the

[6] Heidegger, "Heimkunft/An die Verwandten" (1943), in *Erläuterungen zu Hölderlins Dichtung,* ed. Friedrich-Wilhelm von Herrmann (*Gesamtausgabe,* Vol. 4; Frankfurt-Main: Klostermann, 1981), pp. 29–30. See also Heidegger, *Beiträge zur Philosophie (Vom Ereignis),* ed. Friedrich-Wilhelm von Herrmann (*Gesamtausgabe,* Vol. 65; Frankfurt-Main: Klostermann, 1989), esp. pp. 14–22, and *An Introduction to Metaphysics,* trans. Ralph Manheim (Garden City, N.Y.: Anchor, 1961), esp. pp. 31–32, 37–38, 166.

different strands of his thought during these years, thus allowing them to intersect and occasionally to collide. My endeavor, in any event, is not to replace one monolithic Heidegger (inclined to fascism) with another monolithic figure; for my own purposes, it suffices to show the presence—in the welter of perspectives—of an "other" Heidegger and thus the feasibility of another political reading of his work. This, in brief, is the modestly ambitious aim of the present book.

The opening chapter introduces the reader to the complex topic of Heidegger and politics by providing a broad overview of the phases of his intellectual development as seen from the angle of political relevance. The take-off point for the presentation is Victor Farias's *Heidegger et le nazisme* (1987) (subsequently translated as *Heidegger and Nazism*) together with the heated debate unleashed by this publication. Wary of polemics, I seek in this chapter to keep attention focused on possible lessons to be derived from Heidegger's development, that is, on the prospect of a continuing learning experience. In pursuing this course, my discussion tends to blend out or steer clear of the array of specific incidents, charges, or allegations with which Farias's book is replete (but which are all surrounded by controversy). As it seems to me, many of these specific points are of only limited intellectual interest and are best left to historians, archival detectives, or prosecuting attorneys (I am neither of these). To make some headway through the thicket of accusations, I rely for guidance on two mentors who are both recognized as experts on Heidegger and known for a certain fair-mindedness: Otto Pöggeler and Jacques Derrida. As it happens, both philosophers wrote accounts relevant to *l'affaire* Heidegger roughly at the time of the first appearance of Farias's book; both Pöggeler and Derrida emphasize the nexus of philosophy and politics in Heidegger's work (although the former features politics and the latter metaphysics). Weaving my commentary around their accounts, I show the ambivalence and multivocity of this nexus and the untenability of reducing Heidegger's thought to a summary verdict (which, in Farias's case, is lifelong fascism). The point of the presentation is not to vindicate or exculpate his involvement prematurely but only to draw attention to the broader context of the story, thereby encouraging more nuanced assessments. The defect of summary verdicts, in my view, is not only their inequity but also their intellectual barrenness; among other things, they shield from view the continued significance of Heidegger's "turning," that is, his effort to extricate himself from traditional metaphysics in its linkage with the ongoing struggle for planetary dominion.

The second chapter moves from the level of a broad overview to the more specific domain of political theory and philosophy. Instead of relying on expert mentors, my endeavor here is to articulate my own views regarding possible Heideggerian contributions to some key areas of political thought. A central guidepost of the chapter is a distinction prominent in the professional literature—that between "politics" and "the political," between politics seen as concrete policy-making, on the one hand, and politics construed as basic regime or paradigmatic frame-work, on the other. Whereas "politics" in the narrow sense revolves around day-to-day decision-making and ideological partisanship, "the political" refers to the frame of reference within which actions, events, and other phenomena acquire political status in the first place. The main thesis of the chapter is that Heidegger's promising contributions to political thought are located on the level of ontology or paradigmatic framework (the political) rather than that of practical policy and ideology (which is the level of his Nazi involvement).

In the third chapter I sharpen the focus further, by concentrating on the political framework that is the dominant regime type in our time: democracy. This topic is particularly hazardous and troublesome in the present context, given the fact that Heidegger has repeatedly expressed his reservations with regard to democracy. As it happens, however, the term "democracy" is by no means unambiguous or univocal; seen as a paradigmatic structure (an expression of "the political"), the meaning of the term depends very much on underlying ontological or metaphysical premises. In traditional formulations, democracy means rule by "the many" or "the people"—where these are viewed as sovereign agents endowed with a unitary identity akin to the sovereignty of kings. The question that needs to be raised, and is raised in this chapter, is whether this construal can still be maintained in an age of "post-metaphysics"— that is, in a time moving (in Heidegger's words) toward an "overcoming" or transgression of traditional metaphysics. If, under post-metaphysical auspices, the cogency of thought can no longer be anchored in stable foundational categories, then the conception of "the people" or "the many" must be reformulated—away from a unified sovereignty or collectivity in the direction of a latent agency in multiple guises or of an "absent presence" of rule. Differently phrased, democracy (as a mode of "politics") is revealed in diverse partisan policies and complex power struggles, activities that simultaneously conceal its status as a regime (on the level of "the political").

Like democracy, the theme of ethics has an elusive status in Heidegger's work. In part, this elusiveness is again due to Heidegger himself, who wrote no treatise explicitly devoted to ethics but persistently—as in the *Letter on Humanism*—subordinated this topic to the "being question." As in the case of democracy, however, appearances are somewhat deceptive—as becomes clear once attention is given to lectures and manuscripts dating from the Nazi period and its immediate aftermath. In Chapter 4 I examine writings dating from those years, in which questions of ethics and justice come to assume a distinct and even prominent place, though a place sharply different from prevalent ethical theories. In contrast to rationalist, rule-governed conceptions of ethics (deriving from Kant) as well as to substantive virtue ethics (traceable to Aristotle), the writings adumbrate a broadly ontological perspective of "letting-be" in which different elements or modalities of being are related without mutual intrusion and by granting each other space in the interstices of presence and absence, arrival and departure. In my interpretation, the writings amount to a sharp indictment of the Nazi regime, given that the latter aimed at an arrogant and brutal dominion over others based on racial-biological grounds.[7]

In the next two chapters I probe the aspect of Heidegger's progressive "inner emigration" after his resignation from the rectorship in Freiburg. Chapter 5 deals with the lecture course (previously alluded to) Heidegger offered in the fall of 1934. The focus of the course was on two of Friedrich Hölderlin's later hymns, "Germania" and "The Rhine." Although the hymns seemingly appeal to patriotic sentiments, their tenor as well as Heidegger's commentary is far removed from any kind of nationalist self-indulgence or chauvinistic triumphalism (which was sweeping the country at the time). On the contrary, both hymns and exegesis are marked by shy reticence and sober renunciation. The basic theme of the two hymns is a subterranean occurrence that Hölderlin viewed as a fundamental experience of our modern age: the experience of the flight or disappearance of the gods. In Heidegger's account, the significance of Hölderlin against this background resides in his opening up a different historical path. Hölderlin, he notes, was both a "poet's poet" (by shaping the very meaning of poetry) and "poet of the Germans"—a poet who "poetically invents the Germans" by propelling them far ahead into the

---

[7] See especially Heidegger, "The Anaximander Fragment," in *Early Greek Thinking*, trans. David F. Krell and Frank A. Capuzzi (New York: Harper & Row, 1984), pp. 13–58. For a curious interpretation of this essay (deviating somewhat from mine) see Hannah Arendt, *The Life of the Mind*, Vol. 2: *Willing* (New York: Harcourt Brace Jovanovich, 1978), pp. 189–194.

"most distant future," the horizon of a possible reconciliation and "wedding feast" of humans and gods.

A sign of deep disillusionment, the lecture course of 1934 was only the first step on the long road of disenchantment and alienation—a road, however, that did not lead into a no-man's land. Alienation from national and cultural settings reached a high point during the war years and continued in modified form in the postwar period. Under the title "Homecoming through Otherness," in Chapter 6 I examine the meaning of estrangement, or experience of otherness, in Heidegger's work while simultaneously differentiating this experience sharply from aimless nomadism. Turning first to the war years, I review two of Heidegger's lectures courses, offered in 1941 and 1942. Both courses were again devoted to the exegesis of Hölderlin's later poetry—this time the hymns "Remembrance" and "The Danube," whose central theme is the encounter between native and alien modes of life and the transformative quality of estrangement, all seen as a gateway to self-discovery or homecoming. Elaborating on the hymns, Heidegger emphasizes that German culture could find itself (or come into its own) only through estrangement or exposure to otherness. Again, Hölderlin emerges in these lectures as the poet of an alternative German future, opposed to a xenophobic nationalism.

Heidegger's concern with estrangement continued after the war, though now projected onto a broader, global horizon: the horizon of Western technological ascendancy or supremacy in the world. I next turn to an essay (of 1953) on Georg Trakl's poetry in which Heidegger seeks to pinpoint the "site" of Trakl's work—which he locates basically in its alienation, or "apartness" (*Abgeschiedenheit*), from traditional modes of life, an estrangement serving as guidepost for a new dawn, another beginning launched in "sacred blueness." Like the wartime lectures, the Trakl essay thus intimates an alternative future, now on a global scale: away from world domination in the direction of a "gentler entwinement" of humankind.[8]

One of Heidegger's more neglected postwar writings, and for several reasons one of my favorites, is *Hebel—the House-Friend*. The essay was

---

[8] From another angle, estrangement and its different modes in Heidegger's work have been explored by Gerald L. Bruns in *Heidegger's Estrangements: Language, Truth, and Poetry in the Later Writings* (New Haven: Yale University Press, 1989). For perceptive interpretations of Heidegger's reading of Hölderlin and other poets, see also Veronique M. Fóti, *Heidegger and the Poets* (Atlantic Heights, N.J.: Humanities Press, 1992); and Susanne Ziegler, *Heidegger, Hölderlin, und die Aletheia* (Berlin: Duncker & Humblot, 1991).

written in memory of the poet Johann Peter Hebel, author of the "Ale-mannian Poems" (1803) and also of an annual almanac published under the heading "Calendar of the Rhenish House-Friend." In Chapter 7 I ponder Heidegger's comments on Hebel and especially on the latter's "Treasure Chest" (*Schatzkästlein*), which assembled some of the best stories and insights from his almanacs. In Heidegger's interpretation, Hebel was not just a parochial figure narrowly confined to a region but rather a poet broadly open to the world, though allowing his work to be nourished by Alemannian dialect. This openness or breadth of vision throws light on Hebel's status as "house-friend"; "house" here does not mean a particular structure or edifice but the world at large seen as the proper place of human "building and dwelling" or (in Heideggerian terms) as the gathering or "in-between" zone between earth and sky, between mortals and immortals, between happiness and grief. The house-friend befriends the world by participating in everyday joys and sorrows, but in a reticent, unobtrusive way. As Heidegger points out, Hebel's friendliness sought to embrace both enlightened knowledge about the world (as offered by modern science) and ordinary experience of nature and world (as captured in poetry). In this respect, his work can still provide a distant inspiration in our own age—an age marked by a steadily widening rift between scientific knowledge and life-world, between technology and ordinary experience, or between "calculable nature" and the (poetic) "naturalness" of the universe.

In large measure, the disparity between technology and life-world can be translated into the division between "developed" and "developing" (or Third World) countries—which, with a few exceptions, matches the distinction between Western and non-Western societies. In this respect, a stark feature of contemporary world politics comes into view: the gulf between the global or universalizing thrust of Western science and the heterogeneity of historically grown cultures, especially those of a non-Western vintage. In this division, too, a house-friend or world-friend is sorely lacking today: someone capable of bridging and reconciling the ambitions of Western modernity with the insights of indigenous traditions. As it happens, Heidegger's work has in many ways provided a bridge or meeting ground between Western philosophy and various non-Western modes of philosophical thought. By way of conclusion I seek to illustrate this mediating role by focusing on a Japanese thinker who, in his own ways, sought to mediate between East and West and who, in doing so, found some inspiration in Heidegger's writings. Accordingly, in Chapter 8 I introduce Keiji Nishitani, a prominent member of the

Kyoto School who endeavored to steer a path between Zen Buddhism and Western existentialism. Here I offer a detailed comparison of the outlook of Nishitani and Heidegger with respect to two crucial philosophical themes, that of nothingness, or nihilating "emptiness" (*śūnyatā*), and that of thinghood, or the experience of the "suchness" of things.

In exploring the affinity of the two thinkers, I am aware that I am only scratching the surface of multiple cross-cultural currents linked with Heidegger's work. As is well known, during the postwar years Heidegger collaborated with a Chinese scholar on a planned German translation of Lao-tzu's *Tao Te Ching* (an effort that did not come to fruition); in addition, his work has provided impulses and resources for numerous thinkers in India and other parts of the Third World. As one should note, however, in these far-flung contacts Heidegger was not only a source of inspiration but also the beneficiary of novel insights; in dialoguing with non-Western partners he was invariably not only the teacher but also the student opening himself up to a new learning experience. In fact, as a thinker exclusively trained in the Western tradition of philosophy, his ventures abroad were bound to require a sustained willingness to unlearn and learn anew. In this respect, philosophers in the non-West may have an advantage due to their simultaneous and steady exposure today to both Western and Eastern modes of thought. This situation is captured well by Nishitani in a passage reflecting on contemporary cross-cultural relations, specifically from his own, Asian perspective:

> For all the splendors of the intellectual history of the East, the present asks something more of us, and in any event there is no way simply to resurrect ideas from the past for a life in the present. A basic acceptance of Western thought, and perhaps even culture, is required. But merely to follow in the footsteps of the West will never lay the foundations for a contribution to world culture, no matter how long we keep at it. Nevertheless, we find ourselves truly in a culturally advantageous position in the world in the sense that we bear a tradition deeply rooted in an Eastern spirit and Eastern culture that people of the West do not have. One way or another, we must find a way to bring it back to life. Left in its time-worn form it is of no use. And the right way to go, in my view, is to resurrect the culture of the East through the culture of the West—in the form of a rebirth through Western culture, if you will, or of a new development of Western culture.[9]

[9] Keiji Nishitani, *Nishida Kitaro*, trans. Yamamoto Seisaku and James W. Heisig (Berkeley: University of California Press, 1991), p. 41. See also Graham Parkes, ed., *Heidegger and Asian Thought* (Honolulu: University of Hawaii Press, 1987), especially these essays in

To sum up, I seek in this book to draw attention to an "other" Heidegger and to the implications of this otherness for both domestic and global politics. I am aware that my presentation is unlikely to persuade many readers or even to induce them to reconsider their beliefs. As I have found, with respect to Heidegger (or *l'affaire* Heidegger), convictions are sometimes held so fiercely and tenaciously that no amount of argument is likely to make much of a dent. Still, I hope to do more than preach to the faithful. On no account should this book be viewed as a vindication of Heidegger's conduct around 1933 or of his silence in crucial matters later; these aspects clearly need to be weighed in the balance. Also, as mentioned earlier, I have no intention of distilling a purely philosophical Heidegger by extricating him from the political context of our age—a context in which he was in any case embroiled on many levels. My purpose will have been fulfilled if I have shown the ambivalence and multivocity of his embroilment and the feasibility of an alternative reading, specifically an alternative political reading, of his work. Such an alternative reading, in my view, is not only important for the sake of fair-mindedness and academic scholarship; it is also crucial for charting the future of politics.

---

that volume: Otto Pöggeler, "West-East Dialogue: Heidegger and Lao-tzu," pp. 47–78; Joan Stambaugh, "Heidegger, Taoism, and the Question of Metaphysics," pp. 79–91; Paul Shih-yi Hsiao, "Heidegger and Our Translation of the *Tao Te Ching*," pp. 93–103; Yasuo Yuasa, "The Encounter of Modern Japanese Philosophy with Heidegger," pp. 155–174; Tetsuaki Kotoh, "Language and Silence: Self-Inquiry in Heidegger and Zen," pp. 201–211. Regarding Heidegger's relation to Indian thought, the same volume contains an essay by J. L. Mehta, "Heidegger and Vedanta: Reflections on a Questionable Theme," pp. 15–45; Mehta's general outlook is more fully developed in William J. Jackson, ed., *J. L. Mehta on Heidegger, Hermeneutics, and Indian Tradition* (Leiden: E. J. Brill, 1992). See further Wilhelm Hallfass, *India and Europe: An Essay in Understanding* (Albany: SUNY Press, 1988). In another context, I have presented Mahatma Gandhi as "mediator between East and West"; see Fred Dallmayr, *Margins of Political Discourse* (Albany: SUNY Press, 1989), pp. 22–38.

CHAPTER ONE

Heidegger and Politics:
Some Lessons

"Why is it that you don't engage in polemics?" Michel Foucault was asked shortly before his death; to which he replied:

> It is true that I don't like to get involved in polemics. If I open a book and see the author is accusing an adversary of "infantile leftism," I shut it again right away. That is not my way of doing things. . . . I insist on this difference as something essential: a whole morality is at stake, the morality that concerns the search for the truth and the relation to the other.

In the same interview, Foucault distinguished sharply between inter-personal discussion or conversation, on the one hand, and polemical strategies or methods, on the other. While in a discussion, he noted, each partner takes pains "to use only the rights given him by the other," the polemicist by contrast proceeds "encased in privileges that he possesses in advance and will never agree to question." Thus, instead of treating the other person as a partner in the quest for "a difficult truth," the polemicist reduces him to an adversary, an enemy "who is wrong" and "whose very existence constitutes a threat"; in doing so, the polemicist relies on "a legitimacy that his adversary is by definition denied." To underscore his point, Foucault drew a parallel between intellectual po-lemics and certain inquisitorial, judicial, and ideological tactics. As in the case of heresiology, he wrote, polemics establishes "the intangible point of dogma, the fundamental and necessary principle that the adversary has neglected," and denounces this negligence as "a moral failing." The judicial analogy resides in the polemicist's acting as judge and jury: instead of dealing with an interlocutor, he is "processing a suspect." The closest parallel, however, exists with ideological partisanship: like the latter, polemics "defines alliances, recruits partisans, unites interests or opinions, represents a party"; it "establishes the other as an enemy, an upholder of opposed interests, against which one must fight until the moment this enemy is defeated and either surrenders or disappears."[1]

These comments seem apropos with regard to Victor Farias's *Heidegger et le nazisme* (Heidegger and Nazism). By all standards, the book is an intensely polemical work, exuding a prosecutor's zeal; although based in part on historical and archival research, the presentation of findings has the character of a police blotter. Since its first publication in French, the aura of polemics has steadily deepened, as has the range and intensity of charges. In fact, the book and its effects have the earmarks of a publishing event (or media event)—a rare occurrence in the philosophical domain.[2] The target of the book is Martin Heidegger and particularly his political thought and orientation. The theses advanced by Farias are that Heidegger was predisposed toward National Socialism by his background and origins; that his engagement for the regime in 1933 was complete and unqualified; that this engagement persisted unchanged throughout the Hitler years; and that it even remained intact after 1945, as shown by the lack of a clear retraction of Nazi views and the continued talk about a spiritual rebirth of Europe.

In reading this general indictment, one can hardly avoid thinking of Foucault's statements. Throughout Farias's book, Heidegger is never treated as a partner in any common search, only as an enemy who is wrong and whose very existence constitutes a threat. In line with the practice of heresiology, the book proceeds from a superior position or principle that is never fully articulated or defended but whose accuracy is presupposed and in whose name the adversary is judged. Following the prosecutor's model, Farias is content with processing a suspect and collecting proofs of his guilt. As in all polemical battles, the goal (in Foucault's words) is the moment when the enemy is "defeated and either

---

[1] See Paul Rabinow, ed., *The Foucault Reader* (New York: Pantheon, 1984), pp. 381–382.

[2] See Victor Farias, *Heidegger et le nazisme* (Paris: Verdier, 1987); and, for the English version, *Heidegger and Nazism*, ed. Joseph Margolis and Tom Rockmore, trans. Paul Burell and Gabriel R. Ricci (Philadelphia: Temple University Press, 1989). The book has been reviewed by Thomas Sheehan, Richard Rorty, Michael Zimmermann, Jacques Derrida, and Jean Baudrillard, to mention only a few examples. In large measure, the book relies on research done by Hugo Ott and Berndt Martin. In the meantime, Ott has published his findings in a comprehensive work titled *Martin Heidegger: Unterwegs zu einer Biographie* (Frankfurt-Main: Campus, 1988). More judicious and sober in character than Farias's book, Ott's study is unlikely to become a media event.

surrenders or disappears." One of Farias's strongest complaints is the absence of a univocal retraction on Heidegger's part. But would such a retraction—and I mean a complete reversal, since nothing else would do—really have served anyone's purpose? Western intellectual history, from Galileo to Helvetius to Lukács, is replete with profuse recantations—but in a manner that is hardly comforting to defenders of free thought (or the freedom of "spirit").

My point here is not to vindicate or exonerate Heidegger prematurely but simply to raise the issue of fairness. As most commentators agree, Farias's book is a jumble of truths, half-truths, insinuations, and innuendoes—all presented with the same conviction and endowed with the same unquestioned authority.[3] This aspect is particularly disturbing given the general standpoint from which the indictment is launched, which (if I am not mistaken) is that of liberal democracy. A basic pillar of such democracy is respect for due process—something sorely lacking in Farias's book. Nowhere in the book is an effort made to uncover not only evidence against Heidegger but also testimony in his favor or at least mitigating his case. Nowhere is there an attempt or even an inclination to interrogate Heidegger himself as to the motives (or simply the nature) of his views; whenever these views are considered, they are quickly dismissed as tainted while credence is given to every accusing voice.

Given the gravity of the indictment, unqualified attachment to National Socialism, one surely would have expected a careful definition of terms, an expectation that is disappointed. As it seems to me, National Socialism as a doctrine includes at least two basic ingredients: belief in the absolute superiority of the Aryan race and advocacy of the exercise of world dominion (*Weltherrschaft*) predicated on this racial superiority. Yet, as most observers—even those sharply critical of Heidegger—concede, the latter subscribed to neither of these tenets. In recognition of this fact, nuanced critics resort to a variety of alternate labels for Heidegger's supposed position, such as "conservatism," "ultraconservatism," or "cul-

[3] Philippe Lacoue-Labarthe, who by no means exonerates Heidegger, is blunt on his score: "This book is profoundly unjust and I even consider it—weighing my words carefully—dishonest [*malhonnête*]." See Lacoue-Labarthe, *La Fiction du politique* [Paris: Bourgeois, 1987], p. 178. Unfortunately, not all commentators share Lacoue-Labarthe's sense of fairness. While acknowledging the deficiencies in much of the accumulated evidence, Thomas Sheehan proceeds to subscribe basically to the accuracy of Farias's account; he certainly makes no effort to sift the evidence or to introduce additional or countervailing evidence. See his "Heidegger and the Nazis," *New York Review of Books*, June 16, 1988, pp. 38–47, esp. p. 23, n. 5, where he speaks of the "sloppiness of Farias's notes" and the "tendentiousness of the French translations of Heidegger's statements."

tural elitism." Whatever the merit of these labels—and I consider them at best partially correct—none of the views they designate are commonly considered as indictable offenses (at least in a democracy tolerant of a certain measure of dissent).[4]

One of the chief defects or incongruities of Farias's book is its general inattention to Heidegger's philosophical opus, as if the latter was immaterial to the investigation at hand. I do not see how thinker and opus can be disconnected without subverting the book's objective. The fact is that Heidegger without his opus is simply not the *cause célèbre* presented by Farias. As Heidegger cogently remarked (in his comments on the nature of art), the artist is not an artist prior to or independently of his artwork; on the contrary, it is the artwork that constitutes its maker as an artist. The same considerations apply to the philosopher and his work. Viewed outside or independently of his opus, Heidegger is simply one of the thousands or millions of petits bourgeois in Germany who somehow managed to arrange themselves with the Nazi regime; seen in this light, *l'affaire* Heidegger hardly generates special interest. Thus, in an important sense, the prominence of Farias's book is dependent on Heidegger the philosopher, on his philosophical opus—which, however, the account slights entirely.[5]

My argument here is not that Heidegger and his work are completely congruent or identical, that there is no way to differentiate for some purposes between the philosopher and the man. On the contrary, there

[4] As Sheehan writes, "Although he never accepted the party ideology in its entirety, particularly its racism and biologism, he did see Nazism as a movement that could halt the spread of Marxism and realize the untraconservative vision of one of his favorite political theorists, Friedrich Naumann (1860–1919): the vision of a strong nationalism and a militantly anticommunist socialism, combined under a charismatic leader." *New York Review of Books*, June 16, 1988, p. 44. Pierre Bourdieu describes Heidegger as one of the many German intellectuals or radical conservatives of the Weimar Republic calling for a "conservative revolution" that would offer a third way between bolshevism and American capitalism; see *L'Ontologie politique de Martin Heidegger* (Paris: Minuit, 1975). Michael Zimmermann argues that Heidegger's "conservatism" was based on two related beliefs: "(1) that the West was in the final stages of a long decline into industrial nihilism, and (2) that only a radical change could save Germany from this dreaded fate"; but he adds that "there is no *necessary* relation between the conservative Heidegger's philosophy and the violent racism which we associate with Nazism." See "*L'affaire* Heidegger," *Times Literary Supplement*, October 9–13, 1988, p. 1116.

[5] "Where is the 'philosophy' of Heidegger, or rather his thinking, if not in his texts?" asks Lacoue-Labarthe. "And what is at issue here: Heidegger's thinking or something else? If there is a '*cas Heidegger*'—which is not distinguished (to my knowledge) by any 'crime against humanity,' even though his silent complicity is terrifying—it is because there is the 'thinking of Heidegger.'" *La Fiction du politique*, p. 187.

are ample reasons to assume that Heidegger, like many authors, at crucial junctures of his life fell below the level of his philosophy. Even without a detailed personality study, which I leave to others, I suspect Heidegger's conduct to exhibit various character flaws (which were aggravated in the context of a totalitarian regime): fits of megalomania, occasional vindictiveness, and a frequent lack of civic courage (*Zivilcourage*). My point is only that biographical knowledge of this kind is no substitute for familiarity with the philosophical opus.

What particularly chagrins me in this matter is the counterproductiveness of the chosen procedure: its inability or unlikelihood to generate new thought or some kind of learning process. To quote Foucault again, "Has anyone ever seen a new idea come out of a polemic?"[6] The only likely outcome of the book is to confirm Heidegger's accusers in their pristine rectitude or correctness, while driving his defenders into stubbornness. In my view, however, much still needs to be learned from *l'affaire* Heidegger and his encounter with National Socialism—whose specter is far from banished. Precisely because Heidegger at one point exposed himself to the contagion of fascism, his thinking was constrained to wrestle concretely with this infection and to generate antidotes. On my reading, Heidegger's opus after 1933 is a prolonged struggle to expel or subdue the virus, without returning to a traditional orthodoxy. For this reason (if for no other) his work remains instructive today. As I see it, a central issue of our time is the frailty of traditional worldviews—from conservatism to liberalism to socialism—all of which are in some ways linked with a humanist metaphysics. The question is whether a path can be forged beyond inherited ideologies, a path that does *not* end up in fascism.

This question was not resolved in 1945 and is not likely to be resolved in the foreseeable future. To make some headway in this area, and to counterbalance Farias's account, I turn in this chapter to two writers who are well known for their intimate familiarity with Heidegger's opus and for their interpretive skills: Otto Pöggeler and Jacques Derrida. Both

---

[6] Rabinow, *The Foucault Reader*, p. 383. As Foucault adds: "And how could it be otherwise, given that here the interlocutors are incited, not to advance, not to take more and more risks in what they say, but to fall back continually on the rights that they claim, on their legitimacy, which they must defend, and on the affirmation of their innocence? There is something even more serious here: in this comedy, one mimics war, battles, annihilations, or unconditional surrenders, putting forward as much of one's killer instinct as possible. But it is really dangerous to make anyone believe that he can gain access to the truth by such paths."

have written extensively on Heidegger's thought in its broad scope, including its political implications. As it happens, both have explicitly commented on Heidegger's politics in publications that appeared roughly at the same time as Farias's book. My guiding concern is neither acquittal nor condemnation. Can anything worthwhile be learned, I want to ask, from this politics and these commentaries—anything beyond the bounds of vengefulness and the solidification of ill will?

I

Before examining Pöggeler and Derrida, I want to invoke briefly some comments by another philosopher and leading Heidegger scholar, Joseph Kockelmans. In addition to a string of other works, in 1984 Kockelmans published an important study on Heidegger's "later philosophy," that is, on the central themes of his thought as they emerged progressively after *Being and Time*. Kockelmans felt it important to include in this study—focused on theoretical themes—a chapter dealing with the relation between Heidegger's thinking and his politics. Right away, he noted a difficulty: the problem of locating this outlook within traditional political vocabulary. "On the one hand," he wrote, "in order to be able to relate critically to Heidegger's ideas, one must already have a conception about what ideally the relationship between philosophy and politics should be. On the other hand, in formulating these ideas, one must formulate and justify this conception with the help of a metaphysical philosophy, which Heidegger precisely tries to overcome." The difficulty is compounded by another dilemma: the seeming aloofness of much of Heidegger's philosophizing from politics (and his protestation against being viewed as a political thinker), an aloofness that stands in stark contrast to his active engagement around 1933. Was it possible to treat Heidegger's philosophy as pure thought completely uncontaminated by political concerns; or, conversely, could this thought be reduced to his involvement in 1933 (whatever the nature of this involvement might be)? Neither of these alternatives appeared sensible to Kockelmans. In his chapter on politics he distanced himself from the notion that there could be a "genuine form of thinking which would be totally 'apolitical'"; but he also was unwilling to surrender philosophy, particularly Heidegger's philosophy, to partisan politics or ideological platforms. With regard to Heidegger's opus, he observed, conflicting claims had been advanced: either there was no concern with politics in this opus or else Heidegger's thought was "really no more than an attempt to justify National Socialism as a political movement." "It does not take much reflection to realize," Kockelmans concluded, "that neither of these claims can be correct or even remotely relevant to the state of affairs and the actual historical events."[7]

As it seems to me, Kockelmans's observations are still pertinent and worth pondering, even in the face of more recent findings. Clearly, Heidegger's opus is not political theory in any conventional sense (or as practiced by professionals in that field). In particular, this opus can scarcely be compressed into a compact ideological formula, given Heidegger's persistent attempts to escape from all worldviews (metaphysical or otherwise). By the same token, however, his work offers no purely speculative retreat—as is evident from the stress on "being-in-the-world" and the worldliness of human experience (where "world" is inevitably "political world," in a sense still to be explored). In the remainder of his chapter, Kockelmans examined numerous interpretations of Heidegger's politics, interpretations that reveal the broad spectrum of possible construals, ranging from conservatism to anarchism. Among these assessments he reviewed some which in many ways anticipated Farias's approach—and which he described as "tendentious and sometimes even defamatory."

In these writings, Kockelmans noted, Heidegger's rectorial address and other speeches during 1933 and 1934 are claimed to express "a deep-seated and long-lasting affiliation with the National Socialist movement, taken in its worst possible interpretation, and a clear sign of Heidegger's insincerity and irresponsibility." Moreover, this affiliation is said to be unambiguously rooted in *Being and Time* as well as a permanent fixture of the later work, none of which was persuasive to Kockelmans. "It seems to me," he wrote, "that anyone who defends the view that there is an intrinsic link between Nazism and Heidegger's later philosophy or between Nazism and the ideas proposed in *Being and Time* is simply mistaken." As he added, the point was not to condone Heidegger's behavior in 1933 and 1934 (and in some instances afterward), because that behavior was indeed unacceptable on several counts. Yet, by the same token, one could not defend "the thesis that this behavior merely made manifest a political philosophy that had always been there and always would remain there."[8]

---

[7] Joseph J. Kockelmans, *On the Truth of Being: Reflections on Heidegger's Later Philosophy* (Bloomington: Indiana University Press, 1984), pp. 262–263.

[8] Ibid., pp. 264–265. Among the more tendentious works cited by Kockelmans were Paul Hühnerfeld, *In Sachen Heidegger* (Hamburg: Hoffman & Campe, 1961); and Guido Schneeberger, *Nachlese zu Heidegger* (Bern: Suhr, 1962).

In support of his arguments, Kockelmans relied on several earlier analyses, among them writings by Pöggeler. The latter is renowned for his comprehensive and detailed study of the development of Heidegger's thought, *Der Denkweg Martin Heideggers* (Martin Heidegger's Path of Thinking). In its original edition of 1963 (when Heidegger was still alive), the book virtually bypassed political issues or implications. Less than a decade later, however, Pöggeler remedied this gap by publishing a monograph specifically devoted to these issues. Building on the structure of the preceding study, the monograph traced the unfolding of Heidegger's thought through several major phases—highlighted by such labels as "meaning of being," "truth of being," and "topology of being"; in each instance, Pöggeler explored the political relevance of Heidegger's outlook, paying close attention to the linkage with National Socialism and also to affinities with French existentialism, neo-Marxism, and similar movements. As he noted in the opening pages, "Even an initial glance at his work shows that Heidegger did not elaborate a political philosophy but that, in the various stages of his thought, he nonetheless was in diverse ways a politically engaged philosopher." Observations on Heidegger's politics, partially gleaned from this monograph, were incorporated into the second edition of the *Denkweg* study of 1983 (which became the basis of the English translation).[9]

For present purposes, I concentrate on a still more recent and more detailed essay by Pöggeler devoted to Heidegger's political self-understanding, which appeared in the volume *Heidegger und die praktische Philosophie* (Heidegger and Practical Philosophy) in 1988. The objective of Pöggeler's essay, and of the others collected in this volume, is not to engage in partisan polemics or recriminations but rather to explore the difficult nexus of politics and Heidegger's opus. What is at issue, the volume editors state, are the thoughts and perspectives that "guided the *philosopher* Heidegger in such a manner as to motivate his political options and his articulation of goals or aspirations."[10]

From the beginning, Pöggeler's essay places the discussion into the

[9] See Otto Pöggeler, *Der Denkweg Martin Heideggers*, 2d ed. (Pfullingen: Neske, 1983), trans. Daniel Magurshak and Sigmund Barber as *Martin Heidegger's Path of Thinking* (Atlantic Heights, N.J.: Humanities Press, 1987); also, Pöggeler, *Philosophie und Politik bei Heidegger* (Freiburg-Munich: Alber, 1972), pp. 15–16.

[10] See, Annemarie Gethmann-Siefert and Otto Pöggeler, eds. *Heidegger und die praktische Philosophie* (Frankfurt-Main: Suhrkamp, 1988), p. 8. As the editors add, "From this vantage it would be misguided to equate Heidegger's philosophy substantively with certain political consequences, that is, to hold his thinking as a whole rather than the 'man' Heidegger responsible for the debacle whose scope and duration occupy most inquiries."

global, or "planetary," context of our century: the context of the political and ideological struggle for world dominion (*Weltherrschaft*), particularly as seen from the vantage of a disoriented Europe. As Pöggeler notes, this context was the background which, overtly or covertly, always overshadowed and permeated Heidegger's political thought. Heidegger's persistent concern, he writes, was "the attempt to respond philosophically to the crisis of Europe as it had been revealed by the First World War. For Heidegger that war meant the senseless self-destruction of Europe, triggered by the fact that—instead of trying to solve their problems creatively—European nation-states threw themselves into the external battle for world dominion." The task facing Europe in our century, in Heidegger's view, was to reconsider its position in the world and to bring to bear its cultural leverage, a task that was perverted by global military ambitions.

Heidegger was fond of citing the lines penned by Stefan George during and about World War I: "These are the flaming signals—not the message." Heidegger shared with many observers the notion of a crisis of Europe rooted intellectually in the progressive sway of nihilism and surfacing politically in successive military conflagrations. A central question in his thought was whether Europe, which had sown the seeds and spawned the growth of nihilism, would find the internal antidotes to counter the anticipated decay. In pursuit of this goal, Heidegger assigned a crucial role to "Germans" or the "German people" (terms that should not simply be taken in an ethnic or racial sense) for several reasons: because of Germany's central location in Europe, because of her own contribution to modern nihilism and the cultivation of the "will to power," and because of an assumed affinity between German and Greek culture (the latter seen as cradle of the Occident). As he stated in the midst of World War II, in his lectures on Heraclitus: "The planet is in flames; human nature is out of joint. A reflective world-historical reorientation can come only from the Germans—provided that they discover and preserve 'the German' [or what 'German' means]."[11]

Heidegger's commitment to the cultural revival and perhaps hegemony of Europe went through shifts of emphasis. No doubt, initially or during the Weimar period, this commitment was still largely embroiled in the very power-political considerations—the struggle for world do-

---

[11] Pöggeler, "Heideggers politisches Selbstverständnis," in *Heidegger und die praktische Philosophie*, pp. 20–23. See also Heidegger, *Heraklit*, ed. Manfred S. Frings (*Gesamtausgabe*, Vol. 55; Frankfurt-Main: Klostermann, 1979), p. 123.

minion—that he bemoaned in the long run. This is the phase for which the label "cultural elitism" (specifically, cultural elitism under German leadership) is probably most appropriate; it is the same elitism that led Heidegger into the proximity of National Socialism, from which he sought subsequently to extricate himself, with considerable difficulty and ambiguous success. In his essay, Pöggeler offers a condensed tour through the major writings and lectures from the Weimar period to the end of the war, always with a focus on the correlation of philosophy and politics.

As Pöggeler points out, at the beginning Heidegger nurtured sympathies for Friedrich Naumann's vision of a restoration of "Middle Europe" under national and social auspices. But under the impact of the depression and the malaise of Weimar institutions, his thinking was radicalized in an extraparliamentary direction. Then, around 1930, Heidegger fell under the spell of a stark Nietzscheanism, which viewed the world as the arena of irresoluble conflicts and antagonisms—between Dionysus and Apollo, between life and spirit, between nihilism and the overcoming of nihilism (to be accomplished only by a cultural elite). This was also the time when Heidegger underwent the impact of Ernst Jünger's writings, especially his essay "Total Mobilization" (1930) and his book *The Worker* (1932). What Jünger tried to show in these writings was that World War I had ushered in an era of world revolution and struggle for world dominion in which only the total mobilization of all available resources (material and human) could promise success; rigorously disciplined in military fashion, instrumental-industrial labor was destined to spearhead this struggle. As Pöggeler reports, Heidegger discussed these writings "in a small circle" and "sought to grasp that planetary history was now placed under the universal sway of the will to power—whether this occurred under the auspices of communism, fascism, or world democracy."[12]

From this radical Nietzschean and Jüngerian conception the road was not far to the embroilment with Hitler's movement, which Heidegger greeted as a possible ally and instrument in the desired cultural revival of Europe (vis-à-vis Russia and America). Among the motives undergirding this embroilment, Pöggeler mentions patriotic sentiments aiming at a German resurgence as well as social concerns about the overcoming of large-scale unemployment in the wake of the great depression; he also points to certain speeches of Hitler, especially the so-called peace talk of May 1933—which were liable to encourage illusions about his goals.

---

[12] Pöggeler, "Heideggers politisches Selbstverständnis," pp. 27–29.

"The 'resurgence' [*Aufbruch*] Heidegger joined in 1933," he writes, "was nationalist in character, designed to restore the dignity of Germany and . . . to be part and parcel of the Wilsonian program of the self-determination of nations." In his rapprochement with National Socialism, one should also note, Heidegger was at least in part guided by the belief that he would be able to steer Hitler and his movement in the appropriate (cultural-elitist) direction. It is now that Heidegger's personal megalomania, which subsequently exacted a heavy price, comes to the fore. In his reminiscences after the war, Karl Jaspers expressed the view that it was Heidegger's ambition to guide or lead Hitler (*den Führer führen*)—probably an accurate assessment which, if true, reveals Heidegger's stark political naiveté as well as his lack of modesty. Heidegger's own speeches and pronouncements during this time were more idiosyncratically Heideggerian in character than reflective of strict party ideology; this is particularly true of the address "The Self-Assertion of the German University" that inaugurated his ill-fated service as rector in Freiburg. As Pöggeler reports, relying on Heidegger's own postwar elaborations on the period, immediately after the address the National-Socialist minister in attendance chided Heidegger for cultivating a "private [or idiosyncratic] National Socialism," an idiosyncrasy evident in the nonacceptance of the racial idea and the rejection of the complete politicization of the university.[13]

The content of the rectorial address has been the target of numerous analyses and interpretations; although relatively brief on this topic, Pöggeler mentions a few relevant points. As he observes, the theme of university reform had been a persistent concern of Heidegger since at least 1919 (when he first lectured on the topic), although the address of 1933 greatly accentuated the aspect of structural or administrative elitism. He also notes the favorable reception of the address among many intellectuals such as Werner Jaeger and Jaspers (who, in September of that year, praised the speech as the "so far only document of a contemporary academic will-power"). In its basic thrust, the address bore the

---

[13] Ibid., pp. 19, 31–32. On Karl Jaspers, see the latter's *Notizen zu Martin Heidegger*, ed. Hans Saner (Munich: Piper, 1978), p. 183; also Pöggeler, "Den Führer führen? Heidegger und kein Ende," *Philosophische Rundschau* 32 (1985): 26–67. On the rectorial address, see Heidegger, *Die Selbstbehauptung der deutschen Universität* (1933), republished with *Das Rektorat 1933–34* (Frankfurt-Main: Klostermann, 1983); also "The Self-Assertion of the German University," trans. Karsten Harries, *Review of Metaphysics* 38 (1985): 470–480, and "The Rectorate 1933–34: Facts and Thoughts," trans. Karsten Harries, *Review of Metaphysics* 29 (1975–76): 481–502.

imprint of Jünger's "total mobilization"; but, whereas Jünger extolled the importance of labor service and military service, Heidegger added as a third and equivalent pillar the function of "knowledge service" (*Wissens-dienst*) to be performed chiefly by universities.

The rectorial period following the address is on the whole a dismal story and the hub of the polemics surrounding *l'affaire* Heidegger. In Pöggeler's account, the evidence is bleak and at best deeply ambivalent—a mixture of subservience and partial nonsubservience to the dictates of the regime; his general conclusion: "Precisely as a leader [*Führer*] Heidegger was a complete failure." After resigning the rectorate in the spring of 1934, Heidegger began the difficult process of disentangling himself not only from Hitler's movement but also from some of his own cherished beliefs, particularly his infatuation with Jünger and with an extreme type of Nietzscheanism. In turning to Hölderlin and the pre-Socratics, Pöggeler observes, Heidegger moved steadily "beyond the horizons confining Jünger's attempts to conceptualize his age." Five years later, in his lecture script for the summer of 1939, Heidegger castigated "total mobilization" as "the organization of absolute senselessness on the basis of the will to power and in the latter's service." During the winter of that year, at the beginning of the war, Heidegger discussed with a small group Jünger's *Worker* and complained that this book "fails entirely to grasp Nietzsche's metaphysics philosophically. It does not even point the way; on the contrary: instead of treating it as questionable [*fragwürdig*], it renders this metaphysics self-evident and thus apparently redundant."[14]

In comparison with Jünger's work, his departure from Nietzsche proved to be more complicated and halting, mainly because of the greater depth of the latter's insights. Immediately after resigning the rectorate, in the summer of 1934, Heidegger offered a lecture course on Heraclitus with a focus on *polemos* and conflict—a treatment in which Nietzsche's "agonistics" was curiously distanced or rendered in alien garb (*verfrem-det*), thus permitting ontological or metaphysical scrutiny. Subsequent lecture courses on Nietzsche bear the earmarks of intense personal struggle. The lectures of 1936 and 1937—on "the will to power as art" and "the eternal recurrence of the same"—still present Nietzsche's thought as a viable and innovative critique of Platonism, though a critique formulated itself in traditional metaphysical terms. By contrast, the course on

---

[14] Pöggeler, "Heideggers politisches Selbstverständnis," pp. 21, 30, 32–33. For a perceptive interpretation of the rectorial address, see Graeme Nicholson, "The Politics of Heidegger's Rectoral Address," *Man and World* 20 (1987): 171–187.

European nihilism, offered in 1940 after the outbreak of the war, exudes a somber and even hostile mood: Nietzschean will to power is now portrayed as an outgrowth of an aggressive anthropocentrism in which humankind is reduced to the level of brute animality or bestiality.

As Pöggeler indicates, this progressive distancing from Nietzsche was paralleled by the steady emergence of Hölderlin in Heidegger's opus, that is, by the accentuation of poetic "world disclosure" (which eludes human control or manipulation) in lieu of radical conflict and willful self-assertion. A lecture course of winter 1934 was devoted to a discussion of Hölderlin's hymns "Germania" and "The Rhine"—seemingly patriotic themes. But instead of serving as a chauvinistic symbol, "Germania" in the lectures was a synonym for the reflective turn to the disclosure (or truth) of being and the origins of Western culture; in Hölderlin's own vision, Germany was meant to be not an imperial power but an unarmed heartland preparing the ground for a cultural or spiritual renewal. These themes were reiterated and intensified in courses on Hölderlin during the war years. Thus, in lectures presented during the summer of 1942, Heidegger differentiated sharply between the classical conception of *polis* and modern or contemporary politics with its ideological politicization of life in general. Whereas the classical *polis* was a place of questioning and unsettled openness, modern politics aims at the implementation of historical plans: "Since it denotes the technical-historical certainty of all action, politics or 'the political' is marked by its own absolutely unquestioned status. This status of politics and its totality go together."[15]

Throughout these years, Heidegger's political thought was preoccupied, with growing urgency, with the issue of world dominion seen as the goal of competing global ideologies. The lecture course of 1935, titled *Einführung in die Metaphysik* (Introduction to Metaphysics), turned philosophical attention to the pre-Socratics and also to Sophoclean tragedy (as interpreted by Hölderlin); but the political concern or frame of reference was entirely contemporary: human destiny in a world steadily instrumentalized and closing in on itself. Heidegger talked at the time of a "darkening of the world" (*Weltverdüsterung*) connected with the crisis or

---

[15] Pöggeler, "Heideggers politisches Selbstverständnis," pp. 33–35, 39. See also Heidegger, *Hölderlins Hymne "Der Ister,"* ed. Walter Biemel (*Gesamtausgabe*, Vol. 53; Frankfurt-Main: Klostermann, 1984), p. 118. Regarding the lecture course on "Germania" and "The Rhine," see Chapter 5 in this volume. According to Hannah Arendt, Heidegger's so-called *Kehre* (turning) surfaced primarily in the shift of mood separating the lectures on Nietzsche of 1936/37 from the wartime lectures on nihilism. See *The Life of the Mind*, Vol. 2: *Willing* (New York: Harcourt Brace Jovanovich, 1978), pp. 172–173.

decay of Europe, a crisis induced by the European spirit itself, especially by Western metaphysics. "This Europe," he stated, "which in its ruinous blindness is forever on the point of cutting its own throat, lies today in a great pincers, squeezed between Russia on one side and America on the other. From a metaphysical vantage, Russia and America are the same: the same dreary technological frenzy, the same unrestricted organization of the average man." Similar assessments of Russia and America were recurrent in Heidegger's writings and lectures of the period, always with an edge against technology and mass organization (both united through the will to control). Generally speaking, Heidegger differentiated among three major instrumentalizations of culture or spirit: Marxism, positivism, and fascism. Whereas the first relegates culture to a redundant superstructure and the second (prevalent in America) is content with the scientific replication of given states of affairs, fascism aims at the organizational control of a people under racial auspices. The latter aim, to be sure, is quite removed from the view that led Heidegger into the proximity of National Socialism. As the same lecture course (in its printed version) affirmed, "The stuff which is now being bandied about as the philosophy of National Socialism—but which has not the least to do with the inner truth and greatness of this movement (namely, the encounter between global technology and modern man)—is casting its net in these troubled waters of 'values' and 'totalities.'" More than any other passage, this phrase has been strongly attacked by critics—and understandably so given its reference to an inner truth and greatness of the regime. Moreover, research has shown that the phrase in parentheses was not part of the original lectures but rather a later addition, perhaps inserted to attenuate the harshness of the claim. However this may be, one can hardly deny that Heidegger's concern with planetary strategies and the struggle for world dominion antedates 1935 and can in fact be traced to his involvement with Jünger.[16]

Apart from these and other lecture courses, Pöggeler also discusses at some length the so-called *Beiträge zur Philosophie* (Contributions to Philosophy) written between 1936 and 1938, which he describes as Heidegger's crowning work. According to his essay, the *Beiträge* was a deep philosophical inquiry seeking to uncover the truth of being as a "happening" (*Ereignis*) not amenable to human control, as a "clearing" pointing the

---

[16] Pöggeler, "Heideggers politisches Selbstverständnis," pp. 35–38. See also Heidegger, *Einführung in die Metaphysik*, ed. Petra Jaeger (1935; *Gesamtausgabe*, Vol. 40; Frankfurt-Main: Klostermann, 1983), pp. 40, 208; trans. Ralph Manheim as *An Introduction to Metaphysics* (New Haven: Yale University Press, 1959), pp. 37, 199.

way toward spiritual recovery. In stark contrast with this clearing, the treatise outlined the dominant features of our age, concentrating on mass organization, the unleashing of technology, and the general instrumentalization and ideological politicization of life. Among the ideologies criticized in the study were bolshevism with its planned social progress, liberalism with its treatment of ideas and culture as "values to be implemented," and "folkish" ideology with its focus on political training and racial breeding. To the extent that the term was to be used, Heidegger argued at the time, "folk" should refer not to a given race or empirical entity but only to a common search or aspiration. The general goal of the *Beiträge* was to encourage a renewed philosophical reflection, particularly a recollection of buried cultural origins that heralded a better future. As Pöggeler points out, philosophizing in Heidegger's sense was authoritative (*herrschaftlich*) because it turns back to the origins in contrast to the decay of later times; however, authority in this case did not equal dominion, since its chief exemplars were said to be not rulers but marginalized thinkers and artists (such as Hölderlin, Nietzsche, and van Gogh). Philosophy of this kind, Pöggeler comments, is "useless in that it cannot be placed in the service of historical self-assertion (as Heidegger had still assumed in 1933). Such philosophizing means opposition and resistance to a National Socialism which at that time was preparing for the struggle for world dominion and which, in lieu of reflection, was seeking the unquestioned sway of a total ideology and total politics."[17]

By way of conclusion, Pöggeler points to some of Heidegger's writings and statements after the war. At this time Heidegger disengaged himself almost entirely from prevalent political orientations and ideological formulas, including the restorative tendencies in postwar Germany. His thinking now focused increasingly and stubbornly on the effects of modern nihilism and on the prospect of technology as global human destiny. In this respect, World War II appeared to him not as an end or even turning point but as a stepping stone to planetary instrumentalization. As he observed in *Was heisst Denken?* (What Is Called Thinking?) (1951–52), "That world war has not decided anything, provided we take decision here in that broad and crucial sense where it concerns the basic human destiny on this planet." Similar sentiments were also echoed in the *Spiegel* interview of 1966. As Heidegger stated in response to questions about global trends, the past several decades had shown "that the planetary movement of modern technology constitutes a power whose

17 Pöggeler, "Heideggers politisches Selbstverständnis," pp. 42–47.

determining historical significance can hardly be underestimated." In the same context, Heidegger also pondered the issue of the political order or regime appropriate to this technological age—and he questioned that it was democracy (as commonly understood).

A striking feature of the postwar years was the appropriation of Heidegger's thought by various intellectual movements, such as French existentialism and Western neo-Marxism—developments Heidegger observed with curiosity but without active support or other concrete engagement. Although not discouraging adjustment to political trends, Heidegger—in Pöggeler's account—persisted in his ontological-metaphysical "radicalism," seeking the antidote to modern nihilism in recollective-meditative thinking, in poetic world disclosure and particularly in Georg Trakl's post-metaphysical (or postmodern) poetry. In an effort to correct or at least counterbalance this radicalism, Pöggeler at the end stresses the importance of practical-political judgment—which Heidegger generally lacked—and the need for a nonradical, prudential politics: "If there is a European responsibility—as Heidegger insisted in his own way—then this responsibility (after the self-destruction of Europe as former heartland) must reside in the effort to accentuate the limited chances of a prudent politics which still remain possible."[18]

II

Pöggeler's account accords major weight to political factors and particularly to the struggle for planetary dominion, sometimes in a manner that overshadows philosophical issues. Although probing the nexus of philosophy and politics, his essay alludes only briefly (if at all) to such key Heideggerian themes as the being-question and the departure from, or overcoming of, metaphysics. Virtually the reverse is the case in Derrida's interpretation as it is developed in his study *Of Spirit*, subtitled *Heidegger and the Question* (whose French version appeared in 1987). Although not entirely neglected, political struggle and its drama take a back seat there to searching philosophical and "deconstructive" queries.

---

[18] Ibid., pp. 23–24, 48–51, 54–57. See also Heidegger, *Was heisst Denken?* 3d ed. (Tübingen: Niemeyer, 1971), p. 65; trans. J. Glenn Gray as *What Is Called Thinking?* (New York: Harper & Row, 1968), p. 66; and "Only a God Can Save Us: The Spiegel Interview (1966)," trans. William J. Richardson in Thomas Sheehan, ed., *Heidegger: The Man and the Thinker* (Chicago: Precedent, 1981), pp. 45–67, at p. 55.

Not formally a student or disciple of Heidegger, Derrida seeks to explore unsettled issues in Heidegger's work, issues that are still "suspended, undecided, and thus in movement" in his texts.

A major issue of this kind is the meaning and status of spirit (*Geist*), a topic that surprisingly (to Derrida) has not received any attention in the massive literature surrounding these texts. His study aims to remedy this inattention, for reasons he lists in his opening chapter. On the one hand, the theme of spirit enjoys an extraordinary authority in the tradition of German philosophy, particularly in German idealism, an authority that is bound to affect or reverberate in Heidegger's thinking. On the other hand, the theme tends to be inscribed in Heidegger's writings into a highly politically charged context—in the sense that it usually surfaces in discussions on such topics as "history, nation, gender, the Greek or the German." Moreover, as Derrida adds, references to spirit are not merely loosely or accidentally related to political contexts that somehow remain external to the theme; rather, the linkage is more intimate: "Perhaps this thinking [of spirit] determines the very meaning of the political itself; at least it can indicate the locus of such a determination (if one is possible). Hence its not yet fully recognized privilege regarding questions of politics or the political that animate so many debates around Heidegger today."[19]

Like Pöggeler's essay, *Of Spirit* offers a tour through Heidegger's successive writings and lectures, in this case with the accent on the shifting role of spirit and spirituality. Taking his point of departure from *Being and Time*, Derrida notes that Heidegger at the time emphasized the need to avoid or bracket the term "spirit" (*Geist*), together with such related terms as "subjectivity" and (transcendental) "consciousness." Some twenty-five years later, in his comments on Trakl's poetry, Heidegger resumed this strategy of avoidance, stating that the poet had always steered clear of *Geist* and *geistig*, preferring instead the word *geistlich* (spiritual). In the interval between *Being and Time* and these comments, however—a period that was not "just any quarter-century"—Heidegger

---

[19] Jacques Derrida, *Of Spirit: Heidegger and the Question*, trans. Geoffrey Bennington and Rachel Bowlby (Chicago: University of Chicago Press, 1989), pp. 4–6, 8. (In the above and subsequent citations, I have slightly altered the translation for purposes of clarity.) The title is adapted from Helvetius's well-known work burned in Paris in 1759 and regarding which Helvetius subsequently wrote an elaborate retraction or recantation (as Derrida mentions, p. 14, n. 1). The subtitle refers to the question of being and the shifting role of questioning in Heidegger's opus.

repeatedly contravened his own counsel, not only neglecting to avoid but rather explicitly invoking *Geist* and related vocabulary. "What has happened?" Derrida asks.

> How can we explain that, in a time period of twenty-five years which lies between the two counsels or *warnings* (of avoidance), Heidegger himself made a frequent, regular, marked (if not remarked) use of this vocabulary, including the adjective *geistig*? How do we account for the fact that he often not only spoke about *Geist* but also in the name of *Geist*, occasionally carried away by his emphasis?

In Derrida's view, both the use and the nonuse or attempted avoidance of *Geist* are symptomatic of Heidegger's philosophical development; in a sense, they demarcate a nodal point at which different strands of his thought are interwoven in a particularly dense and revealing fashion. Among the intersecting strands, Derrida mentions primarily four: the issue of questioning in its relation to being; the status of technology in its contrast to thinking; the meaning of "animality" as compared to *Dasein;* and the epochal character of the history of metaphysics. "As we shall see," he writes, "these epochal divisions may be tied up with the kind of 'difference' which . . . separates the Platonic-Christian, metaphysical or onto-theological definition of *Geist* from another thinking which surfaces in the dialogue with Trakl: the thinking of the spiritual [*das Geistliche*]."[20]

Turning back to *Being and Time,* Derrida reminds readers that Heidegger at that point tried to extricate himself from traditional metaphysics, particularly from subject-object or mind-body dualism, which also surfaces as the opposition between spirit and matter (or thing). His "existential analytic" sought to rescue *Dasein* not only from different types of objectification but also, and explicitly, from a subjective definition of spirit. In traditional metaphysics, spirit was part of a string of "non-objects," that is, of concepts that stood opposed to material reality—a string including consciousness, soul (or *psyche*), subjectivity, personhood, and reason. An attempt to elucidate *Dasein* nonmetaphysically required an effort to avoid or bracket the entire string of non-objects, including

---

[20] Ibid., pp. 1–2, 9–12. Translation is complicated by the fact that the English "spiritual" can stand for both *geistig* and *geistlich.* The difference might be elucidated as follows: if *Geist* captures the Greek *logos*, *geistig* might be rendered as "logical" or "*logos*-related." In contrast to the coincidence of *logos* and being in *Geist* and *geistig,* *geistlich* expresses the openness of thinking to the disclosure and otherness of being. In the following, I use "spiritual" for *geistlich* and "spirituality" for *Geistlichkeit.*

particularly the concept of spirit. According to Heidegger, the defining characteristic of *Dasein* was not so much consciousness or spirit as rather its openness to being or to the "question of being"; among other beings or entities, *Dasein* was differentiated as that mode or modality for which its own being (and being as such) is questionable, or raised to the status of a question.

Seen from this vantage, *Dasein* was not simply an objectively given and ascertainable entity (in the sense of *Vorhandenheit*); but neither was it merely a non-thing. In fact, categories like spirit and consciousness were not helpful gateways but rather obstacles obstructing access to *Dasein* seen as the locus of the questioning of being. Such terms as "existence" and "being-in-the-world" were used to obviate misunderstandings. As *Being and Time* stated, the assertion that *Dasein* is an inquiry meant that "the 'substance' of man resides not in spirit construed as synthesis of soul and body but in his existence." Heidegger also distanced his work from several disciplines and investigations predicated on this Cartesian metaphysical basis, including mental sciences (*Geisteswissenschaften*) and the host of philosophical anthropologies and theories of personality animated by the traditional vocabulary.[21]

Before departing from *Being and Time*, Derrida turns to the later chapters devoted to the status of space and time, and especially to Hegel's conception of history. As he notes, Heidegger at this point reintroduces the concept of spirit—but places it in quotation marks. Thus, apparently, "something signified by *Geist* in quotation marks can be salvaged"; *Geist* is simultaneously distanced and reappropriated. Regarding space, Heidegger insists that *Dasein* is not simply spatial in an external sense, namely, due to the spatial character of the body (as part of extended matter); by the same token, *Dasein* is not an inner, mental quality (after the fashion of *res cogitans*). Rather, *Dasein* has its own distinctive mode of spatiality; likewise, not being a mere object, *Dasein* is in a sense also "*geistig*"—although the term now appears in quotation marks: "Precisely because it is '*geistig*' (the word now obviously in quotation marks)," Derrida comments, "*Dasein* is spatial, endowed with an original spatiality; *only* because of this kind of '*Geistigkeit*'—Heidegger underscores the point—is *Dasein* a spatial being."

The same issue recurs in the discussion of Hegel's conception of time and history. Although presenting history essentially as the history of spirit (its unfolding in time), Hegel nevertheless maintained that spirit also "falls into" time, that is, lapses into something mundane or sensual. According to Heidegger, Hegel here himself lapsed into something non-philosophical—into a vulgar notion of temporality seen as external clock time, thereby showing his indebtedness to Newtonian physics. Only by clinging to this clock time could temporality and history be opposed to spirit and the latter be said to fall into the former. In seeking to overcome this opposition, Heidegger again invokes the term *"Geist"*—again in quotation marks. In his own words, " *'Geist'* does not merely fall into time, but exists as the original temporalization of time itself." To the extent there is still a falling, it denotes a lapse from one time into another, from original into vulgar temporality—which is an endemic possibility of spirit viewed as temporalization. In this manner, Derrida states, *Geist* is only half-heartedly accepted; with a "reticent hospitality" it is greeted at the door—and kept there in quotation marks.[22]

Leaping ahead six years, Derrida turns to the rectorial address of 1933 and discovers a surprising fact: the return of *Geist*—this time in full regalia and no longer constrained by quotation marks. Suddenly, he writes, "the curtain rises, the quotation marks disappear—making room for a powerful effect: *Geist* itself comes on stage." Undisguised, spirit now asserts itself, as an integral part of the "self-assertion of the German university." What induced this change, Derrida asks, this resort to "passionate rhetoric" in the name of spirit? Self-assertion in Heidegger's usage involves a *geistig* order supported by a leadership (*Führung*) that itself is guided by a *geistig* mission or commission. As Heidegger himself states in the opening paragraph, "Assuming the post of rector means to take on the task of the *geistig* leadership of this high school of learning." This leadership, however, is possible only if the leaders (*Führer*) allow themselves to be led—"by the inescapability of that *geistig* mission which molds the fate of the German people into the distinctive shape of its history."

Overstepping his usual caution (and certainly his earlier counsel of avoidance), Heidegger later in his address proceeds to offer a definition of spirit, one in which several crucial aspects of his thought are conjoined. In contrast to mere cleverness, wit, or analytical intelligence, *Geist* "is the originally tuned and knowing resoluteness in the pursuit of the essence of being." Accordingly, the *Geist* or "*geistig* world" of a people is not a mere cultural superstructure or arsenal of usable values but an existential

---

[22] Derrida, *Of Spirit*, pp. 23–29. See also Heidegger, *Sein und Zeit*, pp. 428–436 (par. 82).

power (*Macht*) arising from chthonic forces and the deepest testing of its historical *Dasein*. As Derrida comments, this definition and its elaboration combine the highest and the lowest, spirit and chthonic yearnings. He also points to the marked philosophical ambivalence evident in the definition. For, treated as a concrete historical force, *Geist* no longer fits the metaphysical model governing modernity; in line with *Being and Time*, *Geist* is "not equated with subjectivity, at least not in its psychic and egological construal." At the same time, however, it is at least arguable that the "massive voluntarism" of the address still remains hostage to the age of subjectivity.[23]

Linked with and hidden behind this philosophical quandary is a more important, political ambivalence. In invoking *Geist* and *geistig* mission, Derrida observes, one might say that Heidegger spiritualizes National Socialism, thereby legitimating its policies (even its worst). But in shouldering this risk of spiritualization, Heidegger may also have pursued the aim of cleansing and thus salvaging National Socialism (from its worst inclinations). In that case, Heidegger's address opened a breech between *Geist* and biological racism or naturalism; at least the address no longer *appears* to belong to an ideological discourse that "appeals to dark forces— forces which are not *geistig* but natural, biological or racial forces (corresponding to a non-*geistig* construal of the 'blood-and-soil' theme)." Seen in this light, however, Heidegger's spiritualization exacted a price: the price of a relapse (at least in part) into traditional metaphysics rooted in spirit and subjectivity.

In Derrida's portrayal, this price seems unavoidable—because "one can extricate oneself from or *oppose oneself* to biologism, naturalism, or racism in its genetic form only by stipulating spirit as the opposite pole, by equating the latter again with subjectivity (if only a voluntaristic mode of subjectivity)." Commenting on a crucial dilemma of our age, as highlighted by fascism, Derrida observes that the pressure exerted by this dualism is powerful:

> It reigns over most of the discourses which today—and probably for a long time to come—oppose themselves to racism, totalitarianism, National Socialism, fascism and the like, and which do so in the name of *Geist*, in the name of freedom of spirit, or in the name of axioms directly or indirectly indebted to the metaphysics of subjectivity (such as the axioms of democracy and the "rights of man").

[23] Derrida, *Of Spirit*, pp. 31–37. See also Heidegger, "The Self-Assertion of the German University," pp. 470, 474–475.

In Derrida's view, the alternatives available in this scenario—the options for or against *Geist*—are all "frightfully impure and contaminated." One always has to ask oneself which option or "type of complicity" is less grievous; in any event, "the urgency and importance of the question cannot be taken seriously enough."[24]

As far as the rectorial address is concerned, Heidegger mixed the two options in many ways, thereby compounding their ill effects: he "vouched" for National Socialism by employing a "still metaphysical gesture." The same ambivalence persisted, though with modified accents, in the *Introduction to Metaphysics* (1935). Heidegger himself alluded there to this aspect when he stated, in the opening pages, that "every essential form of spirit hovers in ambivalence." The treatise sought to provide an introduction or guidance (*Einführung*) into philosophy construed as a mode of questioning, more specifically, as the "questioning of the basic question." This guidance was not meant to lead into a substantive domain or to yield various types of information but only to arouse wonder and questioning; moreover, the guiding introduction could not rely on any other form of external leadership (*Führung*) but had to entrust itself entirely to questioning. Thus, unguided and uncontrolled, a questioning guidance forms the gateway to philosoophical questioning—and "this is precisely what characterizes spirit; it is the nature of *Geist* itself."

By using the vocabulary of leadership Heidegger seemed to accede to dominant fascist formulas. Derrida, however, writes, "one should be honest enough to admit: at the very moment when he seems to place the theme of *Führung* in the service of a certain kind of politics, Heidegger shows that he entirely distances himself from this politics, that he cancels his service." To be sure, this distancing or retreat from politics was not complete or unambiguous. For one thing, questioning here was still connected with a will to know and thus with assertive resoluteness (familiar from earlier writings). On the other hand and more important, the *Introduction* placed itself into a new political or geopolitical context: the planetary context of the struggle for world dominion. According to Heidegger, Europe and particularly Germany were held in a great pincers, threatened on two sides by Russia and America (both seen as technological powers bent on global mastery). The question was whether Europe could recover the strength of her origins, which required the

---

[24] Derrida, *Of Spirit*, pp. 38–40. The reference to spiritualization is a straightforward translation of the French *spiritualiser*; it should not be taken in the sense of "spiritual" as *geistlich*.

"unfolding of new historical-*geistig* forces from the middle" (or heart-land). As Derrida comments, geopolitics here takes the form of a "world politics of the spirit"; this politics is to counter the "darkening of the world [*Weltverdüsterung*]: flight of the gods, destruction of the earth, massification, rule of mediocrity."[25]

In the *Introduction to Metaphysics*, the darkening of the world was connected or equated with a progressive disempowerment (*Entmachtung*) of the spirit, a process that was not an external accident but a feature endemic to spirit itself. In Heidegger's account, this disempowerment took several forms, including the misconstrual of spirit as wit or intel-ligence, its reduction to a superstructure (in Marxism) or to a formula for racial mass organization (in fascism). Countering this process of decline, Heidegger presented spirit as strength or force, as "an originally unifying and obligating power." In this context, the *Introduction* reinvoked the definition of *Geist* offered in the rectorial address, adding these com-ments: "Spirit is the empowerment of the powers of being as such taken as a whole; wherever spirit rules [*herrscht*], being as such becomes steadily more essential." As Derrida notes, Heidegger's formulations at this time were still strongly (though ambiguously) indebted to traditional meta-physics with its focus on spirit as self-possession and self-identity (or *logos*). In subsequent writings or lectures, however, these moorings were loosened or displaced, making room progressively for new vistas.

In his lecture course on Schelling of 1936, Heidegger still emphasized the unifying or gathering nature of spirit, calling *Geist* the "originally unifying unity." But he added that, as this unity, "spirit is *pneuma*," that is, a wind or breeze, a mode of respiration or aspiration. From where does this wind arise? Following Schelling, Heidegger pointed to the potency of love, stating, "For even *Geist* is not the highest; it is only the spirit or breeze of love. But love is the highest." The same Schelling lectures also broached the topic of evil (*das Böse*), seen as the falling away and self-enclosure of existence in rebellion against the unifying spirit of love. Derrida also refers to some of Heidegger's lecture courses dealing with Hölderlin, particularly to the 1942 course on "The Danube." There Heidegger presents the soul (*Gemüt*) of the poet as the receptacle and nourishing soil for spirit. Spirit, however, is now seen as fire or flame, in accordance with the opening of Hölderlin's hymn: "Come now, fire!" As fire, spirit no longer denotes self-possession or self-identity but rather a

[25] Derrida, *Of Spirit*, pp. 40–46. See also Heidegger, *An Introduction to Metaphysics*, pp. 9, 21, 36.

continuous movement or yearning, a perpetual process of expropriation and reappropriation. By offering his soul, Hölderlin the poet is put afire; he is "almost incinerated, turned to ashes."[26]

The last stage reviewed in *Of Spirit* is Heidegger's intense postwar engagement with language, and particularly his commentary (1953) on Trakl's poetry. Heidegger again raises the question, "But what is spirit?" And now he replies, "*Geist* is the flaming [or enflaming]" or more simply "*Geist* is flame." In this phrase, *Geist* is both what enflames, by laying fire, and what goes up in flames. In Derrida's view, the passage does not merely paraphrase Trakl, it reflects or captures Heidegger's own thought. What one should note, however, is that, as used in the sentence, *Geist* no longer belongs to traditional metaphysics (and thus does not succumb to a strategy of avoidance). This becomes clearer in Heidegger's comments on Trakl's verse: "But the soul is strange [that is, a stranger-sojourner, *ein Fremdes*] on earth." As Heidegger insists, the term "strange" here does not mean that the soul is banished into a bodily, earthly prison in which it does not belong—in accordance with an old-fashioned type of Platonism. Instead, "strange" here signifies a wayfar-ing-sojourning quality, the fact that the soul is still "in search of the earth" which it does not yet inhabit.

The yearning of the soul points to the future, but to a future in the sense not of ordinary clock time but of a mode of temporality in which the "later" anticipates the "earlier," where evening is prior to morning and death prior to life. For this kind of temporality and its earth world, Trakl uses the term *geistlich*, as when he writes of the "spiritual twilight" and the "spiritual night" as the concealing disclosure of the sun's path. In pointing forward, *geistlich* temporality has the character of a promise, the promise of a morning or dawn before night and day, before evening-land

---

[26] Derrida, *Of Spirit*, pp. 63–68, 76–82. Derrida also alludes to Heidegger's lectures on Nietzsche, but without pondering the progressive shift of accents in these lectures: "During these same years [1930s]," he writes (p. 73), "Heidegger's interpretive strategy is also concerned with Nietzsche. Its goal is to extricate Nietzsche from biologistic, zoolo-gistic or vitalistic appropriations. This interpretive strategy is also a mode of politics; the extreme ambiguity of the gesture resides in the attempt to salvage a thought by surrender-ing it" (to metaphysics). See also Heidegger, *An Introduction to Metaphysics*, pp. 37–41, 48; *Schellings Abhandlung über das Wesen der menschlichen Freiheit* (1809), ed. Hildegard Feick (Tübingen: Niemeyer, 1971), pp. 153–154; and *Hölderlins Hymne "Der Ister,"* pp. 157–170. Regarding the Schelling lectures, see Fred Dallmayr, "Ontology of Freedom: Heidegger and Political Philosophy," in Dallmayr, *Polis and Praxis* (Cambridge: MIT Press, 1984), pp. 104–132, at pp. 121–127.

and morning-land construed as Occident and Orient. "Evening-land" (*Abendland*) in Trakl's poems, Heidegger states, must be carefully distinguished from Western civilization or the "idea" of Europe in Plato's sense (and largely assimilated by Christianity). Trakl's evening-land, he writes, is "older, namely earlier and thus more promising than the Occident conceived along Platonic-Christian and especially along European lines."[27]

In adopting Trakl's use of *geistlich*, Heidegger distances himself again, as in his early work, from traditional metaphysics and its vocabulary. As Derrida observes, "Although after 1933 the term had been employed regularly and for a long time without quotation marks, the adjective *geistig* is now brusquely rejected"; Heidegger acts as if for twenty years he had not eloquently "celebrated the *Geistigkeit* of *Geist*." Instead, these terms are now relegated to the "Platonic-metaphysical tradition"—or rather the Platonic-Cartesian tradition—of the West. In his commentary on Trakl, Heidegger himself is quite explicit on this point. Why, he asks, does Trakl "avoid the term *geistig*? Because *geistig* means the opposite of the material. This contrast highlights the difference between two spheres of being and, in Platonic-Occidental language, designates the gulf between the suprasensible (*noeton*) and the sensible (*aistheton*)." Understood in this way, however, *Geist* and *geistig* have in the meantime been leveled into the "rational, intellectual and ideological" and thus belong together with their opposites to a decaying age. The latter condemnation (of the "rational, intellectual and ideological"), Derrida notes, corresponds roughly to views voiced in *Introduction to Metaphysics;* but now the critique proceeds from the vantage of *Geistlichkeit* (not *Geistigkeit*). Yet, as he concedes, the distinction does not amount to a radical dismissal—for *Geistlichkeit* is earthly temporality illuminated by *Geist*, the latter construed as fire or flame, and fire is also the source of the spirit as *pneuma* or *spiritus* (as well as *ruah*). More important, even under the auspices of *Geistlichkeit* Heidegger does not abandon the unifying quality of *Geist:* as he still maintains in his commentary on Trakl, *Geist* is "as such the gathering." By way of conclusion, Derrida returns to the political connotations of the reviewed journey, of the various options for or against *Geist* (with or without quotation marks):

---

[27] Derrida, *Of Spirit*, pp. 83–85, 87–90, 92–93. See also Heidegger, *Unterwegs zur Sprache* (Pfullingen: Neske, 1959), pp. 35–77; trans. Peter D. Hertz as *On the Way to Language* (New York: Harper & Row, 1971), pp. 159–198.

What is at issue here is not something abstract. Rather we are dealing with past, present and future "events," with a constellation of forces and discourses which seem to wage a merciless war on each other (roughly in the period from 1933 to today). We are faced with a program, a combination of possibilities whose power is abysmal. Strictly speaking, no discourse that participates in this power struggle can be described as innocent.[28]

III

So far, I have juxtaposed two accounts of the trajectory of Heidegger's thought. In many ways, the two accounts—Pöggeler's and Derrida's—complement each other by accentuating, respectively, more overtly political (or geopolitical) and more recessed metaphysical issues. Although different in style and general orientation, both authors seek to correlate politics and philosophy, that is, to interpret Heidegger's political views in light of his opus. In doing so, they add new dimensions to *l'affaire* Heidegger, dimensions that counterbalance Farias's polemical approach. Pöggeler's account in particular is helpful in recalling concrete historical contexts or background factors which (while not explaining or warranting) at least render some of Heidegger's motivations more plausible. Among these factors are Heidegger's disaffection with the stalemate of Weimar politics (a disaffection shared by many intellectuals at the time); the fascination exerted by an extreme or conflictual Nietzscheanism (as articulated chiefly in Jünger's writings); the concern with the fate of Europe in the midst of the struggle for world dominion (a concern promoting cultural revivalism and elitism); the attempt to guide Hitler's movement in the direction of a cultural or *geistig* resurgence (an attempt giving rise to an idiosyncratic National Socialism); the progressive disenchantment with the biologism and racism of Hitlerism and with the growing brutalization of the hoped-for resurgence (a disenchantment entailing, at least philosophically, a kind of "inner emigration"); and the preoccupation with the "darkening of the world" due to the decline of Europe under the onslaught of planetary technology (a decline sealed by the outcome of World War II). Pöggeler also points to reasons ungirding Heidegger's aloofness from concrete politics after 1945, tracing it to a distrust in merely "restorative" tendencies (reminiscent of the Weimar

---

[28] Derrida, *Of Spirit,* pp. 95–96, 106–107, 109. See also Heidegger, *Unterwegs zur Sprache,* pp. 59, 66; and *On the Way to Language,* pp. 178, 185.

period) as well as to his overriding absorption with issues of planetary technology. Regarding the retraction of earlier pro-Nazi views—a prominent point in the accusations leveled at Heidegger—Pöggeler offers some personal testimony: "By stating forcefully at least in conversation that he was completely wrong in 1933 and that nothing could excuse this mistake, Heidegger also supported efforts to avoid such mistakes in the future."[29]

To be sure, the preceding comments cannot (and are not meant to) simply exonerate Heidegger's conduct in 1933 and later, both on a personal and a broader intellectual level. In personal terms, Heidegger's moments of pettiness, immodesty, and occasional vindictiveness caused grief to many people. In addition to acts of commission, there were important omissions, particularly his persistent silence on Auschwitz and the holocaust. In this respect, Pöggeler states correctly that the comparison of Auschwitz with wartime mass killings neglects the fact that the inmates of concentration camps were "killed before their death, namely, by being stripped of human dignity." Along with Pöggeler (and many others) I am troubled by Heidegger's continuous self-distancing from modern democracy, although on this score one can speculate more readily about reasons for his reticence. From Heidegger's vantage, democracy or "popular rule" very likely signified a collective type of anthropocentrism or a collective will to power along humanist-metaphysical lines. Perhaps his scruples would have been eased by nonfoundational or post-metaphysical conceptions of democracy such as have been advanced in recent times from various quarters. Clearly, the issue of anthropocentrism was at the heart of Heidegger's complaint about planetary technology, which he probably construed in too all-embrasive or monolithic terms. This construal or misconstrual is particularly evident in his assessment of America and Russia as purely technological powers. In my own view, Heidegger was largely ignorant of America and American culture, where fascination with technology is circumscribed by a host of historical and *geistig* factors. Generally speaking, I tend to agree with Pöggeler's assessment regarding the deficiency of prudential judgment in Heidegger's outlook—although heightened political judgment probably does not need to be purchased with the loss of philosophical radicality.[30]

---

[29] Pöggeler, "Heideggers politisches Selbstverständnis," p. 52.
[30] Ibid., pp. 52, 56–57. Invoking a distinction familiar in French discussions, one might say that prudential judgment operates on the level of *la politique* (politics as policy) whereas philosophical radicality is more appropriate to *le politique* (politics understood as polity or

There is another point, however, in which I concur with Pöggeler's assessment, namely, his counsel not to be too quickly done with *l'affaire* Heidegger by pronouncing a summary verdict. Are political invectives, he asks, not also the attempt "to escape from those questions which Heidegger effectively posed for our time?" It is at this point, I believe, that polemics is counterproductive—or productive only of self-congratulatory conceit while undercutting the task of learning (even and especially from mistakes). Regarding world politics, how can one be sanguine about planetary technology, at a time when through "star wars" the struggle for world dominion is extended into outer space? And for what purpose or in whose name is this contest being waged—in the name of which spirit or non-spirit, *Geist* or *Ungeist?*

As is well known, much of Heidegger's philosophical animus was directed against modern ideologies or total ideological worldviews. Was he simply mistaken in regarding these ideologies as attempts to transform the globe into an instrument of human satisfaction and self-aggrandizement, into an arena for the implementation of a grandiose master plan (or competing master plans)? And has the situation really changed much since the time of his writings? More likely, problems have been aggravated by the linkage of Western ideology—particularly the ideology of rapid global "development"—with worsening ecological conditions. Along these lines, is there not ample reason to be troubled by the reduction of nature and the global environment to a human tool—to the kind of "standing reserve" Heidegger deplored in his comments on technology and "technicity" (*Technik*)? In all these respects, is it reasonable to put Heidegger summarily aside; can we afford not to learn from, or at least ponder, his thoughts?

Similar considerations apply to Heidegger's broader philosophical orientation. He is sometimes chided for having initiated or invented nihilism, or at least for having compounded Nietzsche's nihilistic outlook. But is this not blaming the messenger for the message? Are there not grounds for holding that—transformed into values or goals to be

---

as paradigm or framework). On post-metaphysical conceptions of democracy, see, for example, Claude Lefort, *Democracy and Political Theory*, trans. David Macey (Cambridge: Polity Press, 1988); and Ernesto Laclau and Chantal Mouffe, *Hegemony and Socialist Strategy: Towards a Radical Democratic Politics*, trans. Winston Moore and Paul Cammack (London: Verso, 1985). On the latter, see Fred Dallmayr, "Hegemony and Democracy: A Review of Laclau and Mouffe," *Philosophy and Social Criticism* 13 (1987): 283–296; also Dallmayr, "Hegemony and Democracy: A Post-Hegelian Perspective," in Dallmayr, *Margins of Political Discourse* (Albany: SUNY Press, 1989), pp. 116–136.

implemented—traditional metaphysics is progressively depleting itself, thereby making room for an existential or ontological void (independently of the role of individual philosophers)? Moreover, for both Nietzsche and Heidegger, nihilism was not simply a fact to be accepted but something to be wrestled with and overcome—although the latter could not be accomplished, in their view, by wishing it away. Contemporary assaults on nihilism, in this light, are ill advised to ignore Heidegger's (and Nietzsche's) writings, where both the problem and possible avenues to recovery were so tenaciously mapped out and discussed.

The issue of nihilism is closely tied up with the larger question of metaphysics and its status in our time. For several reasons (again not traceable to individual malice), some of the "foundational" pillars of traditional metaphysics have become porous or fragile, particularly such pillars as consciousness, subjectivity, reason, or *Geist* (in the sense of *logos*). As is well known, throughout his life Heidegger struggled with this kind of metaphysics and the possibility of its overcoming, in a manner that remains challenging and instructive far beyond the clamor raised by *l'affaire* Heidegger. In departing, however cautiously, from foundational moorings, his thinking ventured out into uncharted terrain—a move fraught with both promise and perils. By featuring this departure, Derrida's comments accentuate a nodal point and perhaps the crucial thread linking together Heidegger's sprawling opus; they also point to the noncapricious, nonarbitrary character of the departure, to the fact that it does not merely signal a headlong plunge into irrationalism, as maintained by many of Heidegger's critics.[31]

One of the chief merits of Derrida's *Of Spirit* is its reference to the political implications of traditional metaphysics and its attempted overcoming. As Derrida insists repeatedly, the option for or against *Geist* is not politically risk-free; accordingly, Heidegger's halting (and always ambiguous) distancing from *Geist* was not simply a fall from innocence, particularly from the presumed innocence of humanist liberalism. Commenting on the *geistig* aura surrounding modern humanism, Derrida remarks: "It is not my intent to criticize this humanist teleology. It seems to me more urgent to realize that—regardless of attempts to avoid or deny it—this teleology is *until today* (until Heidegger, but time and circumstances have not drastically changed) the price one has to pay for

---

[31] For a critique along these lines, see Jürgen Habermas, *The Philosophical Discourse of Modernity: Twelve Lectures*, trans. Frederick Lawrence (Cambridge: MIT Press, 1987), pp. 131–160.

the ethically and politically motivated denunciation of biologism, racism, and naturalism, and the like." Given the linkage of *Geist* with the mastery of nature (and otherness), the price is not negligible or politically neutral; in any event, one has to weigh carefully the gains and losses entailed by the celebration or else questioning of *Geist*-centered metaphysics: "What is required is a hitherto entirely unknown responsibility of 'thinking' and 'acting'—especially with regard to the feature where the issue remains for us an imminent or impending dilemma." From Derrida's perspective, the difficulties inherent in this dilemma—and illustrated in Heidegger's development in all their weight and complexity—cannot readily be exorcised through bonhomie or a return to time-honored formulas. Only a persistent probing of the problem can make headway in this area, although prospects for a resolution are slim. As he adds: "Are we up against a fatality, can one escape it? Nothing speaks for the latter; there are no indications in its favor—either in the discourses of the 'Heideggerians' or in those of the 'anti-Heideggerians.' Can the dilemma be changed or transformed? I do not know."[32]

Although I generally endorse Derrida's account, I do not mean to suggest an uncritical acceptance. There are several points of detail, and also some broader substantive issues, with which I do not concur. Thus, regarding the so-called crisis of Europe, I am not persuaded that Heidegger's statements on this issue were separated by a radical gulf (excluding even "analogies") from nearly contemporaneous observations by Husserl or from earlier reflections by Paul Valéry—particularly the latter's complaint (in 1919) about an impending *capitis deminutio* of Europe. In my view, many of Heidegger's writings around 1935 were precisely motivated by concern about such a *capitis deminutio*, although his view of Europe obviously differed from Valéry's *geistig*-humanist conception. Another source of uneasiness has to do with Derrida's treatment of the overcoming of metaphysics in *Of Spirit*, a treatment that occasionally intimates a simple exodus from tradition. The intimation is present in the discussion of Heidegger's departure from Platonism and Platonically inspired Christianity, in the direction of an "earlier" promise (beyond morning-land and evening-land). This direction is said to be radically different from traditional metaphysics and especially from historical teleologies of the kind formulated by Hegel, Marx, and "some other thinkers of modernity." Heidegger's departure, we are told, promises "more," invokes something completely "other," than metaphysics—but

[32] Derrida, *Of Spirit*, pp. 40, 55–56.

it does so only seemingly because the transit is blocked or impassable (*ungangbar*): "What is dissimilar from origin in foundation appears from this vantage . . . as foundation, as *Geist* and as essence of Christianity." What these comments neglect is the complex interweaving of departure and continuity, of surpassing and preservation which is the hallmark of Heidegger's path—and which Derrida elsewhere has so eloquently portrayed. The same kind of dichotomization seems to operate in the concluding imaginary dialogue in *Of Spirit* between Heidegger and "certain Christian theologians"—for clearly the attempted post-metaphysical reading of Christianity (and the broader Judeo-Christian tradition) is not simply a negation or denial of Christianity or Western civilization, just as Heidegger's critique of Platonism is not a "destruction" of Plato's teachings.[33]

More important for present purposes is a certain muffling of politics— an occasional tendency on Derrida's part to disengage statements or texts from their contexts. This tendency surfaces particularly in regard to Heidegger's reinvocation of *Geist* in violation of his earlier counsel of avoidance. But are dates not significant and even crucial at this point? The dropping of quotation marks from the term occurred first in the rectorial address of 1933, a public speech held in the midst of rampant political rhetoric. Quotation marks can be nuances, signs of intellectual subtlety—which would have been completely wasted on Hitler's movement. By emphatically invoking the tradition of *Geist*, Heidegger deftly demarcated himself from Nazi biologism. The appeal was intensified in 1935, in the *Introduction to Metaphysics*, when the last remaining quotation marks were removed. But by that time the Nazi regime had become firmly entrenched, and Heidegger had began the difficult process of political disentanglement.[34]

Apart from the rectorial address, incidentally, Heidegger's use of *Geist* at no point signaled a simple return to (Platonic-Cartesian) metaphysics. As indicated, *Geist* was prominently celebrated in the lectures on Schelling of 1936, and precisely as an antidote to biologism and militarism—

[33] Ibid., pp. 107–113; on the "crisis of Europe," see pp. 94–97. Heidegger refers explicitly to Valéry's "La Crise de l'esprit" (1919) in "Hölderlins Erde und Himmel," in *Erläuterungen zu Hölderlins Dichtung*, ed. Friedrich-Wilhelm von Herrmann (*Gesamtausgabe*, Vol. 4; Frankfurt-Main: Klostermann, 1981), pp. 176–177.

[34] Derrida makes much of the fact that the definition of *Geist* in the rectorial address had *Geist* in quotation marks, whereas these marks disappeared two years later when Heidegger cited his own earlier definition. See Derrida, *Of Spirit*, pp. 66–67; also Chapter 6 in this volume (esp. n. 25).

but the term was subtly reinterpreted in the sense of a wind (rather than *logos* or intellect) and as an agency subservient to love. From here the road was not far to the lectures on Hölderlin and to the portrayal of spirit as flame or the outgrowth of fire; and with this notion the path was cleared to the conception of *Geistlichkeit*, in the Trakl commentary, as a modality of time (or space-time) suffused with spirit as fire. Derrida fails to mention that, during the Nazi years, Heidegger did not simply abandon quotation marks in discussing *Geist*. Thus, in his lectures on "The Danube" (1942), Heidegger uses the term *Geist*, often in quotation marks, to designate both the "spirit" of modern technology and the dominant category of German idealism. But, at this juncture, Hitlerism was clearly beyond salvaging, beyond the pale of *geistig* rhetoric, thereby permitting a return to subtlety. My point here is not to overemphasize the role of quotation marks—and thus to compound Derrida's strategy—but to suggest a closer linkage between Heidegger's rhetoric and political context.[35]

In saying this, I do not mean to politicize Heidegger's opus narrowly. In my view, Heidegger's path ever since *Being and Time* was marked by an intensive struggle—the struggle with overcoming metaphysics *and*, as a corollary, with the political implications of this move. Both his early counsel of avoidance and the later (temporary) neglect or suspension of this counsel testify to his endeavor to move beyond a *Geist*-centered metaphysics (where *Geist* equals *logos*, intellect, or subjectivity)—without lapsing into *Ungeist* or irrationalism. At this point it is important to recall Heidegger's indebtedness to Husserl, his former teacher and mentor, and particularly the latter's warnings against the perils of naturalism and historicism. Heidegger's departure, in *Being and Time* and later, from Husserl and transcendental idealism should by no means be construed (I believe) as a simple rejection of these warnings; differently put, the turn to being or the question of being must be read not as a lapse into objectivism but as an attempt to rethink the relationship between consciousness and phenomena, spirit and world. In this respect I am more hopeful than Derrida is when he links the dismissal of naturalism with the endorsement of *Geist* as transnatural spirit—seemingly despairing of any possibility to transcend this bifurcation. In my view, these alternatives are not compelling or conclusive. On the contrary: precisely the effort to rethink mind-matter, spirit-nature dualisms rules out the option

---

[35] Heidegger, *Hölderlins Hymne "Der Ister,"* pp. 66, 157–164. Actually, Heidegger uses *Geist* in these passages with and without quotation marks (virtually interchangeably).

for one of the paired terms. Post-metaphysical thinking in Heidegger's sense cannot possibly subscribe to naturalism or biologism, because the latter depend on intellect as their correlate. Translated into political terms this means that the critique of modern ideologies (deriving from metaphysics) cannot possibly entail support for Hitlerism or National Socialism or any kind of naturalist politics (treating nature or human nature as given). This may well be the most urgent lesson or learning experience to be drawn from *l'affaire* Heidegger.

This learning experience, in any event, is my central concern in the present pages. Safely ensconced in a given ideology, contemporary readers may consider themselves above political learning—thereby mistaking (I am afraid) both their own condition and the point of *l'affaire* Heidegger. For Heidegger, the Weimar and Hitler years were bound to be a time of agonizing soul-searching. Reared in a Eurocentric (and perhaps Germanocentric) culture, he must have been deeply unsettled and disoriented by the crisis and progressive decentering of Europe. His initial response was a rallying call—a call for the resurgence of the *Geist* of Europe, for the reassertion of European hegemony in a manner that might tip the scales in the ongoing struggle for world dominion. Only slowly did he realize the futility of this pursuit.

The reason for this futility was not only Hitler's thoroughgoing perversion of the European spirit (although this was a major factor); the root lay deeper, in the basic incompatibility of *Geist* (in whatever sense) with the striving for power or world dominion. Progressively, in his lectures on Hölderlin, Schelling, and Nietzsche, Heidegger turned away from the concern with resurgence or hegemony toward an acceptance of the disempowerment of spirit—not only as an external calamity but as the proper, indigenous path of spirit. In doing so, he parted company with the long-standing preoccupation of Western thought with rule and dominion and particularly with the spirit's right to rule (epitomized in the Platonic philosopher-king). Only by abandoning the right to rule, by enduring dispersal and submission—he slowly came to realize—could spirit of any kind be salvaged and subsist as a generous source of human empowerment. Given his initial trust in leadership (particularly his own), this realization no doubt was for Heidegger a painful rupture or reorientation, something akin to *metanoia* or else to the internal "highway of despair" described in Hegel's *Phenomenology*. In fact, this rupture is one of the chief meanings one can give to the much discussed "turning" (*Kehre*) Heidegger underwent during these years.

Far from being a merely idiosyncratic feature, this turning has general significance—particularly if profiled against the struggle for world dominion. Given the prospect of world conflagration (through a technological Armageddon), are there not ample motives for such a turning from rule or mastery—and is such turning not bound to be painful for those willing to undergo it? In my view, one of the most damaging effects of the polemical dismissal of Heidegger is the silencing or dismissal of the need for *Kehre* (as it is delineated in his opus). In Heidegger's work, the turning involved first of all a move away from anthropocentrism and a man-centered will to power, as it is reflected in global power politics and planetary technology. At a more concrete level, the turning involved a stand against the domestication of the earth, particularly under the auspices of a native or national culture. For Heidegger, the native culture was German, and he has often been accused of harboring an extreme nationalism. One should, however, recall that during the Nazi years Heidegger portrayed with growing intensity the homeland as a promised land at the distant horizon—far beyond the reach of managerial mastery. In his lectures on Hölderlin he contrasted German and Greek culture, assigning to the former the capacity for clarity and organization and to the latter the openness to the "fire from heaven." As he insisted, the task for Germans was not to be satisfied with their native endowment but to venture abroad, into the diaspora of spirit, as the only path for reaching something like home. Without departing from this insight, Heidegger subsequently expanded its horizons beyond the German-Greek encounter to the search for a new future—beyond morning-land and evening-land, Orient and Occident. Can we afford to silence this search, as an alternative to the quest for world dominion? If not, Hölderlin's "The Danube" (with Heidegger's comments) still bears pondering, particularly its opening lines: "Come now, fire! Anxious are we to see the day."[36]

---

[36] Ibid., pp. 6–9, 155–159. Also consider these comments in the lectures of 1941/42: "The own or proper cannot be proclaimed like a dogma whose dictates can be implemented on command. The own is something that is most difficult to find and most easy to miss." See Heidegger, *Hölderlins Hymne "Andenken,"* ed. Curd Ochwadt (*Gesamtausgabe*, Vol. 52; Frankfurt-Main: Klostermann, 1982), p. 123. Two years later, in 1943, Heidegger spoke openly of the importance of emigration and diaspora for homecoming; *Erläuterungen zu Hölderlins Dichtung*, pp. 29–30.

CHAPTER TWO

Rethinking the Political:
Some Heideggerian Contributions

What kind of political thinking is appropriate to our turbulent age? In comparison with the previous century—an era ruled by *pax Britannica* and various shades of utilitarianism—our age is marked by deep stirrings and epochal ruptures or, in academic terms, by paradigm shifts. Instead of fostering the cultivation of routine practices and orientations, such shifts mark exploratory ventures into new terrain, ventures guided by uncertain rules and fraught with uncommon risks.[1] These features are starkly evident in contemporary Western philosophy. Despite the flourishing of various "neo" movements, from neo-Kantianism to neo-Marxism, philosophical attention has tended to focus increasingly on the premises of such movements and, more generally, on the paradigmatic underpinnings of modern Western thought. Pursued on a broad scale, such inquiry has exposed the fragility of traditional conceptions of subjectivity seen as pillars of the modern "philosophy of consciousness," developments aggravated by the steady inroads of linguistic considerations into the hidden moorings of philosophical reflection. Apart from Ludwig Wittgenstein, no one has explored these paradigmatic upheavals

---

[1] The juxtaposition of paradigmatic and extraparadigmatic ages approximates Charles Péguy's distinction between historical "period" and "epoch"—about which Maurice Merleau-Ponty writes: "When one is living in what Péguy called an historical *period*, in which political man is content to administer a regime or an established law, one can hope for a history without violence. When one has the misfortune or the luck to live in an *epoch*, or one of those moments where the traditional ground of a nation or society crumbles and where, for better or worse, man himself must reconstruct human relations, then the liberty of each man is a mortal threat to the others and violence reappears." See Merleau-Ponty, *Humanism and Terror*, trans. John O'Neill (Boston: Beacon Press, 1969), p. xvii.

more resolutely than Martin Heidegger. From his early formulation of a hermeneutic ontology to his later writings on language and the *Ereignis*, Heidegger's opus revolves persistently about Western metaphysics and its possible overcoming—an effort which, far from yielding a new paradigm or fixed system of thought, seems forever under way or at the margin of established routines.

Similar shifts are occurring in contemporary politics and political theory. Despite the continuity of traditional political orientations or ideologies, a reassessment of these orientations is afoot (and has been for a while) which challenges both their self-understanding and their stable location in the customary left–right spectrum. As a sign of this reassessment, recent decades have seen the emergence (or reemergence) of a distinction within the notion of politics itself—that between politics as a regime or paradigmatic framework and politics as concrete decision-making and action orientation, or, more briefly, between politics seen as polity and as policy. Building mainly on German and French initiatives (and particularly on the differentiation between *la politique* and *le politique*), Ernst Vollrath has formulated the issue by juxtaposing politics (*die Politik*) and the political (*das Politische*), where the former refers to concrete decision-making and the second to "the sphere or realm of politics and the specific modality according to which we may speak of phenomena—events, persons, actions, institutions, etc.—as to their political quality."[2]

For purposes of the present chapter, I accept the distinction made by Vollrath and others, albeit with certain reservations. These reservations have to do mainly with the possible misconstrual of the distinction—its transformation into a rigid bifurcation between structure and superstructure, between foundation and derivations, or between noumenal and phenomenal spheres of analysis. More specifically, the reservations pro-

---

[2] Ernst Vollrath, "The 'Rational' and the 'Political': An Essay in the Semantics of Politics," *Philosophy and Social Criticism* 13 (1987): 19; see also his *Grundlegung einer philosophischen Theorie des Politischen* (Würzburg: Königshausen & Neumann, 1987), pp. 29–56. For a German precedent for the distinction, see Carl Schmitt, *The Concept of the Political* (1932), trans. George Schwab (New Brunswick, N.J.: Rutgers University Press, 1976); for French precedents, see Paul Ricoeur, "The Political Paradox," in *History and Truth*, trans. Charles A. Kelbley (Evanston, Ill.: Northwestern University Press, 1965), pp. 247–270); and Etienne Balibar, Luc Ferry, Ph. Lacoue-Labarthe, J.-F. Lyotard, and Jean-Luc Nancy, *Rejouer le politique* (Paris: Editions Galilée, 1981); and for American precedents, see Sheldon S. Wolin, *Politics and Vision: Continuity and Innovation in Western Political Thought* (Boston: Little, Brown, 1966), p. 43; and Hanna F. Pitkin, *Wittgenstein and Justice* (Berkeley: University of California Press, 1972), p. 215.

ceed from the focus of this chapter on Heidegger's thought and work. As can readily be seen, the distinction relates obliquely to Heidegger's notion of the ontic-ontological difference—but with the proviso that the ontic can never be a derivation or simple application of the ontological dimension.

Irrespective of such caveats (to be amplified later), the distinction between two aspects or levels of politics has relevance for Heidegger's own life and opus. It is my thesis here that Heidegger's promising contributions in this domain are located on the level of ontology, or paradigmatic framework, rather than on that of decision-making, or policy. Conversely, his role on the second plane is dismal, to the point of nearly eclipsing the rest of his work. By common consent (a view I share), Heidegger's entry into partisan-ideological policy-making at the beginning of the Hitler regime was an unmitigated disaster, one for which he offered few excuses and for which probably none can be offered. The literature dealing with this political debacle is by now legion—and I do not further augment this list, except to suggest that, at least in part, the debacle reflects Heidegger's own misconstrual of the ontic-ontological difference and its complexities.[3]

Without trying to belittle the gravity of his mistake, I concentrate here on the other political level, in an effort to uncover the contributions or suggestive clues Heidegger's work provides for a rethinking of the political, that is, for a reassessment of the very notion or meaning of political life. My accent is mainly on four topical areas: the status of the subject or individual as political agent; the character of the political community, that is, of the polity or (in modern terms) state; the issue of cultural and political development or modernization; and the problem of an emerging cosmopolis, or world order, beyond the confines of Western culture. In discussing these topics, I try to shield or disentangle Heidegger from possible misinterpretations; more important, I indicate how, in each area, his thought pointed in the direction of an overcoming of Western political metaphysics.

[3] There is some reason to believe that Heidegger mistook Nazism for an ontological or paradigmatic innovation, even though its chosen label (National Socialism) itself revealed its indebtedness to traditional partisan ideologies, namely, to nationalism or chauvinism and to socialism construed here as populism (a populism demagogically manipulated by a leader). For detailed studies of Heidegger's political debacle, see Victor Farias, *Heidegger and Nazism*, trans. Paul Burrell and Gabriel R. Ricci (Philadelphia: Temple University Press, 1989); and Hugo Ott, *Martin Heidegger: Unterwegs zu seiner Biographie* (Frankfurt-Main: Campus, 1988).

I

In the political domain, the linchpin of modern thought and action has undoubtedly been the individual seen as constitutive source of social life. Historically, this focus on the individual was a reaction against various forms of secular and religious authority (or authoritarianism) seeking to promote social and political conformism. In modern political theory, the focus surfaces prominently in the conception of the "state of nature" construed as an arena populated by isolated individuals facing each other in varying degrees of hostility. Against the backdrop of this presocial condition, government and political institutions were assumed to emerge through the medium of a social contract, a contractual conjunction of individual wills and preferences which by no means terminated individual agency. As formulated by modern liberalism, public life after the contract was preeminently the work of individual initiative, although this role was precariously shared during the nineteenth century by social groups (and even abrogated by social classes viewed as carriers of radical change).

Political conceptions of this kind were powerfully buttressed by parallel trends in modern philosophy and metaphysics. Proceeding from radical doubt, Cartesian rationalism postulated the *cogito* (or individual reason) as the sole warrant of epistemic knowledge and hence as the only reliable guide of human conduct. Continued by Enlightenment thought, the Cartesian postulate was elaborated and further refined by German idealism under the headings of "transcendental subjectivity" or "transcendental consciousness," labels designating foundational categories or pillars of metaphysical insight. In modified form, these notions were still operative as pillars in the work of Edmund Husserl, the founder of phenomenology and Heidegger's early teacher and mentor.[4]

Silhouetted against this modern paradigmatic background, Heidegger's opus signals a decisive break, a break with the constitutive role of the *cogito*. No doubt, steps in the direction of a decentering of the ego were at first halting and at least partially overshadowed by the continued influence of Kantian and Husserlian categories. Thus, existential analysis as presented in *Being and Time* was distantly comparable to a Kantian

[4] In large measure, the individualist outlook of modern rationalism was shared by modern empiricism with its focus on the individual organism as receptacle of sensations and stimuli. To the extent that it departed from the contractual model, empiricism placed the accent on individual socialization or habituation (or else on the deliberate engineering of social environments).

inquiry into the transcendental conditions of possibility (of thought and action). In his critical assessment of Heidegger's work, specifically its place in the "discourse of modernity," Jürgen Habermas has taken this distant resemblance as a vehicle for pronouncing a general indictment: the indictment of a relapse into subjectivism if not solipsism.

Although acknowledging Heidegger's "ontological turn," his turn to ontological "preunderstanding," Habermas finds his analysis guilty of succumbing again to "the conceptual constraints of subjective philosophizing: for the solipsistically construed *Dasein* reoccupies the position of transcendental subjectivity." By approximating *Dasein*'s existential possibilities to a Fichtean act of self-constitution, Habermas finds *Being and Time* to be ultimately in the cul-de-sac of subjectivity. Already flawed by their overly sweeping character, these charges can be readily rebutted. Habermas's indictment is based mainly on the section on the "who of *Dasein*," which disproves rather than supports his argument. As Heidegger points out in that section, the who of *Dasein* should by no means be simply equated with an ego or subject; on the contrary, he writes, ontological inquiry would normally reveal "that the 'who of everyday *Dasein*' is precisely *not* I myself" or the "ego of subjective acts." In *Being and Time*, *Dasein* or human existence is circumscribed as "being-in-the-world," where "world" means not only an empirical context but a lived horizon of modes of being. As a synonym for *Dasein*, being-in-the-world indicates "that there is not initially and not ever a mere subject or I without a world"—a situation that does not change in the case of "authentic" *Dasein*, which is distinguished only by its careful attention to world relations and modes of being.[5]

The nonsubjectivist (or nonegocentric) character of Heidegger's work is evident throughout. As is commonly acknowledged, *Being and Time* is concerned not so much or not primarily with human existence but rather with the question of being or the question of the meaning of being. The basic aim of the study is to make room for a renewed, explicit focus on

---

[5] See Martin Heidegger, *Sein und Zeit*, 11th ed. (Tübingen: Niemeyer, 1967), pp. 115–116 (par. 25); Jürgen Habermas, *The Philosophical Discourse of Modernity: Twelve Lectures*, trans. Frederick Lawrence (Cambridge: MIT Press, 1987), pp. 138–189, 148–152. For a fuller discussion of the section on the who of *Dasein* and of Habermas's critique, see Fred Dallmayr, "The Discourse of Modernity: Hegel, Nietzsche, Heidegger (and Habermas)," *Praxis International* 8 (1989): 377–406, and *Margins of Political Discourse* (Albany: SUNY Press, 1989), pp. 57–58, 60. For a detailed vindication of the nonsubjectivist character of *Being and Time*, see Friedrich-Wilhelm von Herrmann, *Subjekt und Dasein: Interpretationen zu "Sein und Zeit,"* 2d ed. (Frankfurt-Main: Klostermann, 1985).

this question; human *Dasein* is relevant as a gateway to this question chiefly because it is seen as the questioning agent or as the kind of being for whom being itself is at stake. In Heidegger's words: "Elaboration of the question of being means: rendering transparent one entity—the questioner—in his being. . . . That entity which each one of us is or represents and which includes questioning among its possibilities of being, we denote by the term '*Dasein*.'" As a gateway to being or to the question of being, *Dasein* cannot possibly be construed as a self-contained entity and particularly not as a synonym for "subjectivity"—a term deriving from the Latin *subjectum* (the Greek *hypokeimenon*) denoting an underlying foundation or pre-given substance.

Traditionally, Heidegger notes, concepts such as the "I" or the ego have been invoked to explain the coherence or selfsame identity of *Dasein;* the role assigned to these concepts was to serve as underlying ground (that is, as substance or subject). Far from being a reliable guide, however, traditional linguistic practice acted largely as an obstacle to philosophical analysis. One of the first tasks of such analysis, he adds,

> will be to demonstrate that any approach that starts from a pre-given I or subject completely misses the phenomenal content of *Dasein*. Ontologically speaking, every notion of subjectivity . . . continues and replicates the approach relying on the *subjectum* (or *hypokeimenon*), no matter how strenuously one may protest on an ontic level against the concept of "psychic substance" or the "reification of consciousness."

According to *Being and Time*, this verdict applies to the formulations of Descartes and Kant (and even, to some extent, of Husserl). Despite his radical ambitions, we read, Descartes failed to question the starting point of his argument, namely, the ego construed as thinking substance: "With the principle '*cogito sum*' Descartes claimed that he was putting philosophy on a new and secure footing"; but "what he left undetermined in this 'radical' departure was the mode of being of the *res cogitans* or (more precisely) the *meaning of being of the 'sum*.'" This deficiency continued in Kantian thought, despite its refinement of the transcendental premises of reflection. Like Descartes, Kant neglected to offer a "prior ontological analysis of the subjectivity of the subject"; while sharpening the idea of the *cogito*, he persisted "in treating the 'I' as a subject and thus in an ontologically inappropriate manner."[6]

[6] Heidegger, *Sein und Zeit*, pp. 2, 7 (par. 1), 46 (par. 10), 95–96 (par. 21), 318–320 (par. 64). For a fuller treatment of the divergence between *Dasein* and subjectivity in *Being and*

It would not be difficult to multiply passages from *Being and Time* which point in the same direction, an exercise I forego (my point here being simply the correction of a misinterpretation). From these early, occasionally ambivalent formulations, the decentering of subjectivity became a persistent and steadily deepening theme in Heidegger's evolving lifework. To illustrate this persistence I offer two examples, one from Heidegger's middle phase (roughly coinciding with the Nazi period) and the other from the postwar era. The first example is the magnum opus of Heidegger's mature years, the so-called *Beiträge zur Philosophie* (Contributions to Philosophy) of 1936–38. Among the many issues dealt with in this sprawling work, a central topic is the status and meaning of *Dasein*, now seen as participant in the ongoing disclosure and happening of being (a disclosure termed *Ereignis*).

As Heidegger recognizes, the notion of *Dasein* has undergone a profound transformation from its earlier usage in the context of Western metaphysics. In the context of that tradition, he states, *Dasein* was simply "the name for the mode or modality of the *actual* existence of a being and thus designated something like presentness-at-hand [*Vorhandensein*]"; in this sense it was possible to speak of the *Dasein* or actual presentness of objects, animals, plants, and humans. Heidegger's usage, by contrast, is radically different, so different in fact as to prevent a smooth transition or mediation of meanings. *Dasein*, he affirms in the *Beiträge*, "is not the mode of actuality of any being whatever; rather, it is the 'being of the there' [*das Sein des Da*] as such. The there [*Da*], however, means the openness of beings in their totality, the arena of the disclosure of truth (*aletheia*) in its originary sense." Differently phrased, *Dasein* is the kind of being in which being (transitively construed) permeates the spatial-temporal site of thereness; it is the happening of an openness, or "clearing," which simultaneously opens up the "self-concealment" of being and thus manifests ontological truth.[7]

Seen as participant in the happening of being, *Dasein* clearly cannot be equated with subjectivity or the ego in their modern metaphysical sense. The *Beiträge* explicitly underscores and intensifies the decentering of these concepts. As Heidegger indicates, *Being and Time* at least partially gave the *appearance* of fostering an "anthropological, subjectivist and

---

Time, see Fred Dallmayr, "Egology and *Being and Time*," in *Twilight of Subjectivity: Contributions to a Post-Individualist Theory of Politics* (Amherst: University of Massachusetts Press, 1981), pp. 56–64.

[7] Heidegger, *Beiträge zur Philosophie (Vom Ereignis)*, ed. Friedrich-Wilhelm von Herrmann (*Gesamtausgabe*, Vol. 65; Frankfurt-Main: Klostermann, 1989), pp. 295–296.

individualistic" approach; but in reality the aim of the work was the opposite—and this not fortuitously or accidentally but as a necessary corollary of its turn to the question of being construed as the basic question of philosophy. In linking *Dasein* with an ontological occurrence, the *Beiträge* renders the break with metaphysics still more evident and perspicacious. Elaborating on thereness (*Da*) as an open arena or spatial-temporal site of the contest between "earth and world," Heidegger insists that something like human selfhood can emerge only on this ontological site. Yet, selfhood is never an "I": instead, the self-relation of selfhood occurs only as "the intense-attentive acceptance of ontological appropria-tion [*Ereignung*]," and selfhood itself means "belonging to the intimacy of the contest seen as contest over appropriation." Heidegger's verdict regarding the ontological deficiency of foundational subjectivity carries over from the singular to the plural as well as to the correlates of "I" and "we": "Proceeding on its own, no correlation of 'I' and 'Thou' or of 'we' and 'you,' that is , no *community*, can ever reach the level of selfhood; instead, every correlation of this kind misses that level and remains excluded from it—unless it manages to ground itself first of all on *Dasein*."[8]

As my second example I choose the so-called *Zollikon Seminars*, a published volume containing transcripts of seminar sessions conducted by Heidegger with medically trained psychiatrists during the last two decades of his life. Among other things, the seminars again address the question of the status of *Dasein* in *Being and Time* and the difference between that work and earlier philosophy, including Husserl's phe-nomenology—a difference often surrounded by confusion (as shown in Habermas's assessment). The distinction of *Being and Time* from Hus-serl's phenomenology, Heidegger states, resides not in the elaboration of merely "ontic structures of *Dasein*" but rather in the fact "that human being is defined as *Dasein* and this explicitly in contrast to the defi-nitions of humanness in terms of subjectivity and of transcendental ego-consciousness." Existential analysis of *Dasein* does not rule out the dimension of consciousness, provided that the latter is not accorded foundational status. In modern philosophy, consciousness always means consciousness of something, a phrase that reveals the underlying subject-

<hr>

[8] Ibid., pp. 295, 322. The notion of the contest between earth and world contains an implicit reference to the argument in Heidegger's "The Origin of the Work of Art" (1935–36); see *Martin Heidegger: Basic Writings*, ed. David F. Krell (New York: Harper & Row, 1977), pp. 149–187.

object relation, the juxtaposition of consciousness and objects in the world. In the eighteenth century, Heidegger adds, the term "consciousness" acquired the theoretical meaning of a "relationship to the domain of empirical objects," a domain that for Kant was "nature seen as a realm of sense experience." Progressively, philosophy also came to talk of "pure consciousness," a phrase designating a mode of knowledge relating not only to sense perception but to the "conditions of possibility of sense experience" or of the "objectivity" of objects. In addition, consciousness was closely linked with self-consciousness in the sense of a (more or less distinct) awareness of an ego or "I" accompanying all acts of object cognition. In this manner, consciousness emerged as a foundational category of modern Western philosophy.[9]

In Heidegger's account, the modern fascination with ego consciousness was basically inaugurated by Descartes—an initiative which, though often rehearsed in textbooks, should give rise to puzzlement. "How did it happen," Heidegger asks, "that Descartes—such a sensible and rational thinker—should hit upon the strange theory that man exists first of all by himself without relation to things (and world)?" Even "my revered teacher Husserl," he adds, "still clung largely to this theory," although he moved intuitively beyond it. According to the *Zollikon Seminars*, Descartes's outlook was prompted both by historical circumstances and by the newly found prestige of science. Descartes's option, we read, arose from the dilemma of a thinker who "has ceased to accept the definition of his existence from faith, from the authority of the Bible or the church," and who, retreating into utter solitude, has need of a new philosophical anchor (a *fundamentum absolutum inconcussum*).

This search for a new anchor was aided by the rise of modern science with its reliance on conclusive self-certainty modeled on mathematical evidence. In this manner, Descartes arrived at his own mode of self-certainty—"the certainty of the *cogito sum:* I am as thinking substance." Since Descartes, human knowledge was construed basically as the perception and representation of external objects in the mind of the *cogito* or thinking ego; differently and more harshly formulated, modernity witnessed the "insurgency" and self-enthronement of human beings as constitutive "subjects." In contrast to this kind of epistemology (buttressed by modern metaphysics), the *Zollikon Seminars* counsels the approach of

[9] Heidegger, *Zollikoner Seminare*, ed. Medard Boss (Frankfurt-Main: Klostermann, 1987), pp. 156, 189–191.

ontological phenomenology familiar from *Being and Time*, that is, the approach of an intimate engagement of *Dasein* with being and the world (highlighted by the phrase "being-in-the-world"). To proceed along this path, Heidegger observes, we have to "free ourselves from the customary conception of a merely subjective representation of objects inside our heads" and have to "become engaged in the mode of *Dasein* we already are." We have to "deliberately perform this engagement [*Sicheinlassen*] in the mode of being that is ours."[10]

The political connotations of Heidegger's departure from subjectivity, seen as paradigmatic linchpin, are numerous and surface repeatedly in my subsequent discussions. At this point I simply note its implications for social and political agency, construed traditionally as individual or group activity. Paraphrased as being-in-the-world or as engagement in being, Heidegger's notion of *Dasein* challenges or decenters the customary focus of action theory on desire, will, or deliberate intentionality (a focus particularly prominent in Weberian sociology); instead, the accent is shifted to ontological participation in which the actor is released at least partially from the dictates of an instrumental pursuit of objectives. This shift, one should note, does not cancel action or remove moral-political responsibility, but it does highlight the complex preconditions of action beyond the confines of purposive goal attainment.

Clues pointing in this direction, the direction of a released or non-attached mode of activity, are contained in a dialogue Heidegger appended to his essay *Gelassenheit* (Releasement) of 1955. According to the dialogue, releasement is a willingness of *Dasein* to become engaged in a domain transgressing human will power, that is, in being or the happening of being (*Ereignis*). Countering the simple equation of releasement with inaction or passivity, the same dialogue insists that in traditional metaphysical terms released engagement occurs "outside the distinction between activity and passivity" and thus does not coincide with a weak permissiveness "allowing things to slide and drift along." In talking about these matters, Heidegger comments, the impression can easily be created that releasement "hovers in a realm of unreality and thus of nothingness" and that, devoid of any initiative, it implies a "spineless acceptance of everything and basically a denial of the will to live." This impression is, however, incorrect given the peculiar resoluteness of released engage-

---

[10] Ibid., pp. 129, 142–143. For a closer reading of *Zollikoner Seminare*, see Fred Dallmayr, "Heidegger and Psychotherapy," in *Between Freiburg and Frankfurt: Toward a Critical Ontology* (Amherst: University of Massachusetts Press, 1991), pp. 210–237.

ment, which remains distant from instrumental pursuits or ideological programs.[11]

II

Some of the issues raised in these comments become clearer once consideration turns to the second topical area—from subjectivity to intersubjectivity or, in Heidegger's language, from *Dasein* to *Mitsein* ("co-being," "being-with"). As in the case of subjectivity, this field is full of misinterpretation. In Habermas's critical assessment, it is entirely barren or unexplored in Heidegger's opus because of his subjectivist and even solipsistic moorings. Although recognizing that in *Being and Time* co-being is explicitly introduced as a constitutive trait of being-in-the-world, Habermas blames Heidegger for falling short of, or not coming to grips with, the "primacy of intersubjectivity"—a defect ultimately attributed to an outlook "held hostage to the solipsism of Husserlian phenomenology."

Elaborating on this shortcoming, Habermas finds parallel arguments between Heidegger and his former teacher: just as in Husserl's theory intersubjectivity appears as derivative accomplishment of subjectivity, or the "transcendental ego," so co-being in *Being and Time*, is said to be the outcome of the constitutive acts of subject-centered *Dasein*. Only at one point of his life is Heidegger credited with venturing on a different path—a path, however, he quickly abandoned again in favor of a relapse into solipsism (or else a retreat into mysticism). In his 1939 lectures on Nietzsche, Habermas reports, Heidegger in an "interesting chapter" voiced objection to the "monological" style of the philosophy of consciousness, but this time with explicit attention to the role of communicative understanding or agreement. Opposing a merely instrumental or calculating rationality, we read, Heidegger stressed "the non-strategic meaning of intersubjectively achieved agreement on which, indeed, the 'relationship to others, to things, and to oneself' is truly based"; he also seemed to recognize the importance of such consensus for social integration and the viability of social life. Unfortunately, however, this insight

[11] Heidegger, *Gelassenheit*, 6th ed. (Pfullingen: Neske, 1979), pp. 33, 57–58; trans. John M. Anderson and E. Hans Freund as *Discourse on Thinking* (New York: Harper & Row, 1966), pp. 61, 79–80. For an ontological reconsideration of action theory, see also Fred Dallmayr, "Praxis and Experience," in *Polis and Praxis: Exercises in Contemporary Political Theory* (Cambridge: MIT Press, 1984), pp. 47–76.

remained ineffective in Heidegger's later work. This ineffectiveness, Habermas concludes, can be explained only by the fact that, despite objections, Heidegger remained basically "caught in the problems that subject-centered philosophy (in the form of Husserlian phenomenology) had bequeathed to him."[12]

As before, the cogency of these arguments can readily be disproved by a closer look at Heidegger's lifework. Actually, in *Being and Time* such terms as "co-being" or "being-with" are used precisely to forestall the impression of a mere conjunction or juxtaposition of individual subjects (an impression still conveyed in such formulas as "intersubjectivity" or "intersubjectively achieved agreement"). In the section on the who of *Dasein*, the passage (previously cited) denying the existence of subjects without a world continues emphatically: "And in the same manner there finally exists just as little an isolated 'I' without the others." Elaborating on the notion of worldhood, the same section adds a bit later that world is "always a world already shared with others: thus the world of *Dasein* is a co-world; being-in signifies a co-being with others."

The difference from Husserl's "constitutive" approach emerges clearly in Heidegger's comments on empathy seen as a gateway to mutual understanding. In traditional usage (shared by Husserl), he notes, empathy is expected "to provide a bridge, as it were, from one's own subjectivity—which at first alone is given or available—to the initially concealed *alter ego*." In this manner, empathy involves an extension of the ego focus, more specifically, "a projection of the ego's self-reference onto an *alter ego*" by which the other is "a duplicate of the self." For Heidegger, however, this approach manifests a complete reversal of priorities, by neglecting the ontological structure of *Dasein:* "Empathy does not constitute co-being" but rather "arises on its basis." The importance of co-being persists even in that portion of *Being and Time* seemingly farthest removed from it, the sections on death or "being-toward-death." As critics have been quick to point out, Heidegger there speaks of the "nonrelational" character of death, of the fact that death "must be shouldered by *Dasein* alone" and lays claim to *Dasein* "in an individual manner." Yet, at a closer reading, "nonrelational" simply means that death is not transferable and that its inroad ultimately resists human (including cooperative) management. This aspect is underscored by Heidegger in an

[12] Habermas, *The Philosophical Discourse of Modernity*, pp. 136–139, 148–152 (translation slightly altered for purposes of clarity). The reference is to Heidegger, *Nietzsche* (Neske: Pfullingen, 1961), 1:578–580.

elaboration of the term "nonrelational." In the face of death, he writes, "the insufficiency of daily concerns and interhuman solicitude by no means signifies a removal of these modes of *Dasein* from authentic self-hood. As essential structures of *Dasein*, these modes are among the basic conditions of possibility of existence."[13]

With slight variations, concern with co-being permeates Heidegger's later writings as well. Although exhibiting strong Nietzschean over-tones, the *Beiträge zur Philosophie* reiterates the structural modalities of *Dasein*, including the dimension of co-being and solicitude for others. As in the previous context, *Dasein* is not equated with a *cogito* or ego con-sciousness but rather marked by care for or engagement in being. This engagement, in turn, can be more or less genuine or deliberate—a difference harkening back to the earlier distinction between authentic and inauthentic modes of human life. The more genuine the engage-ment, in any case, the more solidly grounded co-being and interhuman attentiveness. In Heidegger's words: "Only by coming into its own [or its selfhood] is *Dasein* sufficiently enabled truly to shoulder solicitude 'for others.' Yet this coming-into-its-own never denotes an isolated ego con-ception but rather acceptance of one's belonging to the truth of being." According to the *Beiträge*, carelessness or lack of engagement fosters indifference, social conformism (the rule of *das Man*), and ultimately the "massification" of human existence. By contrast, genuine care prepares the groundwork for possibilities of undomesticated *Dasein* and of released or nonconformist modes of co-being. In discussing these possibilities, Heidegger speaks of the "impending ones" or "people of the future" (*die Zukünftigen*), those who plant the seeds for possible disclosures of being or its recovery from prevailing oblivion. In opposition to the noisy, domineering thrust of modern calculating rationality, these people are also called "the slow ones and slow-listening founders of the essence of truth," or else "strangers of evenly poised hearts" or "silent witnesses of the deepest silence in which truth is suddenly, imperceptibly restored to its being from the disarray of calculating correctness."[14]

With less Nietzschean élan, the *Zollikon Seminars* recapitulates and

---

[13] Heidegger, *Sein und Zeit*, pp. 115–116 (par. 25), 118, 124–125 (par. 26), 263 (par. 53). As Heidegger adds, "As nonrelational possibility, death individualizes; but, in light of its unsurpassable character [for each existence], it does so only in order to render *Dasein* as co-being sensitive for the others' potentiality for being" (p. 264). For a fuller discussion of co-being in *Being and Time*, see Fred Dallmayr, "Heidegger and Co-Being," in *Twilight of Subjectivity*, pp. 64–61.

[14] Heidegger, *Beiträge*, pp. 96, 320–321, 395.

partially reformulates the analysis of *Dasein* inaugurated in *Being and Time*. As in the latter work, Heidegger criticizes and rejects empathy as a mere extension of the ego focus. In line with Descartes, he states, the theory of empathy "postulates first of all an independently given ego that then places itself in the other's mind and so discovers that the other is a human being just like me, that is, an *alter ego*"; but this approach is a "pure construction." For Heidegger, the notion of relatedness, or inter-human relationship, is dubious and misleading because it suggests the "prior existence of two separate subjects that are then assumed to establish connections between ideas in their respective minds"—a construal that misses the dimension of engagement (*Sicheinlassen*) in genuine co-being. Even the "much-belabored" notion of the so-called "I-Thou" and "We" relationships is said to remain incomplete and on precarious ground, because it "still departs from a primarily isolated ego."

In contrast to these conceptions, the *Zollikon Seminars* reasserts the ontological primacy of being as reflected in the structural modalities of *Dasein*. What does "being together" with someone mean? Heidegger asks, and responds: "It means a co-being or being-with, that is, a co-existence in the mode of being-in-the-world, particularly with respect to a shared involvement with encountered phenomena." Given that every *Dasein* is a being-in-the-world, he adds, being together with someone necessarily means or implies a co-being-in-the-world; such co-being, however, does not involve a relationship of *Dasein* to another subject or *alter ego* but rather a joint placement in the "there," or the arena of "thereness." The commonality of *Dasein* is also evident in the shared character of culture and language, provided that the latter is not reduced to a mere medium of communication or information exchange. Once these points are properly taken into account, Heidegger emphasizes, *Being and Time* can no longer be misread egologically: "The analytics of *Dasein* has nothing whatever to do with solipsism or subjectivism."[15]

Viewed in light of these teachings, Heidegger's opus clearly departs from modern political metaphysics, particularly from the conception of an atomistic state of nature superseded by an artificially or contractually established civil bond. This conception, which held sway in political thought from Hobbes to utilitarianism, is undermined by the primacy

---

[15] Heidegger, *Zollikoner Seminare*, pp. 144–145, 151, 183. Regarding the linkage of co-being and language, Heidegger comments: "Language here is conceived not as a capacity of communication but as the originary disclosure of being, heeded by humans in different ways. . . . Insofar as we are dialogue [*Gespräch*, in Hölderlin's sense], human being implies co-being" (p. 183).

accorded to being and co-being. Actually, to return to a critical point, one might say that Habermas's outlook is much closer to traditional contractualism, especially with his emphasis on intersubjectively achieved agreement (and also on language as means of communication). While opposed to political atomism or radical individualism, Heidegger at the same time is averse to any type of collectivism, particularly since the latter is basically only a disguised subjectivism, a "subjectivism writ large" (with the collectivity replacing the individual as social-political agent).

Heidegger's *Letter on Humanism* of 1946 is explicit on this point. "Every nationalism," we read there, "is metaphysically an anthropologism and as such a subjectivism." Moreover, nationalism is not overcome or "humanized" by a bland internationalism, just as little "as individualism is overcome by an ahistorical collectivism"; for the latter is only "human subjectivity totalized." In view of its historical context—the heyday of the Nazi regime—the *Beiträge zur Philosophie* contains a particularly revealing and noteworthy passage relevant to the issue. Commenting on the obstinacy of egocentrism and its many disguises, Heidegger levels a frontal attack on populist nationalism. The most dangerous and obnoxious of these disguises, he writes, is that

> where the worldless ego has seemingly abandoned and surrendered itself to something else which is "greater" than it and into which it is fused as an integral part. The dissolution of the "I" into the "life" of the people involves an overcoming of the ego—but one that neglects the first precondition of such an overcoming, namely, reflection on selfhood and its essential being.[16]

Besides blatant or totalitarian forms of collectivism, Heideggerian co-being also deviates from subtler modes of holistic integration. Thus, Heidegger's outlook is scarcely compatible with compactly or substantively ethical lifeforms, as found, for example, in the ancient Greek *polis* (held together by a common *ethos*). More important, his view differs from newer and recent models of communitarianism, advanced as antidotes to social atomism and grounded either in the continuity of shared traditions or the unity of political goals. What these and related conceptions ignore is the dimension of negativity, of "nothingness," inherent in being, a dimension that necessarily infiltrates both human *Dasein* and co-being. From Heidegger's vantage, this negativity is a radical abyss that can

[16] Heidegger, *Über den Humanismus* (Frankfurt-Main: Klostermann, 1949), p. 28; *Letter on Humanism*, in *Martin Heidegger: Basic Writings*, p. 221; *Beiträge*, p. 321.

never be fully bridged by positive human arrangements, including social and political institutions.

In terms of human *Dasein*, the abyss effects a decentering of the ego, opening a level of selfhood inconsistent both with fixed self-identity and with pliant social conformism. As he writes in the *Beiträge zur Philosophie*, selfhood is "prior to I and Thou and We," which are derivative phenomena; as such, selfhood arises from the happening of being and more particularly from the agonal contest (*Streit*) between being and nothingness, presence and absence pervading that happening. Carried over to the domain of co-being, this view implies a form of interaction that resists management or manipulation and instead involves an attitude of reciprocal "letting-be"—which is not synonymous with indifference. In *Being and Time*, this attitude is strikingly captured in the notion of "anticipating-emancipatory solicitude" (*vorspringend-befreiende Fürsorge*), a solicitude that aids the other in pursuing his or her potential for being and nonbeing. In contrast to managerial ambitions, we read, "there is the possibility of a kind of solicitude which does not so much displace the other as anticipate his/her existential potentiality for being" and which "helps the other to become transparent in his/her care and to become *free for* it." Anticipation of being also includes anticipation of nonbeing, or death, an aspect that uniquely teaches *Dasein* the lesson "to let co-present others be."[17]

On the level of political institutions, Heidegger's thought is at odds with, or relates uneasily to, the structure of the modern state to the extent that the latter denotes a deliberately organized purposiveness or else a vehicle for collective management. The most elevated and philosophically demanding formulations of the modern state have undoubtedly been offered by Rousseau and Hegel, the former seeing the state as embodiment of the general will and the latter as actualization of reason or the "idea" (which is a synonym for actualized subjectivity). Yet, it is precisely the centrality of will and idea that has been rendered dubious by post-metaphysics. At a minimum, Heideggerian co-being invites a reassessment of the Hegelian (and Rousseauan) state.

Heidegger repeatedly provides clues for such a rethinking, particularly in his lectures on Hölderlin (offered during the war). Turning to the issue of political structure, he counsels against equating political life with the state as it has developed in the modern epoch. In lieu of such an

---

[17] Heidegger, *Sein und Zeit*, pp. 122 (par. 26), 298 (par. 60); *Beiträge*, pp. 320–321.

equation, he returns to the Greek notion of *polis*—but in a manner that radically transforms its meaning. In a subtle etymological twist, Heidegger refuses to identify *polis* either with state (*Staat*) or city-state (*Stadt*), preferring instead its translation as "place" or spatial-temporal "site" (*die Statt*), namely, as "site of the historical dwelling of man in the midst of being." Seen as such a dwelling place, *polis* is not a stable habitat or a positive-empirical arrangement but rather the arena of the perennial contest between being and nothingness, life and death—a rift that can be only partially remedied or domesticated by prevailing political structures. "Perhaps," Heidegger writes, "*polis* is the place and space around which everything that is questionable and undomesticated revolves in a preeminent sense. *Polis* then is *polos*, that is, the pole or vortex in which and around which everything turns."[18]

III

Critique of modern metaphysics (including political metaphysics) is linked in Heidegger's writings with a progressive "oblivion of being" and even an "abandonment by being" (*Seinsverlassenheit*)—a point that leads me to the third topical area: the assessment of Western modernity and of cultural and political modernization. More than any other, this topic is heavily clouded by misreadings and hostile recriminations. In attacking the centrality of the *cogito*, Heidegger is said to show his enmity to modern reason and to the rationalization of lifeforms deriving from the Enlightenment. The situation is aggravated by the close connection made in his work between modernity and the sway of science and technology, which exposes him to charges of antiscientific bias and even of antimodernism (that is, a hankering for premodern, purely agrarian conditions).

In Habermas's treatment, Heidegger together with Nietzsche opted to exit from modern reason or rationality instead of continuing and further refining the "discourse of modernity." Following in the footsteps of Nietzsche, he writes, Heidegger aimed to carry out "a radical critique of reason—one which attacks the roots of critique itself." In mounting this

---

[18] Heidegger, *Hölderlins Hymne "Der Ister,"* ed. Walter Biemel (*Gesamtausgabe*, Vol. 53; Frankfurt-Main: Klostermann, 1984), pp. 100–101. On the tradition of the modern state, see Fred Dallmayr, "Rethinking the Hegelian State," in *Margins of Political Discourse*, pp. 137–157.

attack, both Nietzsche and Heidegger were led to regress "behind the origins of Western history back to archaic times" in order to recover there "traces of Dionysian spirit" and thus to gain access to those "buried, rationalized-away experiences" that give meaning to abstract notions like (ontological) being. Moreover, regression in both instances was linked with utopianism, more particularly with a "Dionysian messianism"—as shown in Heidegger's expectation of a new "unconcealment" of being. In lieu of this "destruction" of Western rationalism and its history, Habermas himself offers a revamped evolutionary model which, while not embracing a simple theory of progress, portrays both individual and social development as an evolving and rationally "reconstructible" learning process.[19]

Again, Heidegger's own writings are the best resource for countering or at least sorting out such summary pronouncements. In my own view, his work gives evidence not so much of antiscientism or antimodernism as of an equilibrated stance that carefully weighs the advances and losses of modernity—in a manner not too dissimilar from Max Horkheimer and Theodor Adorno's *Dialectic of Enlightenment*. No doubt, at the center of Heidegger's critique of modernity, seen as a governing framework of social life, stands the issue of scientism and technology, particularly the sway of technological "enframing" (*Gestell*); yet, this sway for him is not simply an aberration or dismal mistake but rather a mode of ontological disclosure and challenge, a mode modern human beings cannot simply bypass but must confront and live through soberly and attentively.

The conception of technology not as a human instrument but as an ontological setting conditioning (or enframing) human life was first articulated in "The Question Concerning Technology," an essay written in the early postwar years. As its opening lines indicate, the question is not meant to conjure up an inescapable destiny controlling or subjugating human life but rather to initiate reflectively a "free relationship" to technology, a freedom achieved by opening *Dasein* to the "essence of technology." This essence, Heidegger emphasizes, cannot be found in

[19] Habermas, *The Philosophical Discourse of Modernity*, pp. 101–102, 104, 136. And consider this comment: "From this vantage Heidegger can so fundamentally de-struct modern reason that he no longer distinguishes between the universalistic contents of humanism, enlightenment, and even positivism, on the one side, and the particularistic, self-assertive conceptions of racism and nationalism, or of retrogressive typological doctrines *à la* Spengler and Jünger, on the other" (pp. 133–134). For Habermas's theory of individual and social development, see his *Communication and the Evolution of Society*, trans. Thomas McCarthy (Boston: Beacon Press, 1979).

utensils or a steadily multiplying gadgetry; nor does it consist in human fabrication by means of instruments. In lieu of instrumentalist or anthropocentric construals, the essay portrays technology as a mode of ontological "bringing-forth" (*poiesis*) and disclosure (*Entbergung*)—but a mode that peculiarly screens or hides being from view by seeking to control or manipulate everything encountered. "The disclosure operating in technology," we read, "involves a challenging [*Herausfordern*] which demands of nature to supply energy which can be extracted and stored as such." Differently phrased, technology challenges by "setting-upon" or enframing nature and world in order to transform everything into a usable resource—hence technology's essential trait of enframing.[20]

In issuing its challenge, however, technology sets not only upon the material environment but also upon human *Dasein*, which is normally seen as architect and master of technical designs. Enmeshed in technology's ontological framework, *Dasein* likewise becomes enframed, but not inexorably or without reprieve: given its intrinsic relationship to being (or to the question of being), *Dasein* can also relate to the concealing disclosure of technological enframing in a questioning mode, which is a gateway not to increased mastery but to ontological liberation. Although challenged and set upon by technology, and set upon "even more relentlessly than natural energies," Heidegger notes, *Dasein* is not utterly or necessarily reduced to a usable resource (or "standing reserve"). The reason resides in the noninstrumental character of technology's essence.

Despite its domineering and exploitative ambitions, technology still remains a mode of disclosure, of the happening of truth (*aletheia*)—with which *Dasein* dimly or clearly resonates. Not identical with fabrication, enframing shows itself as a happening or "mission" of being (*Geschick*), and some such kind of mission always holds sway over human life. Yet, Heidegger insists, this holding sway is "never a fate or destiny that compels; for, *Dasein* becomes truly free only insofar as it belongs to the realm of mission and thus becomes a listener [*Hörender*], though not one who simply submits [*Höriger*]." In terms of the essay, freedom does not merely reside in the exercise of will power or the initiation of causal chains; rather, it means attending to the openness of being, that is, to the happening of disclosure in its various forms. With regard to technology,

---

[20] Heidegger, "The Question Concerning Technology," in *Martin Heidegger: Basic Writings*, pp. 287–288, 294–298 (translation slightly altered for purposes of clarity). See also in this context Silvio Vietta, *Heideggers Kritik am Nationalsozialismus und an der Technik* (Heidelberg: Niemeyer, 1989); and Michael E. Zimmerman, *Heidegger's Confrontation with Modernity: Technology, Politics, Art* (Bloomington: Indiana University Press, 1990).

enframing as disclosure signifies something entirely different from "the frequently voiced notion that technology is the fate of our age (where 'fate' stands for the inescapability of an unalterable course)." Instead, we read, by attending to technology as enframing,

> we are already inhabiting the free space of a mission which by no means darkly compels us to push on blindly with technology (or, what is the same, to rebel helplessly against it and curse it as work of the devil). Quite the contrary: by opening ourselves to the *essence* of technology, we find ourselves unexpectedly addressed by a freeing claim.[21]

Freedom—not in the sense of freedom *from*, but of a free relation *to* technology—is not a foregone conclusion, however, only a possibility of modern and contemporary *Dasein*. Rephrasing the distinction between authentic and inauthentic modes of life, Heidegger acknowledges the alternative possibility that *Dasein* is increasingly absorbed or smothered by technological enframing and thus threatened to be reduced to a "standing reserve." In fact, Heidegger sees enframing as a danger to *Dasein*, and indeed as the preeminent danger in our time. This danger, he writes, manifests itself in two ways. In the first place, enframing pushes *Dasein* "to the very brink of the abyss, namely, to the point where itself will be taken or treated as a standing reserve." Ostensibly, this danger stands in contrast with the prevailing anthropocentrism in which man strikes the pose of "lord of the earth," pretending that everything exists only "due to human fabrication." In fact, however, this pose is pure delusion—because *Dasein* today "in truth nowhere encounters itself (in its essence)." The second, even more pernicious danger consists in the potential exclusiveness of enframing, that is, in its tendency "to eliminate or eradicate every other mode of disclosure," particularly nondomineering or nonenframing modes of "bringing-forth" (*poiesis*). By its challenging and enframing quality, technology threatens to set upon, overwhelm, or drive underground every nontechnological form of bringing-forth—ultimately "even disclosure as such seen as the happening of unconcealment or truth."

Although serious and deeply troubling, these two dangers are not ground for pessimistic despair. Heidegger now invokes Hölderlin: "But where danger is, there rescue grows"; rescue from enframing cannot come from outside our technological age (a regress to premodern, archaic times, as Habermas suggests) but only from a readiness to endure the predicaments of that age. In Heidegger's words, "Precisely the essence of technology must harbor in itself the growth of the rescuing or saving power." Thus, like technology itself, rescue is not simply a human enterprise or machination (although it cannot happen without human engagement). Precisely in enframing that threatens to engulf human freedom, he adds, "precisely in this extreme danger there arises also the innermost, indestructible bond of *Dasein* and the grant (of being)—provided that we, for our part, begin to heed the essence of technology."[22]

The inner bond of danger and rescue is also emphasized in "The Turning," an essay dating roughly from the same period. Turning (*Kehre*) is presented there as crucial possibility latent in the contemporary age of technology. As before, technology is not seen as a set of instrumental gadgets; nor, on the other hand, does it function as external destiny completely constraining human life. In differentiating technology from mere tools, Heidegger asks, does one have to conclude "that *Dasein* is helplessly subjected to technology for better or worse?" And he responds, "No, the opposite is the case; in fact, something more and entirely different is at issue." The difference derives from *Dasein*'s ontological potential, its status as gateway to being, which also allows access to enframing as a mode of disclosure. In terms of this essay, "turning" is basically a transformation of disclosure or ontological mission, namely, from a mode of oblivion and even self-refusal of being (*Verweigerung*) to a renewed revealment of truth. This change is not, however, preordained or automatic; it presupposes unflinching exposure to the stark reality of enframing and to the danger implicit in refusal. In Heidegger's words, presumably *this* turning can occur only once the danger lurking in our age is "first of all seen and recognized as danger." Turning in the sense of an overcoming of enframing is patterned here on the more general overcoming (*Überwindung*) of modern metaphysics, where overcoming is not an exiting from or leaping beyond but a mode of sustained experiencing and suffering through (*Verwindung*) which yields liberating recovery. "For this experiential overcoming of technology," we read, "human *Dasein* is definitely needed—but it is needed in an appropriate sense. It is the being of *Dasein* which has to open itself to the essence of technology—which means something entirely different from a mere affirmation and promotion of technology and its means."[23]

In more explicit fashion, the liberating quality of overcoming (*Verwin-*

[22] Ibid., pp. 307–308, 310, 313–314.
[23] Heidegger, "Die Kehre," in *Die Technik und die Kehre*, 2d ed. (Pfullingen: Neske, 1962), pp. 37–40.

dung) is delineated in *Gelassenheit*, written nearly a decade later; at the same time, the essay rejects any simple antiscientism or denigration of the technological age. At this point, the latter age is renamed the "atomic age"—the age marked by atomic energy and the atom bomb; atomic power, in turn, is traced to the unfolding of modern science and thus to the structural process of enframing whereby nature is transformed into "a gigantic power station, an energy source for modern technology and industry." The same development progressively sets upon and enframes human *Dasein* in the sense that, in all areas of life, "humans are encircled ever more tightly by the presence of technological gadgets and automata"; moreover, these gadgets and energies have long since "transgressed the range of human will power and capacity for decision," thus revealing themselves as parts of an ontological structure or matrix.

In *Gelassenheit*, these developments are again seen as harbingers of grave danger, mainly in two respects. First of all, technological enframing sets upon and undermines *Dasein*'s reflective questioning of being, in favor of a purely technical or calculating rationality. As Heidegger recognizes, both types of thought are important in different contexts; what is threatened in our time, however, is not calculation but reflectiveness or thought of being (*Andenken*). In addition, enframing erodes *Dasein*'s spatial-temporal location in being and world—that is, human rootedness or autochthony (*Bodenständigkeit*)—in favor of a general dispersal or dislocation. Again, rescue from these dangers can occur not through sublime neglect but only through sustained attentiveness to technological enframing, which reveals alternative modes of being and disclosure accessible through reflective questioning. "It would be foolish," Heidegger insists, "to attack technology blindly, and shortsighted to condemn it as work of the devil. For, we all depend on technical devices—which even challenge us to ever greater advances." Yet, in the midst of technological enframing, another possibility is latent: that of using technical devices without slavish attachment, of living with technology in a free or released manner. In this fashion, Heidegger says, our relation to enframing becomes simple and relaxed: "We allow technical devices to enter our daily life, and at the same time we leave them outside, that is, we let them be as things exerting no absolute claim." Heidegger calls this option "releasement toward things" (*Gelassenheit zu den Dingen*), an option that even carries the promise of a new autochthony, or dwelling place.[24]

---

[24] Heidegger, *Gelassenheit*, pp. 16–19, 22–24; *Discourse on Thinking*, pp. 49–51, 53–55.

IV

Sounding somewhat strange to our ears, terms like "releasement" and "nonattachment" carry a distinct resonance with Eastern thought (a point not underscored in Heidegger's essay). Actually, resonances of this kind were present in his work from the beginning. In questioning the *cogito* and seeking to overturn Western metaphysics, Heidegger moved imperceptibly in the direction of Eastern—particularly Japanese, Chinese, and Indian—philosophy, although the rapprochement surfaced only slowly in deliberate form. However slow and subdued in character, the rapprochement accounts in good measure for the warm reception accorded his writings in the non-Western world.

This reception deserves emphasis and elaboration, especially in view of another misreading that beleaguers his work. In presenting a *laudatio* for Hans-Georg Gadamer, Habermas credited the latter with the feat of "urbanizing" and thus civilizing the backward "provincialism" of Heidegger's opus. In accentuating dialogue and intersubjective understanding, he stated, Gadamer forged a path through which Heidegger's thought could be retrieved from its self-imposed cultural isolation. As it happens, this view was not quite shared by Gadamer himself, familiar as he was with the worldwide echoes and thus nonisolation (but not bland cosmopolitanism) of Heidegger's teachings. In a study devoted to Heidegger's complex "paths," Gadamer in fact praised his former teacher's far-flung impact, noting that "in order properly to assess Heidegger's presence one has to move to a global scale."[25] It is important here to stress the political implications. Given the critique of Western political metaphysics, Heidegger's teachings are significant for the future not just of local but of global politics, particularly in an age when non-Western countries and continents are emerging from the margins of history and beginning to challenge the predominance of Western (or Eurocentric) categories and institutions.

Although implicit in his earlier work, the topic of Eastern thought and

[25] Habermas, "Urbanisierung der Heideggerschen Provinz," in Habermas and Gadamer, *Das Erbe Hegels* (Frankfurt-Main: Suhrkamp, 1979), pp. 13–14; Hans-Georg Gadamer, *Heideggers Wege* (Tübingen: Mohr, 1983), p. 17. As Gadamer added: "Whether in America or the Far East, whether in India, Africa or Latin America—everywhere does one find the reflective impulses issuing from Heidegger. The global destiny of expanding technology and industry has been captured in his work; at the same time, the diversity and multivariety of the global heritage—crucial for the world dialogue of the future—have gained through him new reliance."

of the relation of East and West (in the sense of Orient and Occident) emerged steadily in Heidegger's postwar writings, first of all in the *Letter on Humanism*. In critiquing the centrality of the *cogito* and subjectivity, the letter sought to gain access to a more subdued or nondomineering type of humanism, one in which *Dasein* was poised attentively to the disclosures of being. As indicated, the critique of egocentrism was closely linked with the rejection of a self-contained nationalism or collectivism. Now Heidegger turns to Hölderlin's poem "Homecoming," whose title refers not to a simple geographic repatriation but rather to a renewal of ontological attentiveness.

In his poem, Heidegger comments, Hölderlin did not mean to invite the reader to retreat into "the egoism of his country or nation"; rather, the title refers to a reimmersion in the "ontological mission of the West or 'evening-land' [*Abendland*]." Yet, even the West was "not thought regionally as the Occident in contrast to the Orient, nor merely as Europe, but rather world-historically out of nearness to the source [of being]." As Heidegger adds, "We have still scarcely begun to reflect on the mysterious relation to the East which found expression in Hölderlin's poetry." Heidegger does not explore these mysterious relations further in the letter, except toward the very end when he briefly adumbrates the preconditions of such exploration. In seeking to transgress a geographic East–West confrontation in the direction of common origins, he suggests, thinking or reflection has to move beyond philosophy construed in the sense of Western metaphysics: "Thinking is on the descent into the poverty of its provisional being; it gathers language into a simple saying. In this way language is the language of being, as the clouds are the clouds of the sky."[26]

Roughly at the same time as the letter, Heidegger wrote a commentary on a fragment of Anaximander as part of his broader effort to recover the thought world of the pre-Socratics, a world antedating the rise of philosophy seen as metaphysics. This attempt, one should note, was prompted not by purely academic or antiquarian interest but rather by the possibility that earliest sayings might have an "impending" relevance for the future of humankind. In the commentary, this future is shown to hang in a perilous balance. As an outgrowth of Western metaphysics, Heidegger writes, humankind today is poised "to pounce on the entire earth and its atmosphere, to appropriate the hidden workings of nature in the form of energies, and to subjugate history to the planned order of a planetary government." As a result of this outlook, the world and all beings are "the

[26] Heidegger, *Über den Humanismus*, pp. 25–26, 47; *Letter on Humanism*, pp. 218, 242.

target of a single strategy of conquest"; by contrast, being as such in its simplicity "is buried in complete oblivion."

Dealing with the simple order of being, Anaximander's fragment could be the occasion for a rethinking of this situation, opening up the prospect of a different future. "Are we the late-born products of a history [of metaphysics]," Heidegger asks, "which is rapidly moving toward its conclusion by leveling everything into the steadily bleaker order of uniformity?" Or are we the early-born witnesses of an impending dawn after the night? As members of the West, the evening-land, are we stationed "in the evening of a night presaging another dawn? . . . Is the land of the evening perhaps only coming or dawning?" Sharpening and further deepening his questions, Heidegger adds: "Beyond Occident and Orient and transgressing Europe from within, is this evening-land perhaps the site of an impending, more originarily disclosed history? Are we who arc living today already Western or evening-people in the sense which dawns in our entry into the present night of the world?"[27]

The issue of an alternative global future remained a prominent theme in Heidegger's later writings and reflections. About a decade after the Anaximander commentary, the issue resurfaced again in the essay "On the Question of Being," initially titled "Over the Line." Taking his departure from the struggle for planetary dominion, a struggle proph-esied by Nietzsche and completely overshadowing our century, Heideg-ger pondered the possibility of a different "planetary thinking," one that would allow a global building and dwelling:

> No prophetic gifts or gestures are needed in order to realize that such global dwelling is going to face encounters for which the participants on neither side are at all prepared. This holds true for European language and in the same way for East-Asian language, and it holds true especially for the domain of their possible dialogue; for neither side can on its own constitute or inaugurate this domain.[28]

As it happens, Heidegger himself had a few years earlier ventured at least a few steps into this domain, in his "Dialogue on Language." In venturing in this direction, Heidegger was keenly aware (as was his

---

[27] Heidegger, "Der Spruch des Anaximander," in *Holzwege*, 4th ed. (Frankfurt-Main: Klostermann, 1963), pp. 300, 343; "The Anaximander Fragment," in *Early Greek Thinking*, trans. David F. Krell and Frank A. Capuzzi (New York: Harper & Row, 1975), pp. 17, 57.

[28] Heidegger, "Zur Seinsfrage" (1955), in *Wegmarken* (Frankfurt-Main: Klostermann, 1967), p. 252; *The Question of Being*, trans. William Kluback and Jean T. Wilde (New Haven, Conn.: College and University Press, 1958), p. 107.

Japanese interlocutor) of the pitfalls of such an undertaking: the absence of the rudiments of a common language. "I do not yet see," he observed, "whether what I try to delineate as essence of language *also* captures the essence of East-Asian language, whether in the end (which would be a beginning) the essence of language can be thought in a way which would make it possible for Western-European and East-Asian thought to enter into a dialogue nourished by and resonating with a common source"—a source "still hidden from both thought worlds." As Heidegger recognized, the venture was seriously obstructed by the progressive Westernization of the world, a process coupled with the rise of Western culture to a dominant position imperialistically imposed on other cultures. As in the case of technology and Western metaphysics, this process could not be obviated or overcome by fiat or a facile cult of exotic lifeforms. In lieu of both imperialism and a cultural leap, Heidegger for his own part preferred patient engagement with the heritage of Western culture, with the aim of testing and stretching its limits. As he stated in the *Spiegel* interview published after his death: "In my conviction, only the very site which nurtured the world of modern technology can prepare a change or turning of this world (which cannot happen through a simple reception of Zen Buddhism or other Eastern modes of life). . . . Thought can only be transformed by a thought proceeding from the same origin and orientation."[29]

In the meantime, Heidegger's foray into global dialogue is no longer a purely solitary venture; it has been joined by thinkers in many parts of the world. An example is J. L. Mehta, an Indian philosopher equally at home in Eastern and Western thought worlds. A close student of Heidegger, he accepts as given the relentless Westernization of the world which derives from the sway of science and technology. Together with the former, he sees Western metaphysics (dating back to the Greeks) as "pregnant with the entire development which, through its culmination in the scientific and technological mode of thinking dominating the man of today, has assumed a planetary importance, far exceeding the limits of a

[29] Heidegger, "Aus einem Gespräch von der Sprache," in *Unterwegs zur Sprache*, 3d ed. (Pfullingen: Neske, 1965), pp. 94, 103; "A Dialogue on Language," in *On the Way to Language*, trans. Peter D. Hertz and Joan Stambaugh (New York: Harper & Row, 1971), pp. 8, 15; "Nur noch ein Gott kann uns retten," *Der Spiegel* 30 (May 31, 1976): 214, 217; "Only a God Can Save Us Now," trans. David Schendler, in *Graduate Faculty Philosophy Journal* 6 (1977): 24. See also Heidegger, "Hölderlins Erde und Himmel" (1959), in *Erläuterungen zu Hölderlins Dichtung*, ed. Friedrich-Wilhelm von Herrmann (*Gesamtausgabe*, Vol. 4; Frankfurt-Main: Klostermann, 1981), pp. 176–178.

geographically or historically localized 'culture' or 'civilization.'" Following Heidegger, Mehta accepts the challenge of "belonging, irretrievably and inescapably, to this 'one world' of the *Gestell*"—but in the hope of an alternative global future: "There is no other way open, to us in the East, but to go along with this Europeanization and to go *through* it. Only through this voyage into the foreign and strange can we win back our own selfhood; here as elsewhere, the way to do what is closest to us is the longest way back."[30]

These comments are echoed in the writings of Keiji Nishitani, whose own thought tradition is Buddhism, particularly Zen Buddhism, with its emphasis on emptiness and radical doubt. As a member of the Kyoto School, Nishitani basically accepts the statement of his teacher Kitaro Nishida, who differentiated East and West in this manner: "In contradistinction to Western culture which considers form as existence and formation as good, the urge to see the form of the formless, and hear the sound of the soundless, lies at the foundation of Eastern culture." Yet, in line with Heidegger, Nishitani has exposed himself rigorously to Western culture, to the Westernization of the world—again, not in despairing submission but for the sake of initiating a global dialogue. "We Japanese," he writes, "have fallen heir to two completely different cultures. . . . This is a great privilege that Westerners do not share in; but at the same time this puts a heavy responsibility on our shoulders: to lay the foundations of thought for a world in the making, for a new world united beyond differences of East and West."[31]

[30] See J. L. Mehta, *Martin Heidegger: The Way and the Vision* (Honolulu: University of Hawaii Press, 1976), pp. 462–463, 466.

[31] Keiji Nishitani, ed., *Gendai Nippon no tetsugaku* [Philosophy in Contemporary Japan] (Kyoto: Yukonsha, 1967), pp. 2–4; Kitaro Nishida, *A Study of Good*, trans. V. H. Viglielmo (Tokyo: Japanese Government Printing Bureau, 1960), p. 211. See also Nishitani, *Religion and Nothingness*, trans. Jan Van Bragt (Berkeley: University of California Press, 1982), pp. xxv–xxviii; and Wilhelm Halbfass, *India and Europe: An Essay in Understanding* (Albany: SUNY Press, 1988), pp. 169, 440–442. As Halbfass observes: "In the modern planetary situation, Eastern and Western 'cultures' can no longer meet one another as equal partners. They meet *in* a Westernized world, under conditions shaped by Western ways of thinking" (pp. 440–441)—which conjures up the paradox of simultaneous globalization and parochialization. Echoing Heidegger, Halbfass opts for a nonparochial path: "We have to transcend 'what is European' ['*das Europäische*']; we have to reach 'beyond Occident and Orient.'" See also the thoughtful comments of Leo Strauss: "The West has first to recover within itself that which would make possible a meeting of West and East: its own deepest roots, which antedate its rationalism, which in a way antedate the separation of West and East." "An Introduction to Heideggerian Existentialism," in *The Rebirth of Classical Political Rationalism: An Introduction to the Thought of Leo Strauss*, ed. Thomas Pangle (Chicago: University of Chicago Press, 1989), p. 43.

The reference to Eastern culture, to the form of the formless and the sound of the soundless, leads me back to a distinction made at the beginning of these pages—the distinction between politics and the political. As I have tried to show, Heidegger's contributions to political thought reside basically on the paradigmatic level, the level of a reassessment of Western metaphysics, including Western political metaphysics. It is on this level, I have suggested, that the beginnings of a new global dialogue might emerge—one with clear implications for our contemporary planetary politics. Yet, despite this concrete relevance, paradigmatic reflection is peculiarly nonpractical in the sense of not being directly usable for partisan policies or designs. Differently put, politics as framework or regime is not a purely positive setting but one hovering on the boundary of being and nonbeing, of presence and absence, that is, on the gateway to the form of the formless and the sound of the soundless.

To this extent, such politics resists direct application—which means that, at least politically, there cannot be an "applied Heidegger." Wilhelm Halbfass is quite correct when he writes: "The enigmatic future 'dialogue' with the East, to which Heidegger refers, cannot be planned and organized. What we may have to learn above all is *Gelassenheit*, a serene willingness to wait, and *not* to plan for this future." Still, Heideggerian thought is not simply nonpolitical or beyond politics (in a transcendental and hence metaphysical sense). Instead, paradigmatic reflection infiltrates and pervades politics on all sides, but in an oblique and noninstrumental way; to this degree, it injects into politics a playful and liberating dimension, one particularly crucial in our age wedded to planetary planning and control. As Heidegger himself states in "The Turning," "Danger implies or yields rescue"; to rescue, however, is "to release, to set free, to liberate" as well as "to guard, to care for, to keep whole."[32]

[32] Heidegger, "Die Kehre," in *Die Technik und die Kehre*, p. 41; Halbfass, *India and Europe*, p. 170.

CHAPTER THREE

Post-metaphysical Politics:
Heidegger and Democracy?

Nicht mehr für Ohren . . .: Klang.
                                    —Rilke

Ours is an age of endings and beginnings. Contemporary literature is strewn with the vocabulary of departure from the past, departure commonly highlighted by the prefix "post-": from "postmodernism" and "post-metaphysics" to "post-foundationalism" and "post-history." Although these labels are fashionable, their meanings are elusive. Frequently the labels are treated as exit markers from the past, as signposts of a radical closure; hence such expressions as "end of metaphysics," "end of history," and even "end of man." With a slightly different accent, termination is seen as negation, antithesis, or reversal—with the result that post-metaphysics signals the lack or erasure of metaphysics, and post-foundationalism a leap into the abyss. Curiously, this array of endings is matched in our time by a new beginning or affirmation, particularly in the political domain. I am referring here to the upsurge of democracy and democratic institutions in recent years, an upsurge stretching from Latin America and parts of Africa to Eastern Europe, the former Soviet Union, and the Far East. How can one make sense of this conjuncture of farewells and new initiatives, of denials and dramatic endorsements? What passage subterraneously links these disparate events?

No single clue is likely to suffice to disentangle this puzzle. A major complicating factor is the ambivalent character of the democratic upsurge, an ambivalence equal to the ambivalence marking postmodernism and post-metaphysics. As it happens, "democracy" is easily one of the most slippery words in political terminology, notwithstanding its long tradition. For some time now, political theorists have been accustomed to differentiate and contrast several types of democracy; in particular, following C. B. Macpherson, we have learned to distinguish between a "liberal" and a more popular or "populist" variant—with the first type relegating democracy to a subsidiary adjunct of individual (possibly inegalitarian) rights, and the second type insisting on uniform (or egalitarian) popular rule.[1]

In the first type, democracy is subsidiary and elusive because private-individual rights may well concur with a monarchic regime. Matters are not, however, simplified or resolved in the second type. In line with classical teachings, democracy is frequently defined as the rule of "the people" or "the many"; but the meaning of such rule is baffling. Can the people or the many be given a uniform identity, can they be erected into a "subject writ large" capable of overarching and comprising the separate identities of individual citizens? Can the people exercise popular sovereignty in a manner akin to the sovereignty of kings? Quandaries of this kind have spawned a tendency, especially among postmodern writers, to reject the idea of popular rule as a feature of democracy and to equate the latter with a kind of anarchy or else with conflicting power strategies of competing political agents. Yet, how can the lack of rule be treated as a form of rule or regime and, in particular, how can democracy be said to reside in the nonpower or lack of power of an absent or nonexistent people? Alternatively, why should conflicting power strategies be seen as an emblem of democracy, and not rather as a synonym for civil war (possibly between contenders for a throne)?

By all accounts, then, the recent upsurge of democracy is the upsurge of a paradox, the upsurge of something that seems theoretically impossible while it is practically affirmed. This paradox surely deserves further inquiry. Conceivably (or so I claim) some headway can be made in this area by relying on the distinction between regime and agency or, to use a handy formula, between "polity" and "policy."[2] This distinction, I believe, has strong implications for democracy, implications differing from

[1] See C. B. Macpherson, *The Life and Times of Liberal Democracy* (Oxford: Oxford University Press, 1977).

[2] See in this context Paul Ricoeur, "The Political Paradox," in *History and Truth*, trans. Charles A. Kelbley (Evanston, Ill.: Northwestern University Press, 1965), pp. 247–270; also Fred Dallmayr, "Politics and Power: Ricoeur's Political Paradox Revisited," in *Meanings in Texts and Actions: Questioning Paul Ricoeur*, ed. David Klemm and William Schweiker (Charlottesville: University of Virginia Press, 1993), pp. 176–194.

those obtaining in other regimes. Postmodern writers are not mistaken in criticizing the notion of popular rule or sovereignty; but they are mistaken in deriving therefrom a simple absence of regime or else its submergence in policy contests. What needs to be grasped here, it seems to me, is a peculiar confluence of absence and presence, of revealment and seclusion: democracy is revealed or manifested in partisan policies and power struggles, activities that simultaneously conceal its status as regime.

In this chapter, I seek to explore this confluence by enlisting the aid of prominent political theorists and philosophers. In traditional political theory, the concepts of regime and sovereignty are closely linked with the notion of representation, the term taken in its metaphysical-transcendental sense. In the first section, I examine the issue of such a representation of regimes, particularly as this theme has been articulated in Eric Voegelin's *The New Science of Politics*. Voegelin's study does not address the question of democracy. To remedy this deficiency, I move to Claude Lefort, and chiefly to his *Democracy and Political Theory*, which broaches, without fully developing, the correlation of democracy and metaphysics or post-metaphysics. Finally, to deepen and corroborate Lefort's insights, I invoke the thought of Martin Heidegger, paying special attention to a work of his middle years, the *Beiträge zur Philosophie*. Given the character of regimes and their representation, readers will not be surprised to find that the arguments of all three authors carry theological-political overtones.

I

The notion of representation is frequently used in a narrowly circumscribed sense whereby it refers to electoral procedures and elective institutions as found chiefly in contemporary Western contexts; from a still more specialized vantage, the term serves to differentiate one type of modern democracy (the representative type) from other variants. What this focus neglects is the broad sweep of the notion in traditional political thought, a sweep evident in the ascription of representativeness to emperors and princes as well as to kingdoms and political regimes. It is one of Eric Voegelin's lasting merits to have reminded political theorists of this broader tradition and of what one may call the depth quality of the concept.

In large measure, Voegelin's *New Science of Politics* is a treatise on representation, more particularly on "representation and truth"—the title originally intended for the book—where "truth" does not have an epistemological but rather an ontological or metaphysical status. Without deprecating the role of electoral procedures—what Voegelin terms the "elemental" mode of representation—he places the accent squarely on meaning and symbolization, on the domains of existential experience and transcendental significance. In adopting this stance his book, at the time of its first publication, sounded a rallying call in an academic discipline threatened increasingly by scientistic myopia. The effects of this call continue to reverberate today—which does not place the text beyond deserved criticism. For one thing, one cannot ignore the frequent points of unevenness, above all a somewhat extreme or one-sided Augustinianism coupled with displays of non- or antipolitical bias (a bias jeopardizing the proffered "new" approach to politics). Voegelin's argument has in the meantime been augmented, modified, and partially corrected by numerous studies in this field, including Ernst Kantorowicz's magisterial *The King's Two Bodies*. Nonetheless, for purposes of general orientation and broad overview, *The New Science of Politics* still deserves a place of honor in recent theoretical literature.[3]

As indicated above, Voegelin's work focuses on the depth dimension of representation—in his language on its "existential" and "transcendental" modes. Whereas the first mode captures the inner meaning and self-understanding of a political community, the second relates this meaning to a transcendental referent. In each case, representation is closely linked with "articulation," the generation of public meaning or the constitution of society as a political entity. In the existential type, articulation leads to the emergence of a representative figure or institution embodying society's experiential *telos;* in the second type, this figure (and/or its public regime) is seen as representing a transhuman order or design. The two kinds of representation cannot be neatly distinguished; throughout the study, the two modes tend to intermingle—as Voegelin freely admits. The two senses of representation, he writes, "refer to aspects of one problem" insofar as "the existential representative of a society is its active leader in the representation of (transcendent) truth."

Regarding transcendental representation (or representation of truth),

[3] See Eric Voegelin, *The New Science of Politics: An Introduction* (Chicago: University of Chicago Press, 1952); also Ernst Kantorowicz, *The King's Two Bodies: A Study in Medieval Political Theology* (Princeton: Princeton University Press, 1957). For a review and assessment of Voegelin's later opus, see Fred Dallmayr, "Voegelin's Search for Order," in *Margins of Political Discourse* (Albany: SUNY Press, 1989), pp. 73–94.

Voegelin distinguishes three main variants, derived in each case from the specific kind of truth in question. Whereas "cosmological truth" originates in mythic accounts of the universe, "anthropological truth" is said to arise in classical Greece, with the discovery of the soul as the "sensorium of transcendence"; "soteriological truth," finally, is seen as the hallmark of Christianity with its stress on divine salvation (through Christ). The three variants reflect a crescendo or ascent of epiphany, but again their boundaries are blurred. The cosmological type stands relatively separate, but anthropological and soteriological truths tend to intersect because of ambivalences of the man-God correlation. Although treated as anthropological and hence not salvationist, Greek philosophy is said to find its measure or sensorium not in man as such but only in man viewed as "representative of divine truth"—an insight expressed in Plato's formula "God is the measure." Conversely, soteriology cannot abstract from the incarnate character of the Savior and hence cannot entirely dismiss an anthropological component.[4]

In Voegelin's account, cosmological representation, or representation of cosmic truth, was prevalent in preclassical and pre-Christian times in the empires of the Near and Far East. "All the early empires," he writes, "understood themselves as representatives of a transcendent order, of the order of the cosmos." Seen as cosmic analogues, empires were stand-ins for the divinely and mythically sanctioned pattern of the world, with the emperor or ruler representing "the transcendent power which maintains cosmic order." Voegelin refers in this context to the Persian Empire, especially the so-called Behistun Inscription, and also to an edict of the Mongol court which reads (in part): "God is high above all, He himself the immortal God, and on earth Genghis Khan is the only Lord." Features of this cosmic model were preserved in the Roman Empire, where the emperor long continued to serve as *pontifex maximus* of the official Roman cult; moreover, with the expansion of imperial rule, efforts were made to integrate diverse cults and religions into the worship of a supreme deity paralleling the supremacy of the emperor—an endeavor called syncretism or "summodeism." In the meantime, however, cosmological truth had already been challenged and undermined by

---

[4] Voegelin, *The New Science of Politics*, pp. 67–68, 75–77. As he states: "If now the Platonic terminology be adopted, one may say, therefore, that the anthropological principle in a theoretical interpretation of society requires the theological principle as its correlate. The validity of the standards developed by Plato and Aristotle depends on the conception of a man who can be the measure of society because God is the measure of his soul" (p. 70).

Greek philosophy with its accent on human reason and the soul as the locus of true order. For Greek thought, political society still had the character of an "ordered cosmion," but not at the neglect of the human; the *polis* henceforth was to be not only a "microcosmos" but also a "macranthropos." In Platonic theory, the *Republic* could serve as measuring rod of political communities or organized regimes because it reflected the true order of the soul, with the philosopher-king epitomizing this order and hence representing "the truth about human existence on the border of transcendence." Christianity further intensified the upward move toward transcendence while simultaneously emphasizing God's descent toward humankind—which is the heart of "soteriological truth."[5]

Under Christian auspices, the idea of a public representation of truth persisted in new guises, and this despite antipagan and even antimundane and antipolitical impulses (I return to this point shortly). Moves in this direction surfaced quickly during the period of syncretism. As Voegelin notes, the hope to link Christian faith with imperial summodeism "could be entertained with reason because it found support from a Christian tendency of interpreting the one God of Christianity in the direction of a metaphysical monotheism." Tendencies of this kind were shored up by the influx of Greek speculation into Christian faith, a mode of reasoning encapsulated in Aristotle's statement (in his *Metaphysics*) that "the rule of many is not good, one be the Lord." Voegelin alludes at this juncture to the pseudo-Aristotelian *De mundo*, a first-century text correlating imperial rule with divine world monarchy, and also to Philo Judaeus, who sought to erect Yahwe God into an imperial "king of kings" to whom all other gods would be subordinated as subrulers.

Following in these footsteps a few centuries later, Eusebius of Caesarea enlisted Christianity for representational purposes, by portraying Constantine's imperial rule as stand-in for the heavenly monarchy and the *pax Romana* as anticipative analogue of the kingdom of God. In Eusebius's view, the Roman emperor fittingly represented the one god who rules as "king in heaven" and who is also "the one *Nomos* and *Logos*." Representational speculation did not cease with the invasion and subjugation of Rome by Nordic invaders, whose tribal customs and traditions were replete with representational imagery. In Voegelin's words, "Throughout the historiography of the migration, from the fifth to the eighth centuries, the historical existence of a political society was consistently

[5] Ibid., pp. 54–58, 61, 67, 83, 96–98.

expressed in terms of acquisition, possession, or loss of the *rex*, of the royal representative. To be articulate for action meant to have a king." These leanings were given Christian blessing and sanctification with the instauration of the Holy Roman Empire under Othonian and Frankish kings, a structure whose continuity with the pagan empire was not radically broken by its system of dual representation anchored in emperor and pope. A more monistic solution was adopted in Byzantium, where the principle of caesaropapism enshrined the Eastern ruler as direct heir of pagan Rome.[6]

Voegelin's *New Science of Politics* does not closely examine medieval thought and practice. The book barely mentions the Holy Roman Empire; it gives little or no attention to Albertus, Thomas Aquinas, or other leading theologians. Instead, Voegelin focuses on Joachim of Flora, the twelfth-century monk, portrayed as the instigator of a sinister heresy which, over the course of subsequent centuries, encouraged a progressive "immanentization" of the divine. Curiously, this study extolling "transcendental" representation (as a mode of the representation of truth) treats Christianity as basically nonrepresentational or unrepresentable precisely because of its transcendentalism, a treatment that flies in the face both of historical evidence and of the close God-man relation ascribed to soteriological truth. The reason for this baffling procedure resides (as far as I can see) in an extreme Augustinianism, that is, in the endorsement of a two-world theory that radically separates church and *polis*, the city of God from the earthly city.

Voegelin stresses this separation repeatedly. "The truth of Christ," he asserts in the discussion of syncretism, "cannot be represented by the *imperium mundi* but only by the service of God. These are the beginnings of a theocratic conception of rulership in the strict sense," where theocracy means submission to the truth of God. This conception was fully articulated by Saint Augustine, for whom, Voegelin notes, "the order of human existence had already separated into the *civitas terrena* of profane history and the *civitas coelestis* of divine institution." Somewhat later, Voegelin ascribes to Christianity a "revolutionary substance" strictly opposed to worldliness or immanentism, a substance paving the way to an "uncompromising, radical de-divinization of the world." Augustine's view of the two cities, we are told, heralded "the end of political theology in orthodox Christianity. The spiritual destiny of man in the Christian sense cannot be represented on earth by the power organization of a

[6] Ibid., pp. 47, 102–104, 114.

political society; it can be represented only by the church. The sphere of power is radically de-divinized; it has become temporal."[7]

Although boldly stated, these assertions appear dubious—and hardly congruent with the book's representational argument. As can readily be seen, radical transcendentalism undermines the conception of political society as a "cosmion" illuminated inwardly by existential meaning; in doing so, the stance tends to rupture the linkage of existential and transcendental representation affirmed throughout the text. More important, Augustinian dualism jeopardizes the nexus of anthropological and soteriological truth, especially the "experience of mutuality in the relation with God" which is highlighted as "the specific difference of Christian truth." Still more crucial, dualism contradicts the historical record of Christianity's representational role, a role in no way diminished by the supernaturalism of grace or by trinitarian doctrines.[8] As is well known, Thomas Aquinas favored monarchic rule for both philosophical and theological reasons: such rule agreed with Aristotelian metaphysics (regarding a prime mover) and simultaneously provided an analogue to Christ's divine rule (in the unity of three persons). A generation later, Dante in his *De Monarchia* extolled the Holy Roman emperor of the time as *rex pacificus* and as stand-in for Christ's monarchy—even and precisely to the extent that imperial power could curb papal ambitions.

An invaluable aid in understanding representational issues during the late Middle Ages and early modernity is Ernst Kantorowicz's *The King's Two Bodies*. As Kantorowicz points out, the notion of the two natures of Christ (divine and human) gave rise in medieval times to a Christological concept of representation whereby the monarch was seen both as a natu-

---

[7] Ibid., pp. 85, 88, 100, 106. As Voegelin adds, through Christ "the grace of redemption had been bestowed on man; there would be no divinization of society beyond the pneumatic presence of Christ in his church. Jewish chiliasm was excluded along with polytheism, just as Jewish monotheism had been excluded along with pagan, metaphysical monotheism. This left the church as the universal spiritual organization of saints and sinners who professed faith in Christ, as the representative of the *civitas Dei* in history, as the flash of eternity into time" (p. 109).

[8] Ibid., p. 78. A main reason advanced by Voegelin for the unrepresentable character of Christianity is trinitarianism. As he writes: "With the full understanding of trinitarianism the constructions of the Eusebian type would be finished. . . . Christians believe in the triunity—and this triunity of God has no analogue in creation. The one person of an imperial monarch could not represent the triune divinity" (p. 105). This argument underplays the fact that, according to orthodox doctrine, triunity is still unity (one God in three persons). Moreover, there is no reason to assume that divine triunity cannot find analogues in creation. As Voegelin admits, Joachim's historical speculations were precisely inspired by trinitarianism.

ral or mortal person and as a supernatural or immortal ruler, a concept still reverberating distantly in Thomas Hobbes's phrase of the "mortal God." Kantorowicz's study also records the subtle evolution of representational symbolism in early modernity when the Christ-centered representation of truth was modified—without being completely displaced—by juridical, political, and humanist modes of articulation. In the course of this development, Christian imagery was amplified or reformulated with the help of different transcendental-universal categories such as the universalism of "law" or "right," the absolutism of sovereignty, and the revival of classical anthropology (or a metaphysics of man).[9]

The story of transcendental representation can and should be continued beyond Kantorowicz's work, through Reformation, Enlightenment, and Revolution. In a nutshell, the story would reveal a progressive shift in the locus of representation: first from king or emperor to king and parliament (or king and realm), and finally to the people or nation as such. *The New Science of Politics* offers only a few glimpses and is generally not helpful in regard to this relocation. The study refers briefly to developments in medical England after the Magna Carta when parliament was designated as the "common council" of the realm, supplementing royal authority. "The formula," Voegelin comments, "is characteristic for an epoch where two periods of social articulation meet. In a first phase the king alone is the representative of the realm. . . . In a second phase, communes within the realm, the shires, boroughs and cities, begin to articulate themselves to the point where they are capable of representing themselves for action." A bit later, Voegelin draws attention to Sir John Fortescue, who, at the time of Henry IV, eulogized England as a constitutionally ordered monarchy and who, significantly, transferred the Christian symbolism of the *corpus mysticum* to the political realm. In both instances, however, Voegelin makes no effort to draw out the broader consequences for the "representation of truth."

Clearly, the account would have to be pursued from Fortescue to Hobbes and Locke (who expanded the formula "king and parliament" to include the political community) to liberal Enlightenment thought and later revolutionary upheavals which installed the people as ultimate sovereign. Instead, Voegelin's study deteriorates into a general indictment of modernity, whose "essence" is said to reside in the "growth of

9 See Kantorowicz, *The King's Two Bodies*, pp. 87–97, 207–232, 451–495. See also Marc Bloch, *The Royal Touch: Sacred Monarchy and Scrofula in England and France*, trans. J. E. Anderson (London: Routledge & Kegan Paul, 1973).

gnosticism," that is, in the upsurge of the heretical doctrine inaugurated
by Joachim and aiming at the progressive immanentization of the divine
(or the "re-divinization of man and society"). The sweeping character of
this indictment is evident in the definition of the Reformation as "the
successful invasion of Western institutions by gnostic movements"; in the
depiction of English Puritanism as an instance of gnostic revolution
(largely on the testimony of the "judicious" Richard Hooker); and finally
in the portrayal of recent totalitarian regimes as displays of gnostic
triumphalism.[10]

In my own view, Voegelin's study goes astray here through over-
simplification (and an incipient religious fundamentalism). As it seems to
me, public or political representation is by no means alien to traditional
Christianity nor is it simply the outgrowth of Joachite heresy; by the
same token, modernity cannot simply be grasped as a secularization of
Christian faith (particularly of a heretical doctrine). Generally speaking,
the historical development from the Middle Ages to our time is both
more continuous and discontinuous than Voegelin's account suggests—
discontinuous with regard to the content of Christian symbolisms and
continuous with regard to the metaphysical representation of truth (or
the form of representation). A prominent example of this discontinuous
continuity is modern democracy with its tendency to ascribe representational truth to the people or the nation.

The New Science of Politics briefly alludes to this shift, stating that the
expansion of political articulation may reach the point at which society at
large becomes "representative of itself." At this juncture, Abraham Lin-
coln's formula "government of the people, by the people, for the people"
gains pertinence—where "people" signifies successively "the articulated
political society, its representative, and the membership that is bound by
the acts of the representative." Although promising, however, these
comments are not further developed—for a reason: the identification of
modernity with gnosticism overshadows the issue, preventing a clear
analysis of democracy's representational role. As it appears to me, the
chief obstacle to such an analysis resides in the book's attempted retrieval
of traditional symbolisms (and its castigation of opposing trends as heretical), a retrieval evident in Voegelin's counsel to students of politics to
rely preferably on "the methods of metaphysical speculation and theo-

---

[10] Voegelin, *The New Science of Politics*, pp. 38, 42–43, 107, 121, 126, 132, 134. In the
same vein, Hobbes is said to have outdone the gnostic immanentization by a "radical
immanence of existence which denied the eschaton" (p. 179). At one point in the course of
his indictment Voegelin notes disarmingly, "Obviously one cannot explain seven centuries
of intellectual history by stupidity and dishonesty" (p. 121).

logical symbolization." This outlook renders difficult access to modern and contemporary developments and particularly to a grasp of modern democracy in its relation to post-metaphysics.[11]

II

To get a closer look at modern democracy, we must leave Voegelin's *New Science of Politics* behind—though not forget it. Although restorative in many ways, this erudite discussion of the history of representational truth should be kept in mind, as it retains relevance, in a new guise, in democratic contexts. To explore this new guise, I turn now to Claude Lefort, the eminent French philosopher and political theorist whose work is significant particularly for its contributions to democratic theory. Scholarly as well as engaging, Lefort's writings are impressive for both their philosophical and their political acumen. A close associate of Maurice Merleau-Ponty, Lefort followed his friend's intellectual journey from a transcendental (or metaphysical) brand of phenomenology, inspired by Edmund Husserl, to an existential-ontological and finally to a post-ontological (or post-metaphysical) type of inquiry. At the same time, under the influence of both Merleau-Ponty and Hannah Arendt, Lefort mounted a rigorous critique of totalitarian regimes in favor of a steadily more profiled endorsement of an open-ended and nonfoundational conception of democracy. The formulation and development of this conception stretched over a series of publications, culminating in a set of essays collected under the title *Essais sur le politique* and translated into English as *Democracy and Political Theory*.[12] For purposes of brevity, I limit my comments here to this volume.

An important feature of *Democracy and Political Theory*, one highlighted in the French title, is the elaboration of a distinction prominent in recent Continental thought and closely linked with the tradition of representational truth: the distinction between "politics" (*la politique*) and "the political" (*le politique*), or between policy and polity. In this distinction, politics designates overt political activities and power strategies amenable to empirical research, whereas the political has a more elusive, quasi-

---

[11] Ibid., pp. 6, 40.

[12] Claude Lefort, *Democracy and Political Theory*, trans. David Macey (Minneapolis: University of Minnesota Press, 1988); the French original appeared as *Essais sur le politique* (Paris: Editions du Seuil, 1986). For an earlier work, see Lefort, *The Political Forms of Modern Society: Bureaucracy, Democracy, Totalitarianism*, ed. John B. Thompson (Cambridge: MIT Press, 1986).

transcendental or metaphysical status. Lefort's study is eloquent in out-
lining the gist of the difference. Contemporary political science and
political sociology tend to concentrate on manifest behavior, thus treating politics as an empirical object domain alongside other object domains
(like economics, education, or art). Seen from this vantage, political
phenomena appear as ready-made or immediately given data, amenable
to scientific analysis. What this approach neglects is the constituted
character of data—their insertion into frames of reference and particularly into the generative framework of the polity.

In contrast to empirical observation, inquiry into this framework is the
task of political philosophy and metaphysics. Philosophical inquiry of
this type, Lefort comments, raises the question "of the constitution of the
social space, of the *form* of society, of the essence of what was once termed
the 'city.' The political is thus revealed, not in what we call political
activity, but in the double movement whereby the mode of institution of
society appears and is obscured." Constitutive genesis in this context
involves both the assignment of meaning to political events (*mise en sens*)
and their staging in a public forum or social-political space (*mise en scène*).
In terms of the assignment of meaning, the polity emerges and unfolds as
"a space of intelligibility articulated in accordance with a specific mode of
distinguishing between the real and the imaginary, the true and the false,
the just and the unjust, the permissible and the forbidden, the normal
and the pathological." In terms of the stage metaphor, the polity can be
seen to contain within it "a quasi-representation of itself as being aris-
tocratic, monarchic, despotic, democratic or totalitarian." Differently
phrased, staging relates to modes of the representation of truth.[13]

Representation of this kind partakes in some fashion of a general or
universal quality, whereas empirical actions or events are located on the
level of particulars. In Lefort's view, attention to the political seen as a
constitutive framework or generative space-time schema is anchored in
philosophy's "oldest and most constant inspiration." Philosophers, he
notes, have always refused to "localize the political *in* society," that is, to
reduce it to empirical data while neglecting the constitutive "shaping"
(*mise en forme*) of political life manifested in the assignment of meaning
and staging in a public forum. As he adds, such a shaping of society not
only involves the discrimination between true and false, just and unjust,
but extends to the distinction between the visible and the invisible,
between presence and absence, being and nonbeing. To this extent,

---

[13] Lefort, *Democracy and Political Theory*, pp. 11–12.

inquiry into the political ultimately involves "an investigation into the world, into being as such."

According to *Democracy and Political Theory*, the neglect of generative frameworks is not restricted to empiricism or positivism but is shared by versions of traditional liberalism and radical conflict theories which postulate a prepolitical or extrapolitical space immune from constitutive shaping (something like a state of nature). The flaw of such approaches, however, is readily apparent: what they posit is intelligible only on the basis of what they deny. As Lefort observes, "If we grant to relations of production or the class struggle the status of reality, we forget that *social division* can only be defined . . . insofar as it represents an internal division, insofar as it represents a division within a single milieu, within one 'flesh' (to use Merleau-Ponty's expression)." This means that the terms of social conflict are governed by social relations which, in turn, are "determined by their common inscription within a shared space and testify to a common awareness of their inscription therein."[14]

In exploring the nexus of democracy and representational truth, Lefort takes *Democracy and Political Theory* through two steps: the first vindicates philosophy or metaphysics against a restrictive empiricism; the second challenges some of the assumptions of metaphysics itself. The vindication of philosophy goes hand in hand with a reconsideration and partial retrieval of political theology (which is the topic of an important chapter titled "Permanence of the Theologico-Political?"). In Lefort's account, the link between philosophy and religious thought resides in their common attention to symbolism and the generation of meaning. "Both the political and the religious," he writes, "bring philosophical thought face to face with the symbolic, not in the sense in which the social sciences understand that term, but in the sense that, through their internal articulations, both the political and the religious govern access to the world." As he acknowledges, modernity has witnessed a growing separation of philosophy and theology, and also of politics and religion, church and state—a rift seeking to relegate religion to the realm of purely

---

[14] Ibid., pp. 217–219. Traditional liberalism is more directly taken to task in the Introduction to the study, where, commenting on the waning of Marxism's popularity in France, Lefort writes: "But one wonders about the benefits of sophistication when it results in a restoration of rationalism combined with liberal humanism, in the willful ignorance of the latter's inability between the wars to understand the drama that was unfolding in the world, and in particular its inability to understand the depths from which the collective identifications and death wishes sprang, its inability to grasp the link between the unbridled pursuit of individualism and economic competition, on the one hand, and the attractions of communist or fascist collectivism, on the other" (p. 4).

private belief. From these developments, however, it would be quite illegitimate (in his view) to infer the simple disappearance or erasure of religion or its irrelevance to modern social contexts.

What this inference neglects is the depth dimension of political life, particularly the disclosure of truth on the level of the political—a disclosure crucial to political and philosophical reflection. "What philosophical thought strives to preserve," we read, "is the experience of a difference which goes beyond differences of opinion": namely, the experience of a difference "which is not at the disposal of human beings, whose advent does not take place *within* human history, and which cannot be abolished therein"; a difference "which relates human beings to their humanity, and which means that their humanity cannot be self-contained, that it cannot set its own limits, and that it cannot absorb its origins and ends into those limits." Both traditional philosophy and theology, in their distinct vocabularies, enunciate and preserve this difference from oblivion, thereby creating an open space for human thought and action: "Every religion states in its own way that human society can only open onto itself by being held in an opening it did not create. Philosophy says the same thing, but religion said it first (albeit in terms which philosophy cannot accept)."[15]

Philosophical and theological reflection are thus united in their attempt to articulate a space-time schema overarching and exceeding the empirical space-time coordinates in which concrete activities and events occur, that is, to thematize the "excess of being over appearance." Yet, vindication of this attempt is not synonymous for Lefort with acceptance of the specific terms of traditional formulations. Although modernity does not signal the end of religious symbolism, it does herald its withdrawal from a place of dominance to a more subterranean, oblique mode of implication. The clearest manifestation of this retreat is modern democracy in its connection with the political. According to Lefort, modern democracy "testifies to a highly specific shaping (*mise en forme*) of society," such that "we would try in vain to find models for it in the past, even though it is not without its heritage." The specificity of the democratic shaping is said to reside chiefly in the relocation of sovereign power

---

[15] Ibid., pp. 222–223. What philosophy cannot accept is the specific content of revelation, which does not affect the importance of revelation or disclosure as such: "To simplify the argument to extremes: what philosophical thought cannot adopt as its own, on pain of betraying its ideal of intelligibility, is the assertion that the man Jesus is the Son of God; what it must accept is the meaning of the advent of a representation of the *God-Man*, because it sees it as a change which creates humanity's opening onto itself, in both the senses in which we have defined it" (p. 223).

or the representation of truth—from a site of overt rule to an absent site (or a site of absent presence).

"Of all the regimes of which we know," Lefort asserts, modern democracy is "the only one to have represented power in such a way as to show that power is an *empty place* and to have maintained a gap between the symbolic and the real." Emptiness of this kind is indicated through a discourse that reveals "that power belongs to no one; that those who exercise power do not possess it; that they do not, indeed, embody it." But nonpossession or nonappropriation of power is not yet crucial for democracy's representational status. Such nonpossession still operates on the level of agency (or politics) rather than that of constitutive framework. In Lefort's words, nonpossession involves "the actors' self-representation, as they deny one another the right to take power." By contrast, reference to an empty space "eludes speech (or agency) insofar as it does not presuppose the existence of a community whose members discover themselves as subjects by the very fact of their being members"; it thus points to "a society without any positive determination, which cannot be represented by the figure of a community."[16]

Democracy's peculiar status acquires a distinct profile when compared to predemocratic regimes and forms of representation. *Democracy and Political Theory* draws attention to traditional monarchy, and particularly to monarchic rule of the ancien régime with its close linkage of throne and altar—a linkage testifying to the affinity between political thought and theology with regard to generative staging and the assignment of meaning. Originally developed in a theological-political matrix, Lefort notes, traditional monarchy gave the king sovereign power in a particular territory, making him both a secular agency and a representative of God. Sovereign power at this time was concretely visible and inscribed in the king's body (or rather, in the king's "two bodies"), which does not mean that the king held unlimited power or that his regime was necessarily despotic. Rather, the king was seen as "a mediator between mortals and gods or—as political activity became secularized and laicized—between mortals and the transcendental agencies represented by a sovereign Justice and a sovereign Reason."

As mediator between mortals and gods, the monarch also bridged worldly and otherworldly spheres, existential and transcendental modes of representation. The king's power, we read, pointed "towards an unconditional, otherworldly pole," while at the same time the king served, in his own person, as "the guarantor and representative of the

---

[16] Ibid., pp. 223–226.

unity of the kingdom." The kingdom itself was in fact represented as a body or substantial unity, such that "the hierarchy of its members, the distinction between ranks and orders appeared to rest upon an unconditional basis." Unified in the person of the king, royal representation provided a secure foundational warrant to established beliefs, customs, and practices. Seen from a theological-political vantage, monarchy functioned as "the guardian of the certainty which supports the experience of the world" and also as "the keeper of the law which finds its expression in social relations and which maintains their unity."[17]

In all these respects, democracy inaugurates a sharp break with the past and its conception of the political. What is radical and indeed unprecedented in modern democracy is its shift of sovereign power to an absent site, an empty place—a shift manifested on the level of politics in the perpetual contest (though a rule-governed contest) for power. In Lefort's words, the exercise of power in democracy is subject to "procedures of periodical redistributions," which implies an "institutionalization of conflict." Seen as an empty place, sovereign power cannot be occupied or embodied by any individual or group in society; more important, it cannot be overtly represented. What is visible are only the power strategies, the mechanisms of government, and the individuals or groups wielding political authority at a given time; but the unity or space-time framework of the polity remains hidden.

In contrast with traditional deprecations of disunity, modern democracy installs a regime that shows division to be "constitutive of the very unity of society"; in terms of political legitimacy, this regime involves a "legitimation of social conflict in all its forms" (or at least within certain rule-governed forms). Compared with earlier regimes, democracy in sum entails a kind of disembodiment or disincorporation, that is, the institution of a "society without a body" or of one that "undermines the representation of an organic totality." Together with traditional modes of embodiment (in princes or rulers), democracy also puts an end to existential-intellectual security, to foundational warrants of beliefs and actions. "In my view," Lefort states, "the important point is that democracy is instituted and sustained by the *dissolution of the markers of certainty*. It inaugurates a history in which people experience a fundamental indeterminacy as to the basis of power, law and knowledge, and as to the basis of relations between self and other, at every level of social life."[18]

---

[17] Ibid., pp. 16–17, 228. Most of the above passages are taken from a chapter titled "The Question of Democracy."

[18] Ibid., pp. 17–19. With regard to disembodiment or disincorporation, Lefort notes an

Disincorporation, to be sure, does not mean simply the end of representational symbolism or imagery—something contradicted by modern experience. Literally, democracy means "rule by the people," and the people in modern times are frequently identified with the nation or the nation-state—terms that suggest the presence of a sovereign power. The vanishing of bodily representation (by kings or princes), Lefort notes, leads to the emergence of new regimes in which the people, the nation, and the state take on the status of universal categories. What is crucial, however, is that neither of these categories represents "substantial beings or entities." In this context, the category of "the people" is particularly elusive. During the past century, democracy was closely linked to the establishment of universal suffrage, which was to ensure the expression of popular sovereignty or the popular will. Yet, precisely at the moment when popular sovereignty is assumed to manifest itself and the people to actualize its will—in general elections—precisely then "the citizen is abstracted from all the networks in which social life develops and becomes a mere statistic"; hence "number replaces substance." Thus, although one may grant that the people constitute a "pole of identity," expression of their will dissolves at the moment of electoral manifestation. Accordingly, rule by "the people" is inherently ambivalent: although power is exercised in their name and politicians constantly invoke them, "the identity of the people remains latent."

Similar considerations apply to the nation or nation-state, terms which, like "the people," depend on intrinsically multiple and diverse discursive articulations. Needless to say, efforts have not been lacking to transform all these categories into substantive entities and to endow them with the capacity for solid representation—and so we have the roots of modern totalitarianism. Thus, the idea of popular sovereignty has given rise to "the phantasy of the People-as-One," to the quest "for a substantial identity, for a body which is welded to its head, for an embodying power, for a state free from division." Typically what happens in totalitarianism (of the right or the left) is that a party arises and claims "to be by its very nature different from traditional parties, to represent the aspirations of the whole people, and to possess a legitimacy which places it above the law." At this point a "logic of identification" is set in motion which is also a logic of representational embodiment: the identity of the

---

intriguing parallel with the evolution of the thought of Maurice Merleau-Ponty: "A similar necessity led him to move from the idea of the body to the idea of the flesh and dispelled the attractions of the Communist model by allowing him to rediscover the indeterminacy of history and of the being of the social" (p. 20).

party and its leadership with the people generates the representation of "a homogeneous and self-transparent society, of a People-as-One."[19]

As one should note, however, the vice of totalitarianism is the monolithic streamlining of a category that is not simply vacuous: although ambivalent, "the people" is not merely a fiction or ploy of demagogues. The latter is the assumption of libertarians and radical anarchists. The difficulty of understanding democracy resides precisely in the need to grasp the people as an absent presence, that is, as neither a compact body nor a nullity. To treat democracy or the people as signs of a "pure illusion, as liberal thought encourages us to do," Lefort comments, "is to deny the very notion of (political) society, to erase both the question of sovereignty and that of the meaning of the institution, which are always bound up with the ultimate question of the legitimacy of that which exists." With this erasure, power vanishes as a broadly shared enabling potency and is reduced instead to an "instrumental function" or partisan strategy. More important, the view lends credence to a questionable realism whereby individual or group interests are assumed to exist as real outside any symbolic articulation or space-time framework.

Once the symbolic dimension is bracketed and democracy as a regime or polity is put aside entirely, we read, "a *de facto* conflict will appear throughout society," something resembling a Hobbesian state of war. Here, "the distinction between power as symbolic agency and power as real organ disappears," and the reference to an empty place "gives way to the unbearable image of a real vacuum." In this situation, democracy as a political regime is "put to the test of a collapse of legitimacy" because of the radical conflict between the interests of individuals, groups, or classes and "all the signs of the fragmentation of the social space." According to Lefort, a new specter emerges at this juncture, paralleling the specter of totalitarianism: if we adopt this negative vantage, he states, "we replace the fiction of unity-in-itself with that of a diversity-in-itself" (which is a new kind of totalism).[20]

---

[19] Ibid., pp. 13, 18–20, 230. As one may note, Lefort attributes the rise of totalitarianism to a spurious reembodiment or reincorporation and not, as Voegelin does, to a process of "re-divinization." The difference is alluded to in the text in this passage: "We should, of course, be careful not to reduce the totalitarian phenomenon to its religious aspects, as certain imprudent commentators have done" (p. 234).

[20] Ibid., pp. 232–233. The critique of unity-in-itself and diversity-in-itself is reminiscent of the dialectic of identity and difference or equality and liberty as outlined by Ernesto Laclau and Chantal Mouffe in *Hegemony and Socialist Strategy: Towards a Radical Democratic Politics*, trans. Winston Moore and Paul Cammack (London: Verso, 1985). For a critical review of this important study, see Fred Dallmayr, "Hegemony and Democracy: A Post-Hegelian Perspective," in *Margins of Political Discourse*, pp. 116–136.

Having outlined these dangers to democracy, Lefort returns to the issue of political philosophy or metaphysics and its relation to theology. In the face of modern democracy, political thought is caught on the horns of this dilemma: either it must reinvest democracy with traditional metaphysical symbolism, thereby obscuring its novelty, or else cancel all modes of symbolization, at the risk of ignoring the political (as generative space). As Lefort notes, the first alternative has been a pervasive temptation, perhaps because of a certain affinity of political theory with the (metaphysical) categories of unity, oneness, or synthesis. To exemplify this temptation, Lefort turns to the writings of Jules Michelet, especially his *La Révolution française*. Although an opponent of the ancien régime and a partisan of the Revolution, Michelet resolutely and enthusiastically transferred religious imagery of the past to the emerging popular government—and this while insisting on historical discontinuity between the political regimes.

In Lefort's words, Michelet reappropriated "the image of the king and the idea of the sovereignty of the One in order to celebrate the People, Spirit or Reason, and Justice or Right." Moreover, as a learned historian, he even adopted the notion of the king's "two bodies," by distinguishing between the mortal and immortal, temporal and transtemporal dimensions of the people. On the mundane, temporal level, the people are said to be fallible, divided, and often capricious; but in their transtemporal existence (manifest in the "general will"), they acquire their "true identity" and show themselves to be "infallible" and in possession of "an absolute right." In this capacity, the people occupy the position of the immortal king. The question Lefort raises at this point is whether this religious imagery is congruent with the experience of democracy, or whether such notions as the "royalty of the people" or "royalty of the spirit" are not secretly governed by a unitary metaphysics borrowed from the past. No doubt, after the Revolution, the people and the nation emerged as major reference points of social identity and political articulation. Yet, to assimilate these categories to traditional theology or metaphysics is to forget that the new identity remains at best a "floating representation" and hence "indefinable."[21]

Lefort does not sufficiently indicate how a post-metaphysical notion of democracy might be conceived and formulated and how, in turn, it might relate to theology—given the latter's nexus with symbolization. What is clear from his account is that "floating representation" does not simply mean a vacuum of representation and that "indefinability" does not

---

[21] Lefort, *Democracy and Political Theory*, pp. 232, 236, 240–241.

prevent articulation. He repeatedly opposes the "pure self-immanence" of society as an illusion because it obliterates the locus of meaning genesis (which in some sense was captured by religious thought). Beyond this acknowledgment, however, the text's guideposts are dim. "We must recognize," Lefort asserts toward the end, that "any move towards immanence is also a move towards transcendence," which seems to make room for transcendental representation even under democratic auspices, although such representation cannot be a bodily affirmation but only an emblem of "disincorporation" (or of an absent presence). Once unitary metaphysics and kinglike embodiment are eschewed, modern democracy gushes forth in its multiplicity and heterogeneity—relegating representation to a hidden or subterranean potency at best. So, Lefort queries,

> rather than seeing democracy as a new episode in the transfer of the religious into the political, should we not conclude that the old transfers from one register to the other were intended to insure the preservation of a *form* which has since been abolished, that the theological and the political became divorced, that a new experience of the institution of the social began to take shape, such that the religious is reactivated at the weak points of the social, that its efficacy is no longer symbolic but imaginary and that, ultimately, it is an expression of the unavoidable (and no doubt ontological) difficulty democracy has in reading its own story—and of the difficulty political or philosophical thought has in assuming, without making it a travesty, the tragedy of the modern condition?[22]

III

Lefort's somewhat enigmatic conclusion invites further inquiry. What is the fate of metaphysics in a time of post-metaphysics, and what happens to representation and symbolization under modern democratic auspices? To examine these matters more closely, I turn now to Heidegger. This move may seem strange and even frivolous or provocative to readers, given Heidegger's political reputation and the intense controversy surrounding his politics. In light of this debate and some of Heidegger's own assertions, my move is admittedly unorthodox, and certainly I do not take it lightly. There is, first of all, the record of Heidegger's explicitly

[22] Ibid., pp. 234, 254–255. As one may note, Laclau and Mouffe likewise oppose a complete "laicization" of politics, which does not mean an endorsement of traditional theology; see their *Hegemony and Socialist Thought*, pp. 190–191.

voiced reservations concerning democracy (in the *Spiegel* interview), in response to a question about the appropriate regime for our age. Yet, although disturbing, this response might conceivably have arisen from an identification of democracy with popular sovereignty (that is, with the kind of collective identity rendered dubious in our post-metaphysical time).

More damaging and problematic are some of Heidegger's pronouncements at the beginning of the Nazi regime, pronouncements that tended to endorse a militant populism and thus precisely a regime extolling the "People-as-One" as one with the party and its leader. Such statements were not restricted to nonacademic (and loosely phrased) speeches; they also surfaced in Heidegger's rectorial address of 1933, "The Self-Assertion of the German University," in which he exhorted "the people" to contribute to national resurgence through the services of labor, military training, and learning.[23] What encourages me to proceed, nonetheless, is the belief that populist nationalism of this kind had already suffered shipwreck in Heidegger's thought by 1934 (the time of his resignation from the rectorate), a shipwreck that in large measure undergirded his celebrated *Kehre* seen as both a philosophical and a political turning. My conviction is predicated on numerous lectures and treatises dating from the Nazi period. For purposes of illustration, I focus here on probably the major work of the period, a work bearing all the earmarks of a magnum opus: *Beiträge zur Philosophy*.

Considered in its social-historical context, Heidegger's *Beiträge* seems "out of season" (*unzeitgemäss*). Written at the time of nationalist triumphalism, the work exudes a somber and sobering mood, one completely out of touch with ideological fashion. Heidegger himself accentuates the different mood or texture of the work, where mood is not a psychological emotion or state of mind but rather an ontological tuning

[23] On the *Spiegel* interview of 1966, see "Only a God Can Save Us," trans. William J. Richardson, in Thomas Sheehan, ed., *Heidegger: The Man and the Thinker* (Chicago: Precedent, 1981), esp. p. 55; for the rectorial address, see Heidegger, "The Self-Assertion of the German University," trans. Karsten Harries, *Review of Metaphysics* 38 (1985): 470–480; and, for an instructive discussion of the address, see Graeme Nicholson, "The Politics of Heidegger's Rectorial Address," *Man and World* 20 (1987): 171–187. Heidegger's vulnerability to populism seems to be captured by Lefort, who offers an explanation "as to why so many contemporary philosophers—and by no means only minor figures—have become compromised in the adventure of Nazism, fascism or communism: the attachment to the religious which we noted earlier traps them in the illusion that unity and identity can be restored as such, and they see signs of its advent in the *union* of the social body." See Lefort, *Democracy and Political Theory*, p. 233.

(akin to a musical key). In the opening chapter of the book, titled "Preview" (*Vorblick*), he comments explicitly and in detail on the basic mood or tuning pervading the *Beiträge*—which, as a whole, is meant to prepare the groundwork for "another beginning" (*anderer Anfang*). As Heidegger states, every genuine mode of thought requires that its themes or insights be chiseled out of its basic tuning "as out of a granite block." The basic mood of the *Beiträge* is tentatively circumscribed by several terms: "awe" (*Erschrecken*), "reserve" (*Verhaltenheit*), "reticence" (*Scheu*), "premonition" (*Ahnung*), and "renunciation" (*Verzicht*).

Awe in this context corresponds to the wonder marking the inception of Greek philosophy; it stems from the perplexing realization that beings *are*—but at the same time that being itself has withdrawn from beings. Reserve is quiet composure in the face of this realization, hence the readiness to endure or remain attentive to being's withdrawal (or absent presence). Reserve is said to form the midpoint between awe and reticence, which is not so much shyness or bashfulness as the willingness to "let being be" in whatever mode it may happen or occur (particularly in the mode of absence or withdrawal). Premonition, or surmise, opens the view to the dimensions of disclosure and concealment, and specifically to the sense of being's withdrawal or its happening in the mode of refusal, or self-refusal (*Verweigerung*). Once being is seen to happen as or through refusal, a refusal heralding not a vacuum but an absent mode of presencing, then human acceptance of this refusal can only take the form of renunciation (which signals not rejection or indifference but a radical type of engagement). Viewed jointly, the various accents of the basic mood—but particularly reticence as its crucial key—are said to attune *Dasein* quietly to "the silence of the passover or passing-by of the last god."[24]

As can readily be seen, the basic mood of the *Beiträge* is far from triumphant exuberance; none of the terms circumscribing the mood are congruent with militant activism of any sort. Heidegger is keenly aware of this incongruence. As he notes, the opening of his book may easily lead to the misunderstanding that its basic tenor is one of cowardly weakness; this, indeed, would be the likely judgment of the noisy heroism of the time. In an age of a boisterously displayed optimism, talk of refusal or a withdrawal of being was bound to be denounced as pessimistic. Unper-

[24] Heidegger, *Beiträge zur Philosophie* (*Vom Ereignis*), ed. Friedrich-Wilhelm von Herrmann (*Gesamtausgabe*, Vol. 65; Frankfurt-Main: Klostermann, 1989), pp. 14–17, 21–22, 33–34.

turbed, the book pursues its course toward a new and different beginning of human thought and practice. If there is again to be a genuine history and style of human life, Heidegger writes (disregarding the *Reich* of a "thousand years"), then this can happen only as "the hidden history of the great stillness" in which being discloses itself in and through refusal. Thus, he adds, "the great stillness must first come over the world for the sake of the earth—a stillness which arises from silence which, in turn, proceeds from reticence." The opening chapter exacerbates the book's "untimely" character by portraying German contemporaries (*die Heutigen*) as hopelessly myopic and misguided. These contemporaries, we read, remain excluded from the genuine path of thought; they "seek refuge in 'trendy' doctrines and merely supply the staple of traditional school philosophy with a hitherto unknown decor by dressing it up in the mantle of 'politics' and 'racism.'" By contrast, Heidegger's inquiry is moved by a single or singular question—the only one worth asking but hardly trendy in character. The question regarding "the truth of being," he states, "is and remains *my* own question, and it is my *only* question for it concerns the *most singular* issue."[25]

The question regarding the truth of being is liable to be dismissed as empty or "useless chatter" in an age of maximized utility and growth of production, a time when beings or things are multiplied or amassed while being's absence is no longer even sensed as a deficiency. Heidegger speaks in this context of the "oblivion of being" (*Seinsvergessenheit*), an oblivion grounded in a more basic "abandonment of and by being" (*Seinsverlassenheit*). This abandonment—a major theme of the *Beiträge*— implies that being has withdrawn from (ontic) beings and has left them to their own devices, which means basically to the devices of human usage and manipulation; at the same time, it entails that being conceals itself in the overtness or manifestness of beings and that it assumes essentially the character of refusal, absence, or concealment.

The central issue at this juncture is whether concealment is synonymous with nothingness or nihilism or whether it serves as an invitation to a reticence honoring or respecting being's refusal. In our time, abandonment basically equals termination or cancellation. As indicated, beings or things are left to the devices of human manipulation or fabrication. Everything today, the *Beiträge* notes, appears "makeable" or "doable" given proper will power; seen as objects, beings are integrated as cogs into a grandiose scheme of instrumental production or technical

[25] Ibid., pp. 10, 14, 16, 18, 34.

busyness which Heidegger calls machination (*Machenschaft*, a precursor of the later *Gestell*). This machination triumphs in the preoccupation with calculation, speed (tempo), and massification (or mass production); it also surfaces in the "complete insensitivity" for the ambiguity of phenomena and in the glorification of seemingly solid or univocal entities such as folk, community, race, and nation. Ultimately, machination can trace its roots to traditional metaphysics and theology with their focus on a prime mover or God as maker of the world. In this tradition, we read,

> the cause-effect nexus becomes dominant (God as *causa sui*)—which signals a basic distancing from nature as *physis* and a move in the direction of *machination* as the central mark of beings in modern thought. Both mechanistic and biologistic construals are only derivations from an underlying model of machination.[26]

Of late, Heidegger observes, traditional metaphysics has progressively degenerated into ideologies or worldviews (*Weltanschauungen*) in which transworldly principles of the past are translated into cultural "values," political platforms, or "folkish" programs. This ideological turn means the decay of genuine philosophical thought. For, whereas the latter opens up new vistas and terrains, the former restricts and confines human experience; whereas philosophizing is a "constant beginning" and a process of self-transcendence, ideology always heralds a demise, most frequently a protracted demise. According to Heidegger, ideologies are an outgrowth of modern metaphysics and as such partake in, and even solidify, the relentless sway of machination. This is particularly true of totalitarianism or of totalizing types of worldviews. Such worldviews, Heidegger notes, necessarily lapse into a Manichean friend-foe mentality, by denigrating everything eluding their grasp as hostile, inferior, or decadent. Above all, the endeavor of total worldviews can never lead to self-transcendence, since this would undermine their totalizing claims; hence endeavor is from the very beginning replaced by machination or managerial busyness (*Betrieb*).

Among such totalizing claims, Heidegger singles out biological racism or racist elitism, that is, "the ascending predominance of the 'metaphysics' of Richard Wagner and Houston Chamberlain." A corollary of this ascendancy is the glorification of conflict, or struggle (*Kampf*, resonating with Hitler's *Mein Kampf*), a struggle waged for the sake of sheer

[26] Ibid., pp. 108, 111–112, 115–117, 120–122, 127.

self-preservation and self-enhancement in massive proportions and enlisting even "culture" and "worldview" as its supporting instruments.
What emerges at this point, we read, is the mutation of *Dasein* into
a "technicized animal" that seeks to compensate its waning instincts
through "giant technology." Heidegger also refers to the prospect of
"total mobilization" (a phrase coined by Ernst Jünger), portraying this
program as the triumph of pure activism and as the transformation of
everything in the world into a "standing reserve" for purposes of production and machination—hence as a glaring sign and consequence of radical ontological abandonment (*Seinsverlassenheit*).[27]

One of the many valuable features of the *Beiträge* is the discussion of
metaphysics and post-metaphysics in a manner that completely forestalls
a simple thesis-antithesis model. In Heidegger's treatment, "metaphysics" does not name an academic discipline or school doctrine but broadly
signifies a mode of thinking concentrated on the "beingness" (or essence)
of beings in their objective "presencing," or manifest self-presentation.
In this perspective, being as such is always reduced to beingness which,
as a generic or ideal category, permits the grasp and analysis of determi-
nate objects or beings; hence being is always placed "in the service of
beings." The entire history of metaphysics, accordingly, can be construed as the history of a certain question of being—but a question where
being is always considered "from the vantage of beings and for their
sake." In *Being and Time*, the notion of ontological difference had been
introduced to loosen the focus on generic, conceptual beingness and its
nexus with beings and thus to facilitate a new mode of thinking. As
Heidegger cautions, however, the notion must not be taken as a fixed
doctrine, because in this manner "difference" might still be construed
along metaphysical lines; rather, the central point is to see being itself as
difference (*Unterscheidung*): as the play of absence and presence, concealment and disclosure, and particularly as the generative potency letting
the difference happen (*Ereignis*).

According to the *Beiträge*, this mode of thinking about being heralds
the end, the overcoming, of metaphysics—but not in the sense of its
simple negation or cancellation. As Heidegger insists, talk about an end
of metaphysics must not lead to the mistaken view that philosophy is
now "done or finished" with metaphysics; instead, all metaphysical
teachings must be seriously examined and rethought, though with the
aim of a new beginning. All attempts that merely "react *against* meta-

[27] Ibid., pp. 24–25, 36–38, 40, 98, 143, 174.

physics," he writes, "remain in principle dependent on metaphysics and thus themselves part and parcel of metaphysics." This is particularly true of all kinds of naturalism and biologism that proclaim nature or the non-rational as the foundation engendering everything, as the "life-force [*Al-leben*] in which everything stirs." This problem besets even Nietzsche's focus on life and becoming seen as a flight from metaphysics, and particularly as a reversal of Platonism. For "every reversal is precisely a return and reinvolvement in metaphysical dualism (of sensual-supersensual domains)—a dualism Nietzsche keenly and boldly seeks to undermine."[28]

Instead of denoting a reversal, post-metaphysics as seen in the *Beiträge* involves attentiveness to being in its mode of concealment and withdrawal, that is, to being's refusal (*Verweigerung*). Such withdrawal is not synonymous with simple negativity or disappearance; rather, it testifies to the necessary implication of nonbeing in being (and being in nonbeing). "What if," Heidegger asks, "what if being is itself withdrawal that happens as refusal? Is the latter simply a nullity or not rather the highest or greatest gift?" For Heidegger, refusal is neither simply absence nor presence, "neither flight nor arrival," but rather "something primordial: the plenitude of the largesse of being in the mode of refusal." The happening of refusal occurs through concealment, which, however, is not merely a cover-up; rather, concealment is "the unconcealment or disclosure of refusal," a happening opening the gateway to the otherness or "strangeness of another beginning." Attentiveness to being's withdrawal is at the heart of the so-called turning to which the entire text is devoted and whose emblem is not reversal but the clearing (or present-absent space) needed by *Dasein* for its own self-discovery. In and through this clearing, *Dasein* opens and transgresses itself toward its need, which remains beyond appropriation or domestication.

As one should note, "turning" in this context does not in any way signify a turn toward a compact ontological doctrine or a unified system or synthesis, a move entirely blocked by being's refusal. In the *Beiträge*, Heidegger repeatedly polemicizes against the traditional metaphysical conception of beingness as a general essence or idea dominating and encompassing particular instances or entities. Being, we read at one point, does not mean the greatest possible generality or universality; rather, it occurs precisely as the "happening of singularity." Moreover, dislodged from the sway of metaphysical categories, being occurs as an intrinsic difference or rift (*Streit*)—the rift between presence and ab-

[28] Ibid., pp. 173, 182, 229, 423–424, 426, 466–468.

sence, disclosure and concealment, or between being and beings. Far from being reducible to negation or antithesis, this rift ultimately has its origin in the intimate entwinement (*Innigkeit*) of nonbeing with being—which, in turn, permits the latter's disclosure only through refusal.[29]

Although not a treatise on political philosophy, and certainly not one on democratic theory, the *Beiträge* provides many hints regarding the linkage of post-metaphysics and democracy. For Heidegger, the overcoming of metaphysics also implies the overcoming of "the people" or "folk" as a unitary metaphysical category. Repeatedly and emphatically, Heidegger speaks of the indeterminacy of talk about folk. "How does a people become a people?" he asks. "Does a people or folk only become what it already 'is' [as empirical entity]? If so, what *is* it then and how can this be known?" The question is analogous to the issue of human *Dasein* and its irreducibility to an empirical givenness. Just like individual *Dasein*, the folk in Heidegger's account is defined by, and can only come into its own, through self-transcendence (which precludes any kind of biological or racial determinism). In his words, "The nature of folk can be grasped only from the vantage of *Dasein*—which means that the existing folk can never be a goal or program" (a program that only replaces liberal individualism with a folkish collectivism). Only through self-transgression or openness toward difference can a people escape the danger "of becoming mired in itself and of idolizing the conditions of its existence as something absolute or unconditional."

These comments do not entail the simple elimination of a people as a reference point or public community; but instead of exerting dominance through popular sovereignty this community persists only as an absent presence or in the mode of refusal. According to the *Beiträge*, the nature of the people is its voice (*vox populi*). This voice is not, however, regularly reflected in public opinion; rather, it speaks in the language of silence and reticence. Heidegger appeals in this context to the "rare" and "impending" ones (*die Seltenen, die Zukünftigen*) who may still be able to listen to this language and perceive its cues. Hölderlin in particular is singled out as the "most impending or future" poet because of his most distant listening.[30]

By referring to the language of silence, Heidegger's comments on the people subtly shade over into a theological register (*vox populi vox Dei*), but in a completely new key. Given its present absence or its presence in

---

[29] Ibid., pp. 66, 241, 246, 264, 405, 407.
[30] Ibid., pp. 42, 50, 99, 319, 398, 401.

the mode of refusal, the people can no longer function as stand-in for a supreme power or deity, particularly for a "creator God" wielding sovereignty over the world. Heidegger's allusions to a "last god" or "gods" are predicated on the overcoming of traditional metaphysics, an overcoming intimately linked with the death of God (as creator God); to this extent, his comments stand completely outside the range of traditional theology. As he observes, the phrase regarding a "last god" remains outside the confines of such categories as monotheism, pantheism, and atheism; for "monotheism and all types of theism are anchored in Judeo-Christian 'apologetics' which, in turn, is grounded in metaphysics as its philosophical foundation."

The talk of a god or gods deliberately leaves open the issue of the oneness or plurality of the divine as well as its being status (or relation to being). The term "gods," we read, does not imply the assertion of the existence of a plurality of gods; rather, it highlights the "undecided character of the being of gods, whether there be one or many." This undecidedness also comprises the question "whether something like 'being' can at all be ascribed to gods without destroying the divine as such." Broadly, the term "gods" signals the undecided issue "whether a god— and which god—could yet become, in what manner, a basic need for what kind of human beings." The concluding chapter of the text contains a section titled "How Then the Gods?" (*Wie aber die Götter?*), indicating that they could not be topics of religion or targets of (theological) inquiry but at best partakers in the happening of being (and nonbeing), that is, in the happening of difference that discloses itself mainly in the language of silence. But where are there still ears to hear? In the words of that other distantly impending poet, Rilke, "No more for ears . . .: sound / Which, like a deeper ear, / Hears us, seeming hearers."[31]

Let us return now to the topic of democratic theory: Heidegger's argument is clearly opposed to any affirmative kind of popular sovereignty. As it seems to me, Heideggerian post-metaphysics forces democracy into a quandary, shows it to be caught in a dilemma that cannot be resolved in terms of traditional categories. At the beginning of this

[31] Ibid., pp. 411, 437, 508. See also *Rilke on Love and Other Difficulties*, ed. and trans. John J. L. Mood (New York: Norton, 1975), pp. 82–83. Rilke's poem continues: "Inversion of spaces. Sketch / of inner worlds out in the open . . . , / temples before their birth, / solution saturated with heavily / soluble gods. . . . : gong!" Viewed in the light of the *Beiträge*, Jean-Luc Marion—while accusing Heidegger of "ontologizing" the divine—implicitly or obliquely follows Heidegger's lead in his *God without Being*, trans. Thomas A. Carlson (Chicago: University of Chicago Press, 1991).

chapter I referred to the alternatives of liberal and popular democracy; both options, it has emerged, are embroiled in paradox. By relying on isolated individuals or groups, liberal democracy bypasses the issue of representation, of the *mise en forme* of the political, of the framework making politics possible in the first place. Popular democracy, by contrast, insists on such a framework; it even erects this framework—"the people"—into a unitary foundation and ultimate reservoir of meaning. In doing so, however, popular democracy neglects the fragility of this grounding, the elusiveness of "the people" as political community, the fact that democracy is erected on an "empty space," an "absent site."

Yet, as I have also indicated, absence of unitary power or sovereignty does not simply mean vacuum or sheer emptiness; absence still signals a space, a staging, though a peculiar one: an absent presence. Community of the people shows itself not (or not regularly) in overt rule but rather in the interstices of fragmentation, as the hidden backdrop of the antagonisms of modern society. Following Lefort, we may have to think not quite of an "inoperative community" but of something like a submerged or latent community. In Lefort's presentation, the advent of modern democracy is a "political event with a metaphysical significance: the collapse of an unconditional authority which, in one or another social context, *someone* could claim to embody." What needs to be realized, he says, is that in democracy "the idea of equality, of society, of humanity must remain latent if it is not to become a terrifying fiction" and that democracy "emerges from the coming together of multiple perspectives," of a multiplicity of differences whose unity remains elusive.[32]

---

[32] Lefort, *Democracy and Political Theory*, p. 178. On the notion of an "inoperative community" (*communauté désoeuvreé*), see Jean-Luc Nancy, *The Inoperative Community*, ed. Peter Connor, trans. Peter Connor, Lisa Garbus, Michael Holland, and Simona Sawhney (Minneapolis: University of Minnesota Press, 1991).

CHAPTER FOUR

Heidegger on
Ethics and Justice

Ethics has come into vogue again. After the long interlude of positivism and empiricism, attention has returned—at least in academic circles—to questions of moral rules and right conduct. Under the spell of the fact-value split the latter had been regarded simply as matters of emotive preference, but normative considerations have reemerged as legitimate topics of philosophical (and not merely psychological) inquiry. Still, although a welcome reaction to positivism, philosophy's return to ethics has not been a homecoming free of conflict: it has rekindled deep quandaries submerged throughout the positivistic reign.

Even a cursory glance at contemporary ethics shows a battleground of competing if not incompatible doctrines, most of which draw sustenance from strands of traditional metaphysics. Thus, according to one prominent doctrine, ethics basically coincides with the formulation of universal rules, rules that either are grounded in reason as such or else are derivable from argumentation in a universal discourse. Beholden in some manner to Kantian thought, this view clearly revives problems endemic to rationalist ethics: how can abstractly (or noumenally) conceived rules be at all relevant to concrete human practice? How can rules be transferred to specific instances without engendering an infinite regress of rules (for the application of rules)? In response to these dilemmas, another approach—sometimes styled "virtue ethics"—stresses character formation in concrete historical contexts or traditions, thus making moral conduct prominent. Yet, in the absence of a full restoration of Aristotelian or Thomistic metaphysics, the legitimacy of such contexts or traditions remains opaque. To bypass this restorative need, recourse is occasionally taken to nature and natural inclinations as a basis for a substantive (nonprocedural) ethics; but how can nature still be invoked in the face of its disenchantment by modern science? In an age of technology and scientific biology, how can we still do what "comes naturally"?[1]

Ethical doctrines thus abound (and continue to proliferate), but so do their intrinsic perplexities. In large measure, contemporary ethics resembles a confusing Babel of tongues, a fact lending support to ethical skepticism. In this chapter, I propose to turn for some guidance to Martin Heidegger's opus. This proposal, at first blush, is likely to seem odd or counterproductive. As is well known, Heidegger wrote nothing devoted specifically to questions of ethics, justice, or the like. On the contrary, his work is widely reputed to be rich in ontological speculation but entirely barren or unhelpful regarding moral conduct or social equity (this barrenness being perhaps the result of his speculative bent).

In part, this assessment seemed to be endorsed by Heidegger himself, particularly in his *Letter on Humanism*, in which ethics—or the demand to formulate an ethical theory—is specifically subordinated to the question of being. The situation is further complicated or aggravated (perhaps beyond remedy) by Heidegger's pro-Nazi sympathies at the beginning of the Hitler regime, a topic that dominates much of contemporary literature. According to some observers, these sympathies were not temporary but formed an integral staple of Heidegger's worldview for the rest of his life; although only incipiently present in his early writings, this ingredient emerged into full bloom in 1933 and subsequent years, irrespective of the so-called *Kehre* (turning) in his thought.[2] In view of the

---

[1] Major examples of a quasi-Kantian approach to ethics are John Rawls, *A Theory of Justice* (Cambridge: Harvard University Press, 1971); Alan Gewirth, *Reason and Morality* (Chicago: University of Chicago Press, 1978); and Jürgen Habermas, *Moral Consciousness and Communicative Action* (Cambridge: MIT Press, 1990). On virtue ethics, see especially Alasdair MacIntyre, *After Virtue*, 2d ed. (Notre Dame: University of Notre Dame Press, 1984). For a defense of a quasi-Aristotelian naturalism, see Michael Perry, *Morality, Politics, and Law* (New York: Oxford University Press, 1988). On the Habermasian model of discourse ethics, see Seyla Benhabib and Fred Dallmayr, eds., *The Communicative Ethics Controversy* (Cambridge: MIT Press, 1990). For a critical review of Gewirth (and Karl-Otto Apel), see Fred Dallmayr, "Ordinary Language and Ideal Speech," in *Twilight of Subjectivity* (Amherst: University of Massachusetts Press, 1981), pp. 220–254; for an assessment of MacIntyre's study, see Fred Dallmayr, "Virtue and Tradition," in *Critical Encounters* (Notre Dame: University of Notre Dame Press, 1987), pp. 183–208; and for a review of Perry's book, see Fred Dallmayr, "Nature and Community: Comments on Michael Perry," *Tulane Law Review* 63 (1989): 1405–1421.

[2] See in this context especially Victor Farias, *Heidegger and Nazism*, ed. Joseph Margolis and Tom Rockmore, trans. Paul Burrell and Gabriel R. Ricci (Philadelphia: Temple University Press, 1989); also Heinrich Ott, *Martin Heidegger: Unterwegs zu seiner Biographie* (Frankfurt-Main: Campus, 1988).

monstrous immorality and injustice of the Nazi regime, how can anything ethically instructive or salutary be expected from Heidegger's pen?
Given his embroilment with the Nazi regime, must his work not be
regarded as a seedbed of disease rather than a resource for ethical recovery or renovation?

Admittedly, this background threatens my proposed undertaking—
but it does not completely foil it. Being mindful of warnings may actually induce greater attentiveness to textual nuances, thus preventing
summary verdicts. For my own part, I have for some time been wary
of summary pronouncements, particularly the reduction of thought to
ideological slogans.[3] In Heidegger's case, my wariness has been steadily
deepened by the ongoing publication of his works, especially his lecture
courses and treatises dating from the Nazi period. As it seems to me,
these publications throw an entirely new and revealing light on the *Kehre*
in his thought—which, in turn, provides new guideposts for the reading
of both his earlier and his later texts. Most important for my undertaking, these writings show a growing alertness to ethical questions, where
ethics denotes not simply private morality but the broader arena of social
equity (a field traditionally thematized under the label "justice"). Again,
as previously indicated, my concern here is not with a full-fledged or formalized ethical theory, which Heidegger nowhere offered or attempted,
but rather with clues or suggestions for a transformative and nondomineering way of human life (including its social and political dimensions).

In the following pages I pursue these clues by concentrating on writings conceived during the phase of the *Kehre* (the Nazi period) and its
immediate aftermath. The first section takes its departure from the
magnum opus of that era, the *Beiträge zur Philosophie*, and next turns to a
lecture on Schelling offered at roughly the same time. Both texts adumbrate a vision of equity, articulated under the heading of "ontological
joining or juncture" (*Seinsfuge*), which then serves as a yardstick for the
distinction between good and evil. In the second section I consider an
essay of the early postwar period, the "Anaximander Fragment," in
which the notion of ontological joining is explicitly linked with the issues
of justice and injustice, of right (or righteous) and aberrant modes of life.
In a concluding section, I compare Heidegger's outlook with trends in
contemporary ethical theory, particularly recent post-structuralist initiatives, and assess its broader significance for social and political life.

[3] See Chapter 1 in this volume.

I

Contrary to his speculative reputation (and his own occasional disclaimers), Heidegger's entire opus is suffused with ethical preoccupations. Standing firmly opposed to scientific objectivism, his thought was necessarily led to undercut the positivist fact-value dichotomy and its attendant neglect of human conduct. Thanks to the publication of his early Freiburg and Marburg lectures, we now are familiar with his Aristotelian leanings at the time, particularly his retrieval of prudential judgment (or practical-contextual *phronesis*) as an antidote to abstractly scientific theory construction.[4] Although important as a gateway to later formulations, however, the long-term relevance of these leanings is rendered problematic by the programmatic destruction of Western metaphysics announced in *Being and Time*, a program that was bound to affect the metaphysical underpinnings of Aristotelian ethics.

In *Being and Time* itself, ethical considerations are manifested (or can be inferred) in such notions as resoluteness, authenticity, and the call of conscience—to say nothing of the role of care and solicitude seen as key emblems of human *Dasein*. Notions of this kind are frequently given a narrowly humanist or subjective-individualist reading, a construal that shortchanges the work's ontological thrust epitomized in *Dasein's* openness to being. Still, even when subjectivism is avoided, it is difficult to deny a certain existentialist flavor throughout *Being and Time* which tends to privilege individual decision or authenticity (and perhaps private morality) over concern for social and ontological equity.[5] In this respect, Heidegger's experience with the Nazis seemed to induce a rude awakening whose repercussions reverberated throughout all dimensions of his lifework. Without delving into biographical detail, the experience (I believe) furnished one of the motive forces triggering his much-discussed *Kehre*—which provisionally may be defined as a transformative move occurring simultaneously on philosophical and practical-social levels.

---

[4] Martin Heidegger, *Interpretationen zu Aristoteles: Einführung in die phänomenologische Forschung* (1921–22), ed. Walter Bröcker and Käte Bröcker-Oltmanns (*Gesamtausgabe*, Vol. 51; Frankfurt-Main: Klostermann, 1985); *Ontologie (Hermeneutik der Faktizität)* (1923), ed. Käte Bröcker-Oltmanns (*Gesamtausgabe*, Vol. 63; Frankfurt-Main: Klostermann, 1988).

[5] I am aware that Heidegger termed his analysis in *Being and Time* a descriptive (and not a normative) account; but clearly "description" here means not a positivist or empiricist description but a philosophical or ontological one (which transcends the fact-value split). For a critique of subjectivist readings of the text, see Friedrich-Wilhelm von Herrmann, *Subjekt und Dasein: Interpretationen zu "Sein und Zeit"* (Frankfurt-Main: Klostermann, 1974).

My ambition here is not to offer a comprehensive account of the *Kehre*, an exceedingly complex task that is perhaps still beyond reach (given the state of the *Gesamtausgabe*). For present purposes, I limit myself to a few selected works that illustrate the general direction of the transformation. No work is more suitable to this endeavor than the *Beiträge zur Philosophie*, a study comparable in weight to *Being and Time* and functioning as the crucial link between Heidegger's earlier and later phases. Written during the heyday of Nazi might and self-confidence (1936–38), the *Beiträge* is remarkably free of the ideological zeal marking its context. In fact, the entire study is a call away from dominant metaphysical or ideological formulas, and an invitation to a new and different beginning (*anderer Anfang*) for which its pages seek to prepare a tentative ground.

In sharp contrast to prevailing nationalist exuberance, the book persistently stresses a stark and sobering fact: the "abandonment of and by being" (*Seinsverlassenheit*) characterizing contemporary life, an abandonment nurtured in turn by a long-standing "oblivion of being" (*Seinsvergessenheit*). The basic mood or tuning pervading the study is a subdued sobriety befitting the situation of ontological withdrawal; preserving its subtle nuances, this mood is circumscribed variously by such terms as "awe" (*Erschrecken*), "reserve" (*Verhaltenheit*), "reticence" (*Scheu*), "premonition" (*Ahnung*), and "renunciation" (*Verzicht*)—although reserve is said to be the midpoint joining these terms together. As one should note, however, sobriety in the face of being's withdrawal does not simply signal despair or a leap into nihilism; on the contrary, far from betraying negativism, being reserved means recognizing or honoring being precisely in its mode of refusal (*Verweigerung*), that is, the intimate intertwining of being and nonbeing. According to the *Beiträge*, this recognition supplies the exit from traditional metaphysics (and its ideological offshoots) and the gateway to the new beginning, a gateway eluding human fabrication or control.[6]

It is precisely in exploring this shift that the *Beiträge* first introduces the notion of an ontological juncture (*Seinsfuge*). Basically, the broad move from metaphysics to post-metaphysics, from the "first" to the "other" beginning, is presented as a process of joining or rejoining or, in musical terms, as a fugue (*Fuge*) with interlacing parts and voices. According to to the study, there are four major parts, or "joints," constituting the *Seinsfuge* as it is experienced in our age: first, the "sounding" (*Anklang*),

---

[6] Heidegger, *Beiträge zur Philosophie (Vom Ereignis)*, ed. Friedrich-Wilhelm von Herrmann (*Gesamtausgabe*, Vol. 65; Frankfurt-Main: Klostermann, 1989), pp. 14–16, 20–22, 33–36.

which reveals being in its mode of absence; second, the "play" (*Zuspiel*), which alerts us to the tension between different beings; third, the "leap" (*Sprung*), which signals the exit from metaphysics; and fourth, the "grounding" (*Gründung*), *Dasein's* insertion into the happening of being and nonbeing. The last step, in Heidegger's portrayal, is chiefly the work of "impending" or "future-oriented" individuals (*die Zukünftigen*) whose thought is open to the distant echoes of a "last god."

As one should note and as Heidegger repeatedly emphasizes, *Seinsfuge* must not be confused with a totalizing system or framework, that is, with a structure encompassing a set of empirical elements (or subsystems). What prevents such totalization is the present-absent status of being, implicit in being's withdrawal, which entails that grounding is also an ungrounding and the leap also a leap into nonbeing, or the abyss (*Abgrund*). In terms of the *Beiträge*, being as displayed in *Seinsfuge* is not an entity or essence but rather a source of *agon*, or contest, between presence and absence, revealment and concealment—or else of the interplay of "world" and "earth." Regarding the ethical-political implications of *Seinsfuge*, the *Beiträge* tends to be parsimonious, except for some comments on power, violence, and authority. As a happening of being, we are told, *Seinsfuge* opens up a realm of freedom marked or buttressed by authority (*Herrschaft*), in the sense of an enabling potency. Sustained by such potency, this realm has no need of power and violence (*Gewalt*)—which, by contrast, are definitely required for the maintenance or alteration of empirical conditions under the aegis of human domination.[7]

In discussing *Seinsfuge* and its difference from "system," Heidegger explicitly alerts the reader to other writings of the same period in which the notion is more fully elaborated—particularly the lecture course of 1936 titled "Schelling: On the Essence of Human Freedom." Dealing with Schelling's conception of human freedom in all its dimensions, Heidegger there examines topics not directly relevant here, including the distinction between ontological freedom and the metaphysical doctrine of free will, and the relation between pantheism and fatalism (or unfreedom). For present purposes, the chief importance of the course resides in its endeavor to correlate *Seinsfuge* with the question of good and evil.

Following Schelling's transcendental-idealist vocabulary, Heidegger

---

[7] Ibid., pp. 9, 29, 65, 81–82, 282. On a strictly political level, the text actually contains numerous passages denouncing prevailing ideological beliefs, including the sway of biologism, racism, and folkish nationalism; see pp. 18–19, 61–62, 98–99, 143. (In the above, I ignore peculiarities of German spelling, e.g., *Seynsfuge* instead of *Seinsfuge*.)

portrays *Seinsfuge* as the intertwining of ground (*Grund*) and existence (*Existenz*), where "ground" signifies the dark embryonic latency of God or being and "existence" denotes God's fully developed and "spiritualized" manifestation in creation. Schelling himself designated the juncture as "difference" (*Unterscheidung*), a term that clearly anticipates and resonates with Heidegger's own notion of ontological difference, referring to the nexus of being and beings. Departing from a stable ontology of substances and also from Aristotle's view of a prime mover, Schelling (in his treatise on freedom of 1809) sought to grasp the dynamic differentiation in God and hence the temporal quality of the divine. In Heidegger's words:

> Schelling wants to accomplish precisely this: namely, to conceive God's self-development, that is, how God—not as an abstract concept but as living life—unfolds toward Himself. A *becoming* God then? Indeed. If God is the most real of all beings, then He must undergo the greatest and most difficult becoming; and this development must exhibit the farthest tension between its "where-from" and its "where-to."

The where-to is captured by the term "existence" construed as the stage of revealment or self-manifestation of the divine, and "ground" points to the stage of latent concealment and obscurity: "Seen as existence, God is the *absolute* God or simply God Himself. Viewed as the ground of His existence, God is not yet actually Himself. And yet: God 'is' also His ground." Differently put, ground is that in God which is "not God Himself but the ground for His self-being."[8]

In Schelling's account, ground and existence are not simply identical, nor are they fully divorced; rather, their juncture exhibits a unity in and through difference, that is, a togetherness in and through contest. Most important, ground and existence are not component parts of a system or entities that jointly would constitute "the thing called God." Ground is

---

[8] Heidegger, *Schelling: Vom Wesen der menschlichen Freiheit*, ed. Ingrid Schüssler (*Gesamtausgabe*, Vol. 42; Frankfurt-Main: Klostermann, 1988), pp. 190–191. An earlier edition of the lecture course appeared under the title *Schellings Abhandlung über das Wesen des menschlichen Freiheit*, ed. Hildegard Feick (Tübingen: Niemeyer, 1971); for an English translation of that edition, see *Schelling's Treatise on the Essence of Human Freedom*, trans. Joan Stambaugh (Athens: Ohio University Press, 1985). I have consulted the English translation, but I follow the text of the Feick edition and often substitute my own translation. For a brief summary of the lecture course, see Fred Dallmayr, "Heidegger's Ontology of Freedom," in *Polis and Praxis* (Cambridge: MIT Press, 1984), pp. 121–127. See also Parvis Emad, "Heidegger on Schelling's Conception of Freedom," *Man and World* 8 (1975): 152–174: and Michael G. Vater, "Heidegger and Schelling: The Finitude of Being," *Idealistic Studies* 5 (1975): 20–58.

the latency or not-yet-being of God and thus harbors in itself a "not" or "nonbeing," which resists integration into a synthesis without coinciding with pure negativity. "One forgets to consider," Heidegger observes, "whether the 'not' or 'not-yet-existence' of the ground is not precisely the feature that renders existence positively possible, that is, whether the not-yet is not that element from which self-manifestation or self-transcendence proceeds. One forgets that what becomes is already grounded in and as the ground." Thus, divine becoming does not signify a mere departure from or annihilation of the ground; on the contrary, "existence lets the ground be as its ground." This letting-be or juncture also affects the temporal character of becoming, which does not involve a simple succession of stages measured by ordinary clock time. Ground and existence are not separated as past and future but are interlocking temporalities joined in a differentiated simultaneity. The notion of simultaneity, Heidegger comments, does not mean that past and future vanish and melt into a "pure presence" but rather that they maintain themselves as past and future and "coequally join with the present in the full richness of time itself." Becoming thus does not yield stagnation or the submergence of distinct temporal modes in a "gigantically enlarged Now"; instead, it occurs as the unique juncture of "the inexhaustible plenitude of temporality." It is in terms of the unity of this differentiated dynamic, the lecture course adds, that one has to conceive "the correlation of ground and existence."[9]

The differentiated linkage of ground and existence is also the ultimate source of the distinction between good and evil, which in turn is a crucial emblem of human freedom. According to Schelling, divine becoming aims at progressive spiritualization, that is, at the revealment or self-manifestation of God as spirit. But this revealment requires an otherness, a foil, in which spirit can fully manifest itself. As Heidegger comments: "There must be something other which is not God Himself but which harbors the possibility for divine manifestation. Thus there must be something which originates in God's innermost core and shares His quality as spirit and which yet remains separate or distinct from God. This other being is man [or humankind]." For Schelling, man as creature is rooted in nature and thus in the ground or latency of divine becoming; at the same time, however, this creature is the receptacle of divine revealment, the locus at which God's existence becomes most fully manifested.

Since God as spirit is also the epitome of freedom, divine self-mani-

9 Heidegger, *Schellings Abhandlung*, pp. 132, 135–136.

festation can occur only in a receptacle or conduit that shares God's qualities, that is, in an otherness constituted as free being. "This means, however," Heidegger says, "that the conditions of possibility for the manifestation of the existing God are simultaneously the conditions of the possibility of good and evil, that is, of the kind of freedom in which and as which human *Dasein* exists." The notion of evil at this point signals not a deficiency or pure negativity, but rather an outgrowth or corollary of spirit, that is, of human freedom in its partnership with divine freedom. More important, good and evil are not simply matters of human choice; rather, they occupy an ontological status—by being anchored in existence as the manifestation of spirit and, still more specifically, in spirit's manifestation against the backdrop of nature's ground. In this sense good and evil refer back to *Seinsfuge:* "The demonstration of the possibility of evil hence must take its departure from the *Seinsfuge* as source of this possibility."[10]

In God or divine becoming (as stated before), ground and existence are correlated in a differentiated unity, a tensional harmony—with the accent on harmony. In the case of human freedom, a similar correlation prevails, but with a different accent. If the correlation were precisely the same in God and in humankind, the two could not be distinguished, thus yielding either a simple anthropomorphism or pantheism and foiling the goal of divine manifestation (in otherness). In Schelling's words, as paraphrased by Heidegger: "If in man the identity of the two principles (ground and existence) were just as inseparable as it is in God, no distinction could emerge, which means: God as spirit could not become manifest. Thus, that same unity which in God is indivisible must in man be divisible—and this division is the possibility of good and evil."

In Schelling's account, ground and existence are freely variable against each other and not yoked together in an indissoluble teleology. In human *Dasein*, spirit's manifestation can reach fulfillment—to the point of intellectual conceit; at the same time, however, *Dasein* can seclude itself in the opacity of its peculiar ground or nature—to the point of denying the illuminating drive of spirit. Thus, *Dasein* embraces both dimensions seen as polar extremes: "the deepest abyss and the highest heaven." To the extent that seclusion in the ground means *Dasein's* enclosure in its peculiarity or selfishness, and to the extent that spirit intimates unity or harmony, the polar tension pervading *Dasein* can be viewed as permitting the rebellion of self-centeredness against the openness of letting-be, or of

10 Ibid., pp. 142–144.

self-will against universal will. As Heidegger comments: "Since human self-will is still linked to spirit (as freedom), this will can in the breadth of human endeavor attempt to put itself in the place of the universal will; thus, self-will can . . . as particular-separate selfishness pretend to be the ground of the whole. . . . This ability is the capacity for evil."[11]

The insurgence or arrogance of self-will does not mean the cancellation of *Seinsfuge* but only its perversion into disjointedness. In asserting its supremacy, self-will does not deny the unifying thrust of spirit but rather arrogates this unity to itself. In this manner, the correlation of ground and existence gives way to one-sided usurpation: "In elevating itself above universal will, self-will precisely wants to be the latter. Thus, this elevation yields a distinct mode of unification . . . but a unity that is a perversion of the original constellation, that is, a perversion of the wholeness of the divine world in which the universal harmonizes with the will of the ground." Following Schelling, Heidegger speaks in this context (in lieu of divine becoming) of "the becoming of a reverse or inverted God, of an antispirit," and hence of a rebellion against "primal being."

Again, reversal or perversion should not be seen as simple deficiency or negativity but rather as an assertive negation—more precisely, as a negation that usurps and swallows up the place of affirmation. *Seinsfuge* as such, one may recall, is not merely an ontic-empirical but an ontological juncture, a juncture of being and nonbeing—but one in which being and nonbeing are conjoined by "letting each other be." By contrast, in the reversal of *Seinsfuge*—which is a synonym for evil—nonbeing (or the negation of wholeness) appropriates the entire juncture, thus substituting itself for being. Negation, Heidegger notes, is here "not simply the rejection of something existing"; it is "a No-saying that usurps the place of the Yes." With this usurpation, dissonance holds sway in lieu of tensional consonance, rupture and denial in lieu of sympathy. In Heidegger's vocabulary, what happens is "the reversal of *Seinsfuge* into disjuncture or disjointedness [*Ungefüge*] whereby ground aggrandizes itself to absorb the place of existence."[12]

As an outgrowth of *Seinsfuge* and its disjuncture, good and evil are not simply human preferences or options among other preferences; instead, the capacity for both is constitutive of the being of *Dasein*, reflecting its insertion in some form or other in *Seinsfuge*. "Humans alone," Heidegger states, "are capable of evil; but this capability is not a human property or

---

[11] Ibid., pp. 169–171.
[12] Ibid., pp. 172–173.

quality. Rather, to be capable in this sense constitutes the being of humans." More precisely stated, *Dasein* as such is neither good nor evil but capable of both. On the level of sheer possibility, *Dasein* hence is an "undecided being," hovering precariously in indecision (*Unentschieden-heit*). Yet, as a living being, *Dasein* has to exit from indecision and empty possibility and enter the contest over good and evil. Entering the latter contest means confronting the arena of decision (*Entscheidung*)—which, however, is not an arena of arbitrary choice (and hence not a warrant for pure "decisionism").

In Schelling's account, the transition from capability to living reality is governed neither by arbitrary whim nor by external compulsion but by an ontological disposition (*Hang*) that inclines human conduct in one way or another. Without such a bent, Heidegger comments, decision would be sheer contingency occurring in a vacuum and never human self-determination in freedom, never a self-determination proceeding from an inner need or necessity of *Dasein* (thematized as resoluteness in *Being and Time*). In the case of evil, Schelling traces the ontological bent to a "contraction of the ground" (*Anziehen des Grundes*), that is, to a self-enclosure of particularity which terminates indecision, but in such a manner as to provoke divisiveness and disjuncture. On the other hand, goodness follows the attraction of spirit or existence, which in the most genuine form is the attraction of *eros*, or love (*Liebe*). "Love," we read, "is the original union of elements of which each might exist separately and yet does not so exist and cannot really be without the other." Love is not, however, simply unity or identity but rather a unity in difference or a unity that lets otherness be—including the contraction of the ground and the resulting disjuncture: "Love must condone the (independent or contrary) will of the ground, because otherwise love would annihilate itself. Only by letting this independence operate, love has that foil or counterpoint in or against which it can manifest its supremacy.[13]

Although separated by decision, or "decidedness" (*Entschiedenheit*), good and evil are not merely polar opposites or reciprocal negations—just as *Seinsfuge* and disjuncture do not simply cancel each other but remain linked in and through their reversal. As Heidegger emphasizes (following Schelling), *Dasein* involves a capability and decidedness not so much for good *or* evil as rather for good *and* evil—which is the heart of human freedom. Evil in this sense means the manifestation of both good and evil, just as goodness implies the appearance of both. This view

[13] Ibid., pp. 176–182, 187.

stands in stark contrast with a moralistic or value-oriented outlook according to which good is what ought and evil what ought not to be. In terms of the lecture course, the "and" linking good and evil does not have a moralistic tenor, "as if the alternatives were an ought and an ought not"; rather, "manifesting itself in living reality, evil in human life is simultaneously a display of goodness and vice versa." From the vantage of *Seinsfuge*, evil is not simply a reversal or negativity but rather a present absence (or absent presence), in the sense that self-will preserves even in its negation and perversion the trace of ontological wholeness. By the same token, goodness evokes as its counterpoint and condition of disclosure the rebellious presence of evil. Contrary to moralistic construals, the notion of juncture reveals that "good and evil could not conflict if they were not already constituted as opponents, and that they could not *be* opponents if they did not reciprocally condition each other and thus were not ultimately related in their being." All this does not mean that good and evil are equivalent or the same, which would precisely deny their difference. Evil remains evil in the sense of a perversion of goodness, and goodness finds itself confirmed in the counterforce of evil. Far from supporting indecision or undecidability, *Seinsfuge* in the end attests to the superior bent or attraction of goodness. In a phrase that summarizes Schelling's conception (but is not alien to Heidegger's thought), "The will of love takes precedence over the will of the ground, and this precedence and eternal decidedness—that is, the love of being for being—this decidedness is the innermost core of absolute freedom."[14]

II

Although he commented faithfully and in detail on Schelling's treatise, Heidegger did not necessarily endorse his idealist metaphysics, particularly his teleology of nature and spirit (and its connection with subjectivity). Given the latter teleology, ground and existence were at least potentially dichotomous, notwithstanding their asserted juncture or correlation. In the lecture course, Heidegger refers repeatedly to the shortcomings of Schelling's metaphysics. These defects, he notes, emerged most clearly in the later work where the elements of *Seinsfuge*—ground and existence—became "not only less and less compatible but were polarized to such an extent that Schelling relapsed into the rigid tradition

14 Ibid., pp. 188–193.

of Western metaphysics, without achieving a creative transformation." Equally problematic was the anchoring of ground and existence, non-being and being, in a realm of absoluteness, more specifically a domain of "absolute indifference"—a conception that bypassed the finitude and event character of being (what Heidegger came to call *Ereignis*).[15]

During the same period, Heidegger turned increasingly from German idealism and metaphysics to the dawn of Western philosophy in the pre-Socratic period in an effort to retrieve a pre-metaphysical mode of thought which could serve as guidepost for another beginning (or post-metaphysics). In the decade following the Schelling study, he devoted several lecture courses and essays to pre-Socratic thinkers, particularly Parmenides, Heraclitus, and Anaximander and their conceptions of oneness, *logos* (construed as language), and truth (*aletheia*). In the present context, I turn to an essay of the immediate postwar period, "The Anaximander Fragment," in which Heidegger develops the notion of *Seinsfuge* with specific reference to the issue of social (and cosmic) justice.

The essay deals with a saying ascribed to Anaximander which Heidegger terms "the oldest saying of Western (or Occidental) thought." In its customary and literal translation, the fragment offers this: "Whence things have their origin, there they must also pass away according to necessity; for they must pay penalty and be judged for their injustice, according to the ordinance of time." Read in this manner, the statement is cryptic and elusive. Moreover, a traditional (mis-)understanding of pre-Socratic thought additionally hampers access. Dating back to the early Peripatetic school, this understanding became an integral fixture of Western metaphysics and still reverberated in Hegel's history of philosophy. According to this view, the pre-Socratics were basically nature philosophers, where nature is contrasted with culture, politics, and the like; given this focus, their speculations about nature were later corrected and vastly refined by Aristotelianism and ensuing advances in physical science. From the vantage of science and historical teleology, the pre-Socratics are thus condemned to the status of precursors and hence to obsolescence; for later, more "highly developed" modes of knowledge, their relevance becomes increasingly dubious—outside the range of antiquarian interest.

Heidegger's essay radically challenges and inverts these premises. Historicism, or historical antiquarianism, he asserts, means "the system-

---

[15] Ibid., pp. 194–195. The difference from Schelling's position was more fully spelled out in seminars on Schelling held between 1941 and 1943; see especially pp. 208–210, 215, 218–219, 225–231.

atic destruction of the future and of our historical relation to the advent of destiny or mission [*Geschick*]." Far from relegating them to fossils of the past, Heidegger presents pre-Socratic sayings as anticipations of a distant and impending future. "The antiquity marking the saying of Anaximander," we read, "belongs to the dawn of the beginnings of the Occident or evening-land [*Abendland*]. But what if the dawn outdistanced everything late; if the very earliest far surpassed the very latest?" In that case, the history of the West might involve an evening heralding another dawn. In the same sense, we as the latecomers or lateborn of an advanced civilization might simultaneously be the heralds of another beginning. In Heidegger's words: "Are we the late-comers that we are? But are we at the same time also the precursors of the dawn of an altogether different age, which has left behind our present historicist conceptions of history?"[16]

Given metaphysical prejudgments, the translation of Anaximander cannot proceed directly or literally but must venture a leap, a "leap across a gulf or abyss"—which is not just a gulf of two-and-a-half thousand years but the distance separating us from pre-metaphysical thought. The first thing to be noticed in this venture is the mingling of domains carefully segregated in later philosophy. Although presumably focused on natural phenomena, the fragment speaks of justice and injustice, of penalty, retribution, and judgment; thus, moral and juridical notions are apparently mixed in with natural ones. As Heidegger observes, the fragment does not actually speak of things but rather of beings (*ta onta*) in their multiplicity. "Beings," however, comprises more than "things" (in the sense of objects), and certainly more than just things of nature: "Human beings too, the utensils produced by them, and the situations and circumstances effected through human action or omission—they all belong among beings; and so do demonic and divine 'things.'" Hence, the Peripatetic-metaphysical presumption regarding Anaximander as a nature philosopher concerned with natural matters is "altogether groundless."

---

[16] Heidegger, "Der Spruch des Anaximander," in *Holzwege*, 4th ed. (Frankfurt-Main: Klostermann, 1963), pp. 296, 299–301. For an English version, see "The Anaximander Fragment," in Heidegger, *Early Greek Thinking*, trans. David F. Krell and Frank A. Capuzzi (New York: Harper & Row, 1984), pp. 13, 16–18. As Heidegger adds, "If we think from the vantage of the eschatology of being, then we must someday anticipate the distance of the dawn in the distant future and must learn to ponder temporal distance along these lines" (p. 18; in this and subsequent citations I have slightly altered the English translation for purposes of clarity).

With the removal of this presumption, the notion of an indiscriminate and illegitimate mingling of domains likewise becomes untenable. Anaximander speaks indeed of justice, judgment, and penalty—but not as though these terms were borrowed from specialized academic disciplines of ethics or jurisprudence. In the dawn of Greek thought, such disciplines did not exist, which is not to say that early Greece was ignorant of law and ethics. Translation of the fragment thus requires a complex leap—above all, the abandonment of misconceptions like these: "that the fragment pertains to nature philosophy"; "that moral and juridical notions are inappropriately mixed in," involving a borrowing from "the separate domains of physics, ethics, and law"; that the phrase reflects a "primitive experience which views the world uncritically or anthropomorphically and hence takes refuges in poetic metaphors."[17]

In referring to beings, Anaximander's fragment strikes an ontological theme—a theme which, though lying at the heart of Western philosophy, is nonetheless thoroughly opaque. "Being" and "beings" are terms steadily used, but with little or no reflection; they are commonly employed to signify only the broadest or vaguest generalities. In Heidegger's account, we use the terms as something "approximately intelligible," as part of the common stock of knowledge operative in ordinary language; even when familiar with their Greek precursors, we usually invest no more in their meaning than "the complacent negligence of hasty opinion." For Heidegger, to be sure, the terms are far from empty concepts; they are, rather, keywords or codewords of Western thought and history. Being and beings, he notes, are intimately entwined in the manner of concealment and disclosure. More specifically, being reveals or manifests itself in beings, but in doing so it tends to screen or conceal itself from view.

The latter tendency has marked the development of Western metaphysics, in which concern with beings has emerged as the dominant focus and being has been shuffled aside. As Heidegger comments, beings here "do not step into the light of being; the unconcealment of beings—the brightness granted to them—obscures being's light." Differently put, "As it reveals itself in beings, being itself withdraws." This withdrawal, however, should be seen not simply as a deficiency or lacuna but rather as an emblem of being's absent presence, of its disclosure in the mode of concealment. Using terminology reminiscent of the *Beiträge*, Heidegger states that, in withdrawing, being "holds its truth in reserve. This keeping in reserve [*Ansichhalten*] is the early form of its revealment,"

---

[17] Heidegger, *Early Greek Thinking*, pp. 19–22.

and "its early sign is *a-letheia*" (meaning un-concealment coupled with concealment). Still in the vein of the *Beiträge*, Heidegger adds, "Concealment [of being], however, persists under the aegis of reticent refusal [*Verweigern*]."[18]

In embarking on his own translation, Heidegger starts by probing the meaning of "beings" as employed in the first part of Anaximander's fragment (which speaks of their origin and passing away). As he points out, "origin" (*genesis*) and "passing away" (*phthora*) should not be read simply in an evolutionary or teleological sense but rather against the backdrop of concealment and unconcealment. Accordingly, the first term signifies the arising or coming forth of a being from concealment into the light of unconcealment; correspondingly, the second term denotes not simply decay but a being's retreat or withdrawal from unconcealment into sheltering concealment. Anaximander's fragment, in its first part, thus speaks of arrival and departure, of the interplay of hiddenness and manifestation.

To elucidate the sense of this interplay, Heidegger turns briefly to a passage in Homer's *Iliad* which notes that the seer Kalchas was able to perceive present as well as future and past things or beings (*eonta*). Presentness in this context means manifestness or arrival of a being in the open region of unconcealment in which the being lingers for a while (*Weile*). Past and future are, however, also present in a sense, namely, outside the range of unconcealment or in the sphere of absent presence. Nonpresent being, we read, is "the absent or absently present; as such it remains essentially related to the presently present insofar as the latter either comes forth into or withdraws from the region of unconcealment." Thus, even the absent is present in a fashion, namely, by leaving *as* absence its present trace in unconcealment. Presence or presentness against this backdrop is merely an interval between arrival and departure, manifestness and hiddenness. What arrives into presence lingers or "whiles" (*weilt*) in disclosure while already preparing to withdraw into concealment. Hence presence lingers "in arrival and departure," as the "transition from coming to going." Kalchas perceived this interlocking of

---

[18] Ibid., pp. 24–26. As he adds: "We may call this revealing keeping in reserve of its truth the *epoché* of being. However, this term, borrowed from the Stoics, does not here have the Husserlian sense of objectification or methodical bracketing of acts of thetic consciousness. Rather, the *epoché* of being belongs to being itself; we are thinking it out of the experience of the oblivion of being [*Seinsvergessenheit*]" (pp. 26–27). At a later point, oblivion of being is defined as "oblivion of the distinction of being and beings" (pp. 50–51), an outlook which, in turn, is described as a trademark of Western metaphysics.

presence and absence, an insight that enabled him to be a "truthteller" (*Wahrsager*).[19]

Heidegger next turns to the second part of the fragment, focusing initially on the crucial term "injustice" (*adikia*). It is at this point that his exegesis reinvokes the notion of *Seinsfuge* and its correlate of disjuncture. Quite independently of juridical usage *adikia*, he notes, means basically something out of order. In this manner, however, the term implicitly refers to a proper order or juncture, that is, to justice (*dike*) as an emblem of *Seinsfuge*. In Heidegger's words: "The presentness of beings implies a certain juncture [*Fuge*] together with the possibility of being disjointed. Everything present lingers or stays for a while [*Weile*]—which latter means the transitional arrival into departure." Thus, presencing happens "between coming forth and passing away," or "between a twofold absence" (or absent presence). This "between" is precisely the juncture into which every lingering presence is joined from its arrival to its departure; in both directions presencing is inserted or welded into absence, an insertion that constitutes its proper juncture.

Lingering or "whiling" can, however, also turn into disjuncture. Instead of arriving into departure, a present being can try to prolong and solidify its stay; having arrived into presence, it can insist on its presentness, seeking to transform "whiling" into perdurance. At this point, Heidegger notes, presentness "perseveres in its presencing, extricating itself from its transitory state. It aggrandizes itself into the selfish stubbornness [*Eigensinn*] of persistence, no longer caring about other modes of presence." In this manner, presentness leaves or abandons juncture and enters into a state of disjuncture (*Un-Fuge*), which is the basic sense of injustice or *adikia*. Disjuncture in this context is not only an alternative kind of juncture but a counterjuncture or inverted juncture. An outgrowth of stubbornness, disjuncture signifies in fact an insurgence of presentness in favor of sheer continuance. Differently put, "Presentness happens then without and in opposition to the juncture of the passing while."[20]

Anaximander's saying does not refer only to disjuncture, however, but also to penalty and judgment—terms whose meaning so far is hazy. Regarding the phrase usually translated as "paying penalty," Heidegger fastens onto the Greek text, which is actually something like "giving

---

[19] Ibid., pp. 30–31, 34–37. Actually, Heidegger does not consider the entire first part of the fragment authentic; but this fact does not significantly affect his interpretation.

[20] Ibid., pp. 41–43.

juncture" (*didonai diken*). How should this phrase be understood? Giving, he points out, does not only mean giving away; more genuinely, it denotes giving in, conceding, letting happen or be. As he writes: "Such a giving lets another being have what properly belongs to the other. What properly belongs to every being, however, is the juncture of its passing stay [*Weile*] which joins it into arrival and departure." Properly joined into this interval, every being savors and rightly savors its presence, without necessarily lapsing into the disjuncture of stubborn persistence, which remains a possibility and temptation. Differently phrased, being as such is not synonymous with disjuncture or injustice since it is always already inserted into *Seinsfuge*, which lets it happen and which it lets happen in turn. Conversely, injustice does not absorb or overwhelm being, since *adikia* is not strictly a negation or vacuum but rather justice itself in its mode of withdrawal, in its absent presence. Returning to Anaximander, the passage in question thus may be rendered in this sense: that being (every being) allows juncture or justice to happen in the face of disjuncture—and even in the guise or mode of disjuncture. In Heidegger's words: "It is not in *adikia* as such or in disjuncture that the presence of a present being consists, but rather in the *didonai diken . . . tes adikias*, in the letting-be of juncture. . . . Present being is present insofar as it lets itself belong into the nonpresent."[21]

What still remains unexamined in the second part of the fragment is the allusion to a judgment of sorts. In the Greek original, the reference is not so much to judgment as to estimation or esteem (*tisis*), which Heidegger initially translates as consideration or considerateness. By dwelling in *Seinsfuge*, every being considerately grants to other beings their passing stay; by contrast, stubborn self-persistence involves inconsiderateness toward others. In this stubbornness, Heidegger writes, "present being aggrandizes itself vis-à-vis or against others; neither being heeds or respects the lingering stay of the other. Thus, present beings are inconsiderate toward each other, each dominated by the craving for persistence implicit in or intimated by their presence." Still, Heidegger finds "consideration" too pale and nondescript to convey the full strength of the Greek term. Hence he replaces "considerate" and "inconsiderate" with the more poignant (though unusual) pair "reck-ful" and "reckless"—noting that "reck" (*Ruch*), deriving from the Middle High German *ruoche*, corresponds roughly to the notion of "care" (*Sorge*) as employed in *Being and Time*. Care, he states, is concern with or attention to the being of

21 Ibid., pp. 43–44.

others; such attentiveness, however, is conveyed by the term "reck" (*Ruch* or *tisis*). In Heidegger's exegesis, the two aspects of allowing juncture to happen and showing "reck" or care are closely connected, in that the latter derives from the former. "Insofar as beings," we read, "do not entirely dissipate themselves into the boundless conceit of self-aggrandizing persistence, by trying to eject each other mutually from the space of presencing, to this extent they let juncture be [*didonai diken*]." And "insofar as they let juncture be, they also already show or grant to each other 'reck' or care in their mutual relations [*didonai . . . kai tisin allelois*]." Justice (*dike*) and care (*tisis*) are thus related consequentially: "If present beings let juncture be, this happens in such a manner that, in their passing stay, they show care or 'reck' to each other. The overcoming of disjuncture occurs through the granting of care."[22]

The final passage not yet translated is the phrase "according to necessity" in the first part of the fragment (which corresponds to the concluding "according to the ordinance of time"). In Heidegger's exegesis, the phrase refers not so much to necessity as to the background or nourishing soil in terms of which beings are able to let juncture happen and to show each other care. This background, however, is the "being of beings," the happening of disclosure and concealment as such. Looking more closely at the Greek term usually rendered as "necessity" (*to chreon*,) Heidegger notes that it derives from the Greek word for hand (*cheir*), with the result that the phrase actually has something to do with handling, being to hand, or handing over. Far from denoting an external necessity or constraint, the phrase then refers to "the handing over of presence, a handing over which grants or concedes presence to beings, but in such a manner that it keeps beings in hand, guarding their presence."

Looking for a German equivalent for the Greek term, Heidegger (somewhat boldly) proposes *Brauch*, which in its original meaning signifies an ability to savor, to enjoy, to delight in a being's presence and autonomy without possessiveness or radical separation (thus guarding its stay). Enjoyment in this case, however, is viewed no longer as a human capacity but as a quality of being itself in its relation to beings—which is a relation of handing over and keeping in hand. "*Brauch*," we read, "hands beings over into their presence, that is, into their passing stay [*Weile*]; it dispenses to beings their portion of this stay. The latter, in turn, is grounded in the juncture [*Fuge*] which joins present beings into the twofold absence of arrival and departure." Together with juncture, there

22 Ibid., pp. 45–47.

looms up for beings the possibility of disjuncture as well as the contrast of care and recklessness. These prospects are ultimately anchored in the intertwining of being and nonbeing, where the latter is not a simple denial but inscribed in the former. As Heidegger concludes: "Enjoining juncture and care, *Brauch* hands over beings into their presentness or present stay. This conjures up the constant danger that passing presence is congealed into sheer persistence. Thus, *Brauch* also permits the handing over of beings into disjuncture"—which (we should recall) is only the trace of juncture seen as dispensation of *Brauch*.[23]

III

The writings discussed above clearly have manifold implications for ethics as well as for social and political thought; they also help to correct one-sided polemical dismissals of Heidegger as a Nazi ideologist or persistent apologist for fascism. In my view, these writings can actually be read as an indictment of Nazism to the extent that the latter aimed at an imperial dominion of the world based on racial-biological grounds. As presented in the "Anaximander Fragment," juncture and hence justice is the readiness to let others be and to attend to them with considerate care; by contrast, disjuncture or injustice involves the insurgence of selfish conceit bent on permanently monopolizing the space of presence while shuffling others out of the way. Seen from the vantage of *Seinsfuge*, Hitler's Third Reich—scheduled to last for a "thousand years"—was the epitome of disjuncture and injustice as well as of murderous recklessness. In terms of the Schelling lecture, however, disjuncture is also the emblem of evil—the latter viewed not merely as personal-moral deficiency but as an ontological perversion, as a rebellion against the structure of *Seinsfuge*. Again, Hitler's Reich in its extreme destructiveness was an embodiment of such ontological evil (independently of, or conjointly with, the individual perversities of its agents). Yet, the issue of disjuncture and injustice persists beyond the collapse of Nazism, though perhaps in less aggravated fashion. Today's world is marked by the contrast

---

[23] Ibid., pp. 48–54. At this point (pp. 55–56), Heidegger establishes a close linkage between the Greek term for *Brauch*, *to chreon*, and the notions of *hen* and *moira* as employed by Parmenides as well as the notion of *logos* as used by Heraclitus. See in this context his essays titled "Logos," "Moira," and "Aletheia," in *Early Greek Thinking*, pp. 59–78, 79–101, 102–123. For the German original of these essays, see *Vorträge und Aufsätze*, 3d ed. (Pfullingen: Neske, 1967), pt. 3, pp. 3–78.

between West and non-West (or between North and South), where the West is only a small island in the vast ocean of the non-West, although it manages to monopolize the bulk of the world's economic and industrial resources. Is there not still an issue of disjuncture and injustice, now on a global scale, to which Heidegger's writings remain pertinent?

Apart from this stark political relevance, Heidegger's arguments insert themselves pointedly into ongoing debates about ethics and justice. As I indicated previously, contemporary ethics is largely a battleground between Kantian rationalism and neo-Aristotelian virtue ethics (leaving aside the skeptical variant); in broader political terms, the distinction corresponds roughly to that between liberalism and communitarianism. In the language of academic moral theory, the conflict is commonly expressed in opposing pairs such as these: deontology versus teleology, procedural form versus substance, universalism versus particularism. Although alluring as conceptual categories, the ethical import of these notions remains elusive and confusing.

In the case of rationalist ethics, given the strict separation of "is" and "ought," moral maxims and phenomenal experience, how can universal imperatives be transposed into the domain of practical conduct? Premised on the cancellation of teleology and ontology, how can deontological rules impose their "ought" or "must" on the realm of being? Quandaries of this kind confirm the merits of virtue ethics, but without necessarily vindicating its metaphysical assumptions. As has frequently been noted, classical (including Aristotelian) ethics is predicated on a substantive ontology (or ontology of substances) whereby each element or being is assigned its proper place and status in the universe. Couched in terms of moral conduct, right action here means action appropriate to a person's station and duties in life, a conception that readily supports social conservatism. As is well known, functionalist sociology offers a theory of agency in which role performance is strictly tailored to the efficient functioning of the overall system (which, no doubt, is a caricature of classical ethics). The crucial aspect neglected by functionalism and substantive ethics is the dimension of freedom—ontologically speaking, the correlation of being and nonbeing. By anchoring his argument in this correlation, Heidegger intimates a post-metaphysics that bypasses the form–substance, norm–experience dichotomies. Moreover, in linking justice closely with *Seinsfuge*, his perspective bridges the gulf between rightness and goodness, between justice and "the good life."

Still in the domain of ethical theory, the writings reviewed here are liable to counter misconceptions that frequently beleaguer Heidegger's work. One such misconception, triggered chiefly by passages in *Being and Time*, holds that Heidegger's thought sponsors at best a minimalist and noncognitivist ethics, more specifically a moral decisionism grounded in arbitrary will. Human *Dasein*, in this view, basically involves a choice between authentic and inauthentic modes of life—unless choice is abandoned in favor of inscrutable dispensations of destiny (offered as translation for *Geschick*).[24] Heidegger's lectures on Schelling should dispel this decisionist reading, given the emphasis there on *eros*, or inclination, as ontological mentors of ethical conduct (grounded in *Seinsfuge*). To the extent that such conduct does involve decision, the lectures explicitly differentiate that element from both sheer willfulness and fatalism: "Pure arbitrariness fails to supply a motivational basis for decision; external compulsion, on the other hand, does not furnish a motivation for its presumed target, namely, (free) decision."

In countering or correcting decisionism, the same lectures also take exception to its counterthesis, that of ethical-ontological indecision or undecidability. As I mentioned above, Heidegger does not present juncture and disjuncture, or good and evil, as simply alternatives between which one might maintain a stance of neutrality or indecision. *Dasein*, he insists, cannot in actual life remain neutral but must "exit" from indecision. This exit route is again paved by inclination and, more important, by a certain preponderance or weight built into *Seinsfuge:* evil is not simply the negation of goodness but rather the absent presence of goodness, just as nonbeing is the absent presence of being. To repeat a previously cited passage, "Love's will takes precedence over the will of the ground, and this precedence and eternal decidedness—that is, the love of being for being—is the innermost core of absolute freedom."[25]

Curiously, both decisionism and undecidability are sometimes blended today in versions of post-structuralism. In seeking to dismantle foundationalist metaphysics, post-structuralist writers occasionally drift into a no-man's land where being and nonbeing, ground and abyss (as well as good and evil), appear radically exchangeable—unless preference is directly given to abyss over ground (or to anarchy over *arché*). Thus, Derrida sometimes speaks of the exchangeability or undecidability of metaphysical and ontological categories, including the dimensions of disclosure and concealment, presence and absence. Exchangeability,

---

[24] For an interpretation along these lines, see Jürgen Habermas, *The Philosophical Discourse of Modernity: Twelve Lectures*, trans. Frederick Lawrence (Cambridge: MIT Press, 1987), pp. 138–152.

[25] Heidegger, *Schellings Abhandlung*, pp. 177, 185, 193.

however, signals sameness or indifference—which neglects precisely the differentiation or differentiated correlation of these dimensions. As it happens, differentiation is at the same time the hallmark of post-structuralism (and deconstructionism), where it often signifies or is synonymous with decision, struggle, or incommensurability. Under the influence of a radical Nietzscheanism (stressing will to power), post-structuralists sometimes portray human relations entirely under the aegis of conflict and *agon*—to the point of canceling junctures or common bonds; in an effort to exorcise totality, system, and homogeneity, these theorists sometimes end up celebrating particularism and atomistic dispersal. Heidegger likewise extols difference—but a difference that is not equivalent to antithesis or mutual negation; while bypassing system or identity, he portrays struggle as reciprocal entwinement. To quote again from the Schelling lectures: "According to the old saying of Heraclitus, struggle is the basic principle and moving force of being. But the greatest struggle is love—which provokes the deepest contest precisely in order to be and display itself in its reconciliation."[26]

Returning to political connotations, Heidegger's writings are far from neutral undecidability, although they are equally removed from ideological partisanship. The closing paragraphs of the "Anaximander Fragment" insert the discussion of justice and injustice squarely into the present global context, which is marked by the steadily intensified struggle for planetary dominion. The entire thrust of the essay is directed toward finding antidotes to this scenario and hence resources for another beginning. The distant saying of Anaximander, Heidegger observes, becomes accessible only if we ponder the disjointedness (*Wirrnis*) of the present age. Wherein does this disjuncture consist? "Humans," Heidegger responds, "are on the verge of leaping onto the entire earth and its atmosphere in order to harness for themselves the powers of nature in the form of energy and to subject the course of history to the managerial

[26] Ibid., pp. 195. For the notion of undecidability, see, for example, Jacques Derrida, *Spurs: Nietzsche's Styles*, trans. Barbara Harlow (Chicago: University of Chicago Press, 1979), pp. 59, 107, 117–121, and "Otobiographies," in Derrida, *The Ear of the Other*, ed. Christie V. McDonald, trans. Avital Ronell (New York: Schocken, 1985), pp. 3–38. The aspect of conflict and incommensurability (of life-worlds and language games) has been strongly emphasized by Jean-François Lyotard, especially in *The Differend: Phrases in Dispute*, trans. Georges Van Den Abbeele (Minneapolis: University of Minnesota Press, 1988). Justice or equity, from this vantage, is a kind of arbitration between incompatible games; see Lyotard and Jean-Loup Thébaud, *Just Gaming*, trans. Wlad Godrich (Minneapolis: University of Minnesota Press, 1985). See also Stephen K. White, "Justice and the Postmodern Problematic," *Praxis International* 7 (1987–88): 306–319.

plans of a world government." What is lost in this reckless move toward dominion is *Seinsfuge*—the willingness of humans to let juncture be and to be considerate to one another as well as to nature and being. "Rebellious *Dasein*," he states, "is incapable to say or acknowledge simply what *is*—to say what it means that anything *is*. Rather: the totality of beings is the target of a single will of conquest—while the simplicity of being is buried in complete oblivion." In this situation, antidotes cannot simply be fabricated or engineered; instead, their availability depends on the bracketing of instrumental production and the readiness to undergo a transformation (*Kehre*), both a philosophical and a practical-political turning or *periagoge*. In this change, humans turn from oblivion to the recollection of being, while the latter returns to display its nurturing care (*Brauch*). As Heidegger concludes, paraphrasing Hölderlin, ours is an age of danger. But danger "is" most genuinely, when "being itself takes a final stand [in withdrawal], thus turning about the oblivion it had sponsored."[27]

Beyond the stark issue of planetary control, Heidegger's argument is more broadly relevant to questions of social control and hence of social and political equity. In contemporary western society, questions of equity are typically articulated in terms of rights, which usually means resort to legal processes of adjudication. Legal theory and jurisprudence, in fact, are replete with talk of rights and admonitions to "take rights seriously," coupled with acceptance of the legalization of social bonds. Although valuable in the face of totalitarian abuses, however, the language of rights is elusive unless attention is paid to the carriers of rights and political equity. In contemporary Western society, questions of eq- treat as equivalent the rights of the rich and of the poor, the powerful and the powerless, the victimizer and the victims? Such questions point to the power structure of society, and to its equity or inequity.

Typically, rights are initially acquired through struggle; yet, once social conditions stabilize or solidify, there is a subtle transition from rights to "vested rights"—commonly to the detriment of the under- privileged or outcasts of society. It is at this point that Heidegger's discussion of equity or justice comes into play, with its emphasis on "presencing" and on the "passing while" enjoyed by presentness between a twofold absence of arrival and departure, past and future. Unless mindful of their passing while, present rights claims are liable to deterio- rate into privileges, into the attempt to monopolize social control and to

---

[27] Heidegger, *Early Greek Thinking*, pp. 57–58.

shuffle aside both past and future generations (or social groupings). As it happens, vested rights tend to enjoy the blessing of the legal system, with the result that challenges to control are castigated as unlawful or iniquitous. Although a major acquisition of modern constitutional government, the rule of law hence cannot operate abstractly on the level of equivalence (of rights) but must be constantly open to reinterpretation in the light of changing social conditions and demands for social equity.[28]

From the vantage of Heidegger's writings, the latter demands are not simply willful assertions but an outgrowth of *Seinsfuge* and its linkage of presence and absence. Correspondingly, lawfulness means not only legality in the sense of obedience to given rules but also attentiveness to equity or mindfulness of juncture and disjuncture. As Heidegger writes in the *Letter on Humanism*, only being can yield guideposts that might become rules of human conduct. In Greek, such yielding is termed *nemein*. Hence, he adds, "*nomos* is not merely 'law' but more originally the dispensation latent in the happening of being." Only this dispensation is "capable of 'joining' humans into being, and only such 'juncture' is able to bind and to sustain. Otherwise all law or legality remains a machination of human rationality."

In these comments on law, the *Letter* thus invokes and pays tribute to *Seinsfuge*, though without explicitly developing this theme. The theme also surfaces in the *Letter*'s observations on being and nonbeing, on goodness (or the hale) and evil, and particularly on the difference (or conflictual juncture) of being itself. "Together with the hale," we read, "evil too appears in the clearing of being. The latter's nature does not consist in the mere baseness of human action but rather in the malice of rage [*Grimm*]. Both of them, however, the hale and the rage, can occur in being only because being itself is contestable—by harboring the origin of non-being." It is in light of these passages, I believe, that one should see Heidegger's noted reticence about ethics. The target of this reticence is formalized ethical theory—not ethics seen as reflection on juncture and disjuncture, justice and injustice, good and evil. This conclusion is warranted by a passage in the *Letter* in which Heidegger expresses his

---

[28] See in this context Fred Dallmayr, "Hermeneutics and the Rule of Law," in *Legal Hermeneutics: History, Theory, and Practice*, ed. Gregory Leyh (Berkeley: University of California Press, 1991), pp. 3–22. On rights, see especially Ronald Dworkin, *Taking Rights Seriously* (Cambridge: Harvard University Press, 1978). Heidegger's position is more akin to the notion of natural right as articulated by Leo Strauss (minus the Platonic scaffolding); see Strauss, *Natural Right and History* (Chicago: University of Chicago Press, 1953), esp. pp. 81–119.

view forthrightly: "If, in keeping with the basic meaning of *ethos*, the term 'ethics' should designate a reflection on *Dasein's* mode of dwelling, then that type of thinking which ponders the truth of being as primordial abode of ek-sisting-ekstatic *Dasein* is in itself the original ethics."[29]

[29] Heidegger, *Letter on Humanism* (1947), in *Martin Heidegger: Basic Writings*, ed. David F. Krell (New York: Harper & Row, 1977), pp. 234–235, 237–239 (translation slightly altered for purposes of clarity). As one should note, Heidegger does not simply dismiss legality or moral rules in the ordinary sense. As he writes in the same *Letter*, "Great care must be given to moral rules at a time when *Dasein*, faced with technology and mass society, can maintain reliable steadiness only through an organization of planning and acting which matches technological demands. Who can disregard this predicament? Must we not safeguard and secure existing bonds—which sustain humans today ever so ten-uously in sheer presentness? Certainly. But does this need relieve thinking of the task of being mindful of what still awaits to be thought: namely, being which grants to all beings initially their stay and truth?" (pp. 231–232).

CHAPTER FIVE

Heidegger, Hölderlin, and Politics

Not long ago I was privileged to participate in a conference organized in honor of Albert Hirschman, that eminent economist, sociologist, anthropologist, and student of politics; one of Hirschman's challenging books is titled *Essays in Trespassing*.[1] This chapter is also intended as such an essay in "trespassing." Dealing simultaneously with Martin Heidegger, Friedrich Hölderlin, and politics means moving across significant academic and intellectual boundaries, chiefly those between philosophy, poetry, literary criticism, and political thought; one might also add the boundary between past and present. The objective of my trespassing effort, I emphasize, is not simply to produce an indistinct amalgam of ingredients, which would involve not so much the transgression as the erasure of boundaries; my goal is rather to highlight both the distinctness and the mutual correlation of the respective domains.

Before proceeding, I need to qualify my undertaking in several ways. This discussion does not range broadly over Heidegger's entire opus, which would not only be foolhardy but impossible (given the present state of this opus). Nor do I attempt to comment on all Heidegger's numerous writings devoted to Hölderlin. My focus is more restricted: I intend to concentrate chiefly on one relevant publication, Heidegger's 1934/35 lecture course titled *Hölderlins Hymnen "Germanien" und "Der Rhein"* (Hölderlin's Hymns "Germania" and "The Rhine").[2] There are

A version of this chapter was presented as a lecture at a conference held at the University of Notre Dame on the theme "Criticism without Boundaries."

[1] Albert O. Hirschman, *Essays in Trespassing: Economics to Politics and Beyond* (Cambridge: Cambridge University Press, 1981).

[2] Martin Heidegger, *Hölderlins Hymnen "Germanien" und "Der Rhein,"* ed. Susanne Ziegler (*Gesamtausgabe*, Vol. 39; Frankfurt-Main: Klostermann, 1980).

several reasons—good reasons, I believe—for focusing on this lecture course. Heidegger's courses, particularly those offered between 1923 and 1944, were for the most part previously unpublished and are only now slowly becoming available to the public. Thus, there is the freshness and excitement of a new encounter with Heidegger's thought as one after the other of these works appear in print. There is a better reason, however, which has to do with the author himself. Despite the mountain of pages he has written, one should realize that Heidegger was first and foremost not a writer of books or treatises but a teacher.

The testimony of eye witnesses fully concurs on this point. All his students, even those who later drifted away from him, are unanimous in extolling the spellbinding character of his lectures and the intense fascination of his oral presentations. In his *Heideggers Wege*, Hans-Georg Gadamer ascribes to his teacher a "nearly dramatic appearance, a power of diction, a concentration of delivery which captivated all his listeners." He also recounts how, in his lectures, Heidegger was able to transform Aristotle (among other classics) from a scholastic mummy into a living presence or a speaking "contemporary," thus providing a dynamic illustration of what Gadamer later was to call *Horizontverschmelzung* (fusion of horizons). Hannah Arendt has been no less eloquent on this aspect. In an essay written on the occasion of Heidegger's eightieth birthday she observed that, even before any of his major publications had appeared, his

> name traveled all over Germany like the rumor of the hidden king. . . . The rumor about Heidegger put it quite simply: Thinking has come to life again; the cultural treasures of the past, believed to be dead, are being made to speak, in the course of which it turns out that they propose things altogether different from the familiar, worn-out trivialities they had been presumed to say. There exists a teacher; one can perhaps learn to think.[3]

There is another general consideration which, in my view, recommends the lecture courses to our attention: their discursive and maieutic character. More so than polished texts, the courses offer a glimpse of Heidegger at work, that is, in the laboratory of his thought. Precisely because they were addressed to students rather than a nondescript audience, the courses are more attuned than his books to the need of sustained or progressive learning; they also tend to be more argumenta-

[3] Hans-Georg Gadamer, *Heideggers Wege* (Tübingen: Mohr, 1983), pp. 14, 118; Hannah Arendt, "Martin Heidegger at Eighty," in *Heidegger and Modern Philosophy: Critical Essays*, ed. Michael Murray (New Haven: Yale University Press, 1978), pp. 294–295.

tive, more ready to unpack complex notions and also to confront opposing views in a critical fashion.

Regarding the specific lecture course of 1934, there is an additional motivation for my choice: the fact that it follows on the heels of a notorious episode in Heidegger's life, his service as rector of the University of Freiburg from April 1933 to February 1934. As is well known, this episode has placed a heavy onus, perhaps an indelible stain, on Heidegger's public record, a stain some interpreters like to present as evidence of a permanent commitment to fascism. In these pages I do not enter into a discussion of this unfortunate interlude and of the dense emotional aura surrounding it.[4] The issue I do raise, from a political angle, is rather whether the 1934 course on Hölderlin still reflects the sentiments of 1933 or whether, on the contrary, it manifests a profound disillusionment with, and turning away from, the National Socialist regime—a regime which, during the same months, was steadily tightening its grip on the nation.

I do not propose to tackle this issue directly or frontally but in a more roundabout way. Clearly, the chosen lecture course is not an ordinary political tract or pamphlet, a tract amenable to straightforward political (or ideological) exegesis. The central topics of the course are two poems by Hölderlin dating back to the year 1801. Thus, the questions I need to face initially are of a literary character, and seemingly far removed from politics: why does Heidegger turn to poetry, and particularly to Hölderlin's poetry, at this time? Differently and more elaborately put, what is the meaning of poetry (*Dichtung*) for Heidegger, and why does he choose Hölderlin to illustrate this meaning?

I

The status of poetry in Heidegger's philosophy is a complex problem that resists brief summary; one way to facilitate access is to stress his distance from customary aesthetic assumptions (and from modern subjectivist aesthetics in general). Poetry for Heidegger is not the production

---

[4] I address some aspects of this episode in Chapter 1 of this volume and also in "Ontology of Freedom: Heidegger and Political Philosophy," in Dallmayr, *Polis and Praxis* (Cambridge: MIT Press, 1984), pp. 104–132. The text of Heidegger's "Rektoratsrede" of May 1933 has been republished, together with a retrospective epilogue written by Heidegger in 1945, in Hermann Heidegger, ed., *Die Selbstbehauptung der deutschen Universität* (Frankfurt-Main: Klostermann, 1983).

of nice-sounding metaphors or a purely decorative exercise designed to engender aesthetic delight. Broadly speaking, poetry in his treatment has ontological status: it is a prominent or eminent mode of the epiphany of being, where being does not designate a given object (whose presence could be empirically determined) but rather an ongoing happening, a process of advent and retreat, of disclosure and concealment. Since it is not a fixed entity, being needs to be continuously recreated and re-enacted, although not in the sense of a willful fabrication. Poetry participates in this continuing enactment, or "constitution of being" (*Stiftung des Seins*), by putting it into words—although again not in a direct fashion but through the medium of poetic language that simultaneously reveals and conceals. In the lecture course of 1934, Heidegger also calls poetry the "original voice or language [*Ursprache*] of a people" because such language permits the constitution of the being of a people—by opening up a historical space for its deeds and accomplishments as well as its failures and catastrophes.[5]

Given this conception of poetry, what is the significance of Hölderlin, and especially of his later hymns? From Heidegger's perspective, Hölderlin's work is exemplary or prototypical precisely with regard to the constitution of being. He repeatedly portrays Hölderlin as the poet's poet, not only in the ordinary sense (of distinguished or outstanding poet) but in the deeper sense that his work constitutes the very being or meaning of poetry. To illustrate this meaning, he invokes Hölderlin's poem "As on a Holiday . . ." (*Wie wenn am Feiertage . . .*), which contains these lines: "Yet, it behooves us, poets, to stand bare-headed beneath God's thunderstorms" (*Doch uns gebührt es, unter Gottes Gewittern, Ihr Dichter! mit entblösstem Haupte zu stehen*). As he comments: "The poet captures God's lightning in his words and inserts these lightning-filled words into the language of a people. Rather than voicing his inner experiences he stands 'beneath God's thunderstorms.'"[6]

Heidegger goes on to ascribe to Hölderlin a still more specific significance, namely, as a "German poet," or "poet of the Germans"—although, I should add right away, this phrase must not be taken in a

---

[5] Heidegger, *Hölderlins Hymnen*, pp. 20, 33, 64, 216–217.

[6] Ibid., p. 30. For the English version, see Friedrich Hölderlin, *Poems and Fragments*, trans. Michael Hamburger (Ann Arbor: University of Michigan Press, 1967), p. 375 (translation slightly altered). For a more general assessment of Hölderlin's poetry by Heidegger, see "Hölderlin und das Wesen der Dichtung," in Heidegger, *Erläuterungen zu Hölderlins Dichtung*, ed. Friedrich-Wilhelm von Herrmann (*Gesamtausgabe*, Vol. 4; Frankfurt-Main: Klostermann, 1981), pp. 33–48.

restrictive ethnic, or even a directly referential, sense. Hölderlin is poet of the Germans not merely because he happens to be born among Germans but, more radically, because his poetry constitutes the being of Germans by opening up a historical possibility for them—albeit a possibility they tend to ignore. The Preface to the lecture course describes Hölderlin as a poet "whom the Germans have yet to face [in the future]." In a later passage Hölderlin is portrayed as "the poet who poetically invents the Germans" or, more elaborately, as "the poet, that is, the founder [*Stifter*] of German being because he has farthest projected the latter, that is, propelled it ahead and beyond into the most distant future." In which sense or direction has Hölderlin projected this possibility? Heidegger states the answer repeatedly. "He was able," he writes, "to unlock this far-future distance because he retrieved the key out of the experience of the deepest need or agony: the experience of the retreat and (possible) return of the gods." Using a slightly different formulation, he notes in the Preface that, leaving behind our "historicist pretentions," Hölderlin has "founded the beginning of a different history, a history revolving around the struggle and decision regarding the advent or flight of God."[7]

I return to this issue or struggle later; for the moment I just want to let these phrases linger or resonate. As indicated, the lecture course does not deal with Hölderlin's entire opus but concentrates on two of his later hymns—dating from the period when his mind was slowly beginning to drift toward darkness. In his lectures Heidegger offers a detailed exegesis of the two hymns, which I cannot fully recapitulate here. Nor do I attempt to give a descriptive account of the "content" of these poems (if such a thing were at all possible). I simply pick out a few lines or stanzas to convey the general flavor. In the first hymn, for example, these lines are addressed by an eagle to a priestess named Germania: "It is you, chosen, all-loving one who have grown strong to bear a difficult fortune [*ein schweres Glück*]." And the hymn concludes thus: "On your holidays, Germania, when you are priestess and when defenseless [*wehrlos*] you provide counsel to kings and nations." Finally, some lines from "The Rhine" about half-gods, sons of gods (*Göttersöhne*), poets: "For ordinary man knows his home and the animal knows where to build, but these carry the wound in their inexperienced souls of not knowing where to turn."[8]

---

[7] Heidegger, *Hölderlins Hymnen*, pp. 1, 220.
[8] Friedrich Hölderlin, *Poems and Fragments*, pp. 405, 407, 410 (translation slightly altered).

II

We can begin by reviewing some of Heidegger's major arguments regarding Hölderlin's poems. First, a few words on the reading of poetic texts. In addition to providing a substantive analysis, the lecture course also offers numerous observations on exegesis or literary interpretation in general, observations that seem directly relevant to contemporary literary criticism. As Heidegger emphasizes, poetry—and Hölderlin's poetry in particular—cannot simply be explained in terms of historical influences, environmental conditions, and least of all personal biography. Despite their obvious importance, historical settings cannot be used as a shortcut to interpretation, a shortcut predicated on the assumption that historical periods are more directly accessible to understanding than texts and that the latter can therefore readily be deciphered in terms of the former. Perhaps, Heidegger retorts, we may sometimes have to interpret a period or social context in light of its leading texts.

Heidegger is more adamant in his critique of psychological or biographical approaches to exegesis. Poetry, he insists, is not the outpouring of inner feelings, the expression of personal sentiments or experiences— the teachings of traditional (modern) aesthetics notwithstanding. According to the traditional outlook, he remarks, inner feelings are claimed

> to find tangible outer expression—for instance, in a lyrical poem. These processes and sentiments in the poet's "soul" can then be further analyzed with the help of modern "depth psychology." Along these lines one can compare writers of different genres as [psychological] types—such as epic, lyrical, or dramatic writers; depth psychology thus turns into typological analysis.

As Heidegger bitingly comments, "Expression is also the barking of a dog. . . . This conception places poetry *ab limine* under auspices where even the slightest possibility of real understanding hopelessly disappears."[9]

Contrary to this subjective-expressive view, Heidegger finds the es-

---

[9] Heidegger, *Hölderlins Hymnen*, pp. 6–7, 26–28. With a clear political edge Heidegger adds: "If anything deserves the much abused label 'liberal,' it is this conception. For, on principle and from the outset, this conception distances itself from its own thoughts and beliefs, reducing them to mere objects or targets of opinion. Poetry in this manner becomes an immediately given phenomenon among other phenomena—a phenomenon that is further characterized by the equally noncommittal designation as 'expressive manifestation' of an inner soul" (p. 28).

sence of poetry in complete surrender or exposure. Following Hölderlin's suggestion in "As on a Holiday," he writes that instead of articulating inner feelings, the poet "stands 'beneath God's thunderstorms'—'bareheaded,' defenselessly surrendered and abandoned." When Hölderlin occasionally speaks of the "soul of the poet," the phrase does not designate a "rummaging in inner psychic feelings" or an "experiential core somewhere inside" but rather the "utmost exile of naked exposure." For both Hölderlin and Heidegger, thunderstorm and lightning are the peculiar "language of the gods" which poets are meant to capture "without flinching" and to transplant into the language of a people. As the lecture course elaborates, the "language of the gods" is not a direct mode of speech but rather a set of indirect "winks," cues or traces. Poetry, from this perspective, is "the transmission of these winks to the people"; seen from the angle of the latter, it is the attempt "to place the being of a people under the aegis of these winks"—an attempt that does not mean their transformation into "observable objects or intentional contents." It is precisely by enduring and transmitting the "winks of the gods" that poetry is said to contribute to the constitution of being.[10]

Along with the subjective-expressive approach Heidegger rejects the definition of exegesis as a reconstruction of the *mens auctoris* (author's intention). In his view, the author's mind—provided it could be uncovered—is not a reliable or authoritative guide; actually, it is the poem that constitutes the author as author or poet, rather than the other way around. In reading a poem, he observes, we cannot take refuge in the author's intent as a fixed point; instead, we are drawn into the torrent of the poetic language, into the "cyclone" (*Wirbel*) of the poetic saying. As this observation indicates, Heidegger, in criticizing the subjective or mentalist conception, does not simply opt for a textual objectivism or autonomy, that is, for the timeless, aesthetic essence of a text or opus— such as a "Sophocles in itself, a Kant in itself," or a poem in itself. Rather, interpreting a text requires dynamic participation and involvement on the part of the reader—who, in turn, is not a sovereign master. Accordingly, readers must be willing to undergo the same surrender the poet endured; they must themselves be ready to enter the cyclone of the poetic word. Thus, Heidegger stresses the need to participate in poetry, the need to be drawn into the "power sphere" (*Machtbereich*) of poetry and to let poetry exert its leavening and transforming impact on human life.[11]

[10] Ibid., pp. 30–33.
[11] Ibid., pp. 19, 45, 58–59, 145. Heidegger comments repeatedly in the lecture course on the status of metaphors in poetry, a theme that is important because of the connection

III

To be sure, in offering his exegesis of Hölderlin's poems, Heidegger does not himself speak as a poet but as a thinker or philosopher; his interpretation is a distinctly philosophical endeavor. The lecture course repeatedly portrays the relation between thinking and poetry (*Dichten und Denken*) as one marked by both distance and proximity, that is, as a relation of two enterprises whose boundary is both a connecting link and a line of demarcation. In Heidegger's view, thinking and poetry are neither synonymous nor worlds apart; as he notes in another context, they "dwell close together on high mountain tops separated by an abyss." The lecture course, in any event, is not merely a poetic paraphrase or a literary exercise; instead, it deliberately pursues the task of philosophical penetration, an effort guided by the need for lucid sobriety (*heller Ernst*) as distinguished from calculating wit or academic pedantry. "If any poet," Heidegger writes,

> demands for his work a philosophical approach, it is Hölderlin; and this not only because as poet he happened to be "also a philosopher"—and even one whom we can confidently place next to Schelling and Hegel. Rather: Hölderlin is one of our greatest, that is, most impending *thinkers* because he is our greatest *poet*. The poetic understanding of his poetry is possible only as a philosophical confrontation with the manifestation of being achieved in his work.[12]

Judged in strictly philosophical terms, the lecture course is significant not only because of its analysis of Hölderlin's poems but also—in equal measure—because of the light it throws on Heidegger's own perspective and on the development of his thought. The reader acquainted with *Being and Time* will encounter many themes familiar from that work, especially the theme of the ontological status of *Dasein*, of man as the "witness of being" whose *Dasein* is lodged in the existential tension of "thrownness" and "project" (*Geworfenheit* and *Entwurf*). There are also comments on "being-toward-death" as well as on *Mitsein* and authentic

---

between "meta-phors" and "meta-physics." Thus, referring to the first stanza of "As on a Holiday," Heidegger states that these lines do not offer a "poetic comparison such as an 'image' or a 'metaphor.'" For, in a poetic comparison, "what is compared with what? Typically a process in nature with a spiritual-mental experience. But what do we mean by 'nature' and by 'spirit'? . . . No matter how we construe these terms, what is the point of a comparison if the poet insists that nature itself educates the poet?" (pp. 254–255).

[12] Ibid., pp. 5–6, 8. See also Heidegger, *What Is Philosophy?* trans. William Kluback and Jean T. Wilde (New Haven, Conn.: College and University Press, 1956), p. 95.

"co-being." As he states in the lecture course, "Being directly touches and concerns us—we cannot even exist without being entangled in being. But this being or existence of ours is not that of an isolated subject but rather a historical co-being or togetherness as being-in-a-world." In line with the earlier work, the course also contains significant passages on the meaning of time, particularly the distinction between ordinary time seen as the "mere flux of successive nows" and genuine time as the advent or manifestation of being.[13]

In addition to these more familiar topics, the course moves beyond the perimeters of *Being and Time* in the direction of Heidegger's subsequent works. Thus, the portrayal of *Dasein* as a linguistic event (*Sprachgeschehnis*) and as dialogue (*Gespräch*) foreshadows arguments more fully developed in *On the Way to Language*. "Only where language happens," Heidegger states, "can being and nonbeing disclose themselves; this disclosure and concealment, however, is who we are." Similarly, the description of genuine time as a "waiting for the *Ereignis*" may be said to adumbrate later discussions of this mode of ontological happening (sometimes translated as "appropriation" or "appropriating event"). A prominent feature of the lecture course is also the recurrent reference to creators or creative agents (*die Schaffenden*), a topic which became crucial in some of Heidegger's writings during the immediately following years. In particular, the subdivision of creators into poets, thinkers, and founders of states (*Staatsschöpfer*) is a striking anticipation of an argument familiar from "The Origin of the Work of Art" of 1935–36; the same could be said about passages dealing with the role of conflict or *agon* (*Streit*) as precondition of ontological harmony (*Innigkeit*).[14]

IV

I turn now to another boundary, that connecting poetry and thinking with politics, and I approach it on two levels: a more overt and a more latent or subterranean level. There are a great number of overtly political passages in the lecture course, some quite forthright and brazen if placed

---

[13] Heidegger, *Hölderlins Hymnen*, pp. 55, 61, 173–175. As Heidegger insists, the "ownness" (*Jemeinigkeit*) of *Dasein* and of individual death does not nullify the ontological character of co-being. Accentuating the aspect of "thrownness" in every project, the course establishes a close linkage between being and suffering, associating genuine human existence with the need continuously to "undergo" its own calling (*Leiden seiner selbst*) (pp. 73, 174–175).

[14] Ibid., pp. 51, 56, 69–71, 117–118, 123–128, 144, 275.

in the context of 1934. The opening pages of the course borrow a fragment from Hölderlin's late opus which reads: "About the highest I shall be silent. / Forbidden fruit, like the laurel, however, / Is most of all the fatherland. This [fruit] / Everyone should taste last." Heidegger comments:

> The fatherland, our fatherland Germany—forbidden most of all, removed from everyday haste and busy noise. . . . With this we already indicate what our focus on "Germania" does not mean. We do not wish to offer something usable, trendy, or up-to-date and thereby advertise our lecture course— which would convey the pernicious impression as if we wanted to garner for Hölderlin a cheap timely relevance. We do not seek to adapt Hölderlin to our time; on the contrary: we want to bring us and those after us under the yardstick of the poet.

Our fatherland, forbidden most of all—surely strange words at a time of patriotic and chauvinistic frenzy.[15]

But there is more to come. Commenting on Hölderlin's portrayal of Germania—as a priestess or else as a dreamy maid "hidden in the woods"—Heidegger compares this image with a famous national monument, the statue of Germania in the Niederwald forest. This monument, he notes, depicts "a massive woman [ein Mordsweib] with flowing hair and a giant sword. By contrast, Hölderlin's Germania is by today's standards 'unheroic.'" What makes things worse is the reference to a defenseless Germania offering counsel to nations. Thus, Heidegger adds mockingly, Hölderlin "is apparently a 'pacifist,' one who advocates the defenselessness of Germany and perhaps even unilateral disarmament. This borders on high treason." A little later, during a discussion of the expressive view of poetry, Heidegger directly attacks one of the regime's most representative literary figures, Erwin G. Kolbenheyer. In speeches given at various German universities, the latter had claimed that "poetry is a necessary biological function of a people." Heidegger retorts: "It does not take much brain to realize: this [description] also applies to digestion—which likewise is a biologically necessary function of a people, especially a healthy one."

The same discussion aims a barb at Alfred Rosenberg, the regime's star ideologist, and at the doctrine of biological racism. The expressive view, Heidegger insists, is mistaken regardless of whose sentiments are involved—whether these sentiments are those of a single individual or a

---

[15] Ibid., p. 4; see also *Friedrich Hölderlin: Poems and Fragments*, p. 537 (translation slightly altered).

"collective soul," whether (with Spengler) they reflect the "soul of a culture" or (with Rosenberg) they express a "racial soul" or the "soul of a people." Regarding fascist biologism, another passage should also be mentioned. In light of his stress on "earth" and "homeland," Heidegger has sometimes been assailed as harboring a sympathy for the ideology of "blood and soil" (*Blut und Boden*). Alluding to the practice of literary criticism of his time—to the "dubious arsenal of the contemporary science of literature"—he states: "Until recently everyone was looking for the psychoanalytic underpinnings of poetry; now everything is saturated [*trieft*] with folkdom and with 'blood and soil'—but nothing has really changed."[16]

Here, for good measure, are a few more stabs at pet fascist conceptions or slogans. Advocating a view of philosophy a perpetual questioning, Heidegger writes, in mock self-criticism: "Questioning? But no: the decisive thing is clearly the answer. That much every pedestrian or man on the street understands, and since he understands it, it must be right and the whole outlook is then called 'folkish science' or 'folk-related science' [*volksverbundene Wissenschaft*, the official aim of every academic discipline at the time]." Or again, a little later, Heidegger finds a linkage between the fascist view of culture and bourgeois "culture industry." "Only small times," he observes, "when the whole *Dasein* decays into fabrication—only such times officially cultivate the 'true, good, and beautiful' and establish appropriate state ministries for this cultivation." This confusion is compounded by the mistaken assumption that folk culture can be enhanced "through the expanded institution of professorships for folk science and primeval history." Elsewhere, Heidegger displays his chagrin over ongoing developments in academia and education in general. His turn to Hölderlin, he insists, does not reflect an attempt to salvage a national heritage or to "utilize [the poet] in a direct political manner"—things "which no doubt we shall encounter abundantly in the coming years, following the completed political integration [*Gleichschaltung*], of the humanities." In a sardonic vein, pondering future prospects of philosophy, he notes at one point that "it now appears as if thinking will soon be entirely abolished."[17]

---

[16] Heidegger, *Hölderlins Hymnen*, pp. 17, 26–27, 254. On Heidegger's invocation of "blood and soil" in his "Rektoratsrede" of May 1933, see the sensible comments of Graeme Nicholson in "The Politics of Heidegger's Rectorial Address," *Man and World* 20 (1987):171–187.

[17] Heidegger, *Hölderlins Hymnen*, pp. 5, 41, 99, 221. In another context, Heidegger attacks the portrayal of Christ as *Führer*—a portrayal, he says, that is "not only an untruth but also, what is worse, a blasphemy vis-à-vis Christ" (p. 210).

Although criticizing the political winds of the time, I should add, Heidegger does not depict his own preoccupation with Hölderlin as a simple retreat from politics. On the contrary, his lectures explicitly present this concern as a kind of counterpolitics, signaling a radical change of political course. "Since Hölderlin has this hidden and difficult meaning to be the poet's poet and the poet of the Germans," we read, "therefore he has not yet become a guiding force in the history of our people. And since he is not yet this force, he should become it. To contribute to this task is 'politics' in the highest and most genuine sense—so much so that whoever makes headway along this line has no need to talk about 'politics.' "[18]

V

What alternative does Heidegger's counterpolitics suggest? We approach here, I believe, the deeper or less overt significance of Hölderlin in the context of 1934—and, more broadly, in the context of our age. Heidegger delineates this significance by elaborating on the basic mood (*Grundstimmung*) of the two poems "Germania" and "The Rhine," a mood that underlies and permeates these hymns as a whole. By "mood," one needs to emphasize right away, Heidegger does not mean an inner, subjective feeling or psychological sentiment. Readers of *Being and Time* cannot be misled on this point, which is reiterated in the lecture course: "mood" in Heidegger's usage is a kind of ontological tuning or attunement, the attunement of *Dasein* and being, or the mode in which being is revealed and concealed in *Dasein* or (as here) in poetry. As he says, mood (*Stimmung*) denotes "least of all the merely subjective or the so-called interior of man"; rather, it is "the original exposure into the vastness of beings and the depth of being."[19]

Turning first to "Germania," what—in Heidegger's exegesis—is the basic tuning pervading the poem? According to the lecture course, this tuning derives from a fundamental though subterranean event of our age: the flight or disappearance of the gods. Hölderlin's hymn begins with these lines: "Not them, the blessed ones who once appeared, the images of gods of old, them I may no longer call." This non-calling is not, however, simply an act of resignation, least of all a sign of abandonment or indifference; rather, non-calling is a synonym for the patient en-

[18] Ibid., p. 214.
[19] Ibid., p. 142.

durance of a loss, for a long-standing and profound suffering. The tuning or mood of "Germania" is then essentially one of mourning (*Trauer*). Yet, in the treatment of both Hölderlin and Heidegger, mourning is not identical with mere emotional sadness or melancholy, and certainly not with plaintiff anxiety or distress. Rather, as a mode of attunement, mourning has a sober and almost serene quality; in Heidegger's words, it is not a psychological but a spiritual (or ontological) category. Occasioned by the loss of gods, the mourning pervading "Germania" is in fact a "hallowed" or "sacred mourning" (*heilige Trauer*). Moreover, mourning here does not signify a breach or simple farewell. As in the case of a loved one, the experience of the loss of gods actually nurtures and strengthens the bond of love and the desire for reunion. As Heidegger notes, "Where the most beloved is gone, love remains—for else the other could not at all have gone [as the beloved]." Thus, mourning here is both acceptance of the loss, a refusal to cling, and a determined waiting for reconciliation, an expectant readiness for the return of the gods.[20]

The theme of mourning is further elaborated in "The Rhine," whose focus is on the role of half-gods or demigods as exemplary mourners. In Hölderlin's presentation these demigods are directly guided by a divine mission or destiny (*Schicksal*) and thus are able to chart a course for human life; they include the great rivers (like the Rhine) that create a path for human habitation, and also the poets who carry the gods' lightning to men. In Heidegger's commentary, half-gods are basically "overmen and undergods" (*Übermenschen und Untergötter*). When thinking about the humans, he observes, we necessarily point beyond humans toward a higher region; in thinking about gods, on the other hand, we inevitably fall short and remain at their threshold. Hence the importance of half-gods as mediators and placekeepers of the "in-between" realm. Standing directly under divine mandates, half-gods are particularly vulnerable and exposed; being specially attuned to the withdrawal (and possible return) of the gods, their existence is marked by intense suffering and

---

[20] Ibid., pp. 80–82, 95. As Heidegger adds: "Sacred mourning is ready to renounce the old gods; yet—what else does the mourning heart desire but this: in relinquishing the gods to preserve immaculate their divinity and thus, through a preserving renunciation of the distant gods, to remain in the proximity of their divinity. The not-being-able-to-call the old gods, the acceptance of the loss, what else is it—it is nothing else—but the only possible, resolute readiness to wait for the divine" (p. 95). Together with Hölderlin, incidentally, Heidegger interprets the term "sacred" or holy in the sense of "unselfish"—something that radically transcends the domains of both individual and general interest (or utility) (p. 84).

endurance. In effect, their suffering is the emblem of their mediating and creative role. Thus, as in the case of "Germania," the basic mood or tuning of "The Rhine" is one of hallowed mourning, occasioned by the flight of the gods. In Heidegger's words:

> The manner in which the being of half-gods—the midpoint of being as a whole—is disclosed is suffering. This great and alone decisive kind of suffering, however, can pervade *Dasein* only in the form of that mood that manifests simultaneously the fugitive and approaching power of God and the exposed plight of human life: the mood of sacred mourning and expectant readiness.[21]

VI

One should mark this well: mourning—sacred mourning—as the central mood of Hölderlin's hymns and also of Heidegger's entire lecture course. How incongruous—in 1934, and still today. How much disillusionment and personal agony must have preceded and nurtured this mood in the case of both Hölderlin and Heidegger. How far removed, how radically distant is this outlook from the ebullient self-confidence of the fascist regime in 1934, from the mood of national resurgence (*Aufbruch*) at the inception of the "thousand-year Reich" (1934, one may recall, was the year of the mammoth party congress in Nuremberg which, in a celebrated film, has been glorified as "triumph of the will").[22] How distant is this outlook from our own contemporary life, from our own ebullient self-confidence in the unlimited blessings of technological progress.

Mourning, sacred mourning—about what? About the godlessness of our age, about the withdrawal and absence of the gods. I should add right away that mourning of this kind is not simply a call for moral or spiritual renewal or for a mobilization of religious faith; least of all is it a call for a

---

[21] Ibid., pp. 165–166, 182. For an attempt to find a more overt political meaning in "The Rhine," see Johannes Mahr, *Mythos und Politik in Hölderlins Rheinhymne* (Munich: Fink Verlag, 1972).

[22] Heidegger was well aware of the mentioned incongruence or contrast. As he writes: "The flight of the gods must first become an experience and this experience must push *Dasein* into a basic mood in which a historical people as a whole endures the plight of its godlessness and brokenness. It is this basic mood which the poet seeks to implant in the life of our people. Whether this happened in 1801, and whether in 1934 it has not yet been perceived and grasped—this is not the issue since dates are immaterial at such a watershed" (*Hölderlins Hymnen*, p. 80).

strengthening of church institutions or confessional ties. Godlessness here is not a question of the vitality of established churches or of inner, personal belief. Instead, it has to do with the absence of gods from our civilization and our existence as a people, that is, from our way of life or way of being. It has to do with our relegation of the divine to a decorative status on holidays, to the status of folklore at religious festivals. As Heidegger emphasizes: "The issue is not how an empirically given people handles its traditional religion or denominational faith. Rather, at stake is the genuine advent or non-advent of God in the life of a people out of the agony of its being."[23]

The stress on a common way of life (or ontological condition) highlights another dimension of the key mood of the two hymns: the reference to a homeland or fatherland. For Hölderlin and Heidegger, mourning is not the experience of an isolated individual or a subjective state of mind; rather, it is a mourning "in" and "with the homeland [*Heimat*]" or "with the native earth [*heimatliche Erde*]." But homeland here is not simply a natural habitat or empirical-ecological setting; nor is it a mere abstraction or speculative-metaphysical idea. As interpreted in the lecture course, homeland is rather the site of an ontological mediation—the name for a concrete promise, namely, for a potential dwelling place of the gods.[24] Properly speaking, mourning is possible only on the basis of such a promise. For, how could one talk of their withdrawal or advent if gods lived in an immutable realm separated from humans by an unbridgeable gulf? And how could one sense or experience their loss if human life were invariably wretched? Mourning thus necessarily involves a transgression of traditional metaphysics (predicated on the juxtaposition of two separate "worlds").

VII

Let me slowly come to a close. I have explored Heidegger's exegesis of Hölderlin's hymns and also some of their overt and covert political implications. I do not wish to leave the impression that I find all Heidegger's arguments equally persuasive. Some passages still carry overtones of a youthful exuberance (*Sturm und Drang*) that required further seasoning; some details are not entirely congruent, in my view, with the overall

[23] Ibid., p. 147.
[24] Ibid., pp. 88, 90, 104, 122–123.

direction of his thought. Thus, I find dubious Heidegger's persistent reference to "the people" (*Volk*) in the sense of a homogeneous entity or totality. Precisely his nonobjectivist ontology and his stress on ontological difference should have suggested to him a greater heterogeneity among people (perhaps along the lines of Arendt's notion of "plurality"). Appeals to "the people" or a bland populism are particularly problematic if the people, here the German people, are assigned an eminently poetic or historically creative role; surely subsequent years and decades must have disabused Heidegger of such hopes.

Together with the concept of "the people" I would also question the notion of "the state" as used in the lecture course, especially in the portrayal of founders of states as exemplary historical agents; too heavily burdened with modern metaphysical weight, "the state" does not seem an adequate vehicle for Heidegger's thoughts.[25] Finally, I find disconcerting the excessive emphasis on conflict and *agon* (*Streit, Feindseligkeit*), an emphasis that renders harmony (*Innigkeit*) extremely precarious if not impossible. In the exegesis of "The Rhine," this emphasis is actually so strong and pervasive that Heidegger almost omits to comment on a crucial theme in Hölderlin's poem: the impending wedding feast of gods and men. In this instance the experiences of subsequent years and the outbreak of the war seemed to have a remarkable effect. When Heidegger again offered a lecture course on Hölderlin (in winter 1941/42), his focus and the basic tuning of the course was precisely this wedding feast (*Brautfest*).[26]

Yet, I wish to end on a different note—by returning to 1934. In the midst of fascist triumphalism, Heidegger's lecture course is pervaded by overwhelming grief. What is the significance, then, of Hölderlin in Heidegger's perception? Who is this poet as reflected in the two hymns and in the lectures? He is, simply put, a caller in the desert, a voice in the wilderness of our age, or, as Heidegger says, a "first fruit" or "first born" (*Erstling*) liable to be sacrificed. What does the voice proclaim? Mostly

[25] In all these respects, Heidegger's later works contain important self-corrections. Thus, his *Beiträge zu Philosophie* of 1936–38 sharply questions the broad label of "the people" (*Volk*), introducing instead careful internal differentiations; see *Beiträge zur Philosophie (Vom Ereignis)*, ed. Friedrich-Wilhelm von Herrmann (*Gesamtausgabe*, Vol. 65; Frankfurt-Main: Klostermann, 1989), pp. 42, 50, 99, 319, 398, 401. Likewise, a lecture course held in summer 1942 contrasts the *polis* construed as an ontological site to the modern conception of the state; see Heidegger, *Hölderlins Hymne "Der Ister,"* ed. Walter Biemel (*Gesamtausgabe*, Vol. 53; Frankfurt-Main: Klostermann, 1984), pp. 100–101.

[26] See Heidegger, *Hölderlins Hymne "Andenken,"* ed. Curd Ochwadt (*Gesamtausgabe*, Vol. 52; Frankfurt-Main: Klostermann, 1982), pp. 76–78, 188.

this: prepare the ground, make straight the paths, for a possible return of the fugitive gods, and thus for a possible reconciliation or "wedding feast."[27] Not that through our attitude or activity we could somehow halt their flight or force or fabricate their reappearance; but our grief and expectation may at least serve as an invitation encouraging their return. Mourning thus is preparatory for a different age—for a way of life that is again suffused with lightning and poetic imagination, a life in which young men can again "see visions and old men dream dreams." This is also the meaning of the fatherland as a hallowed or promised land. Heidegger concludes the lecture course by once again invoking the fragment with which he began: "About the highest I shall be silent. / Forbidden fruit, like the laurel, however, / Is most of all the fatherland. This [fruit] / Everyone should taste last."

[27] In Heidegger's words: "The task is to take seriously the long-standing flight of the gods and in and through this seriousness to anticipate their return—which means: to participate in the preparation of their renewed advent and thus to refashion the earth and the land anew" (*Hölderlins Hymnen*, pp. 146, 220–221).

CHAPTER SIX

Homecoming through Otherness

A pervasive theme in contemporary philosophy, especially its Continental variant, is the notion of otherness; under diverse labels, otherness constitutes a crucial link tying together the multiple strands of post-foundational, or postmodern, thought. The focus has (and is meant to have) a critical or subversive edge. Traditional Western philosophy, the argument commonly goes, has had a streamlining or homogenizing bent, manifested in the attempt to subsume all modes of experience under universal categories governed by the standards of identity and rational sameness (*logos*); the bent has reached its apex in modernity with its stress on consciousness and self-enclosed subjectivity. As an antidote to this kind of self-enclosure, contemporary post-foundational writings accentuate otherness, difference, or nonidentity and even the need for a radical exodus or exile. Thus, among many others, Gilles Deleuze celebrates the virtues of "nomad thought," that is, of a nomadic type of thinking and experiencing which, forever "abroad," completely cancels native attachments or any rootedness in a home or settled abode. As he points out, nomad thought is a state of mobility radically opposed to settled structures or to uniform regimes "whose philosophers would be bureaucrats of pure reason."[1]

---

[1] See Gilles Deleuze, "Nomad Thought," in *The New Nietzsche: Contemporary Styles of Interpretation*, ed. David B. Allison (Cambridge: MIT Press, 1986), p. 149. As it happens, a state of nomadic mobility quite outside the range of philosophical discussions is instantiated today by the host of international, "cosmopolitan" experts and corporate executives whose lifestyles indeed involve a denial of any local attachment. On this point, see Ulf Hannerz, "Cosmopolitans and Locals in World Culture," in *Global Culture: Nationalism, Globalization, and Modernity*, ed. Mike Featherstone (London: Sage, 1990), pp. 237–251; also Graham Hancock, *Lords of Poverty* (New York: Atlantic Monthly Press, 1989).

Advanced as antidotes or correctives, post-foundational initiatives have a salutary effect. Against the backdrop of our emerging global society (or global village), otherness offers welcome relief from all forms of self-centeredness, including anthropocentrism and Eurocentrism; wherever identity has turned stale or stagnant, nonidentity clearly signals liberation, provided that it is not a counsel of nomadism. What vitiates the latter, in my view, is its escapist vacuity. Unless proceeding from or in the direction of a human habitat, exodus remains an empty escapade (or else simply a mode of self-indulgence). In the absence of a concrete encounter of self and other, of indigenous and alien lifeforms, "estrangement" cannot possibly happen—that is, otherness cannot really be undergone in a manner yielding a learning experience. By claiming to elude all human settlements, nomadism proceeds in a no-man's land devoid of contrasts and possibilities for sustained engagement.

The interconnection between self and other, identity and difference, is a topic not unknown to traditional philosophy—which is sometimes too quickly dismissed as unitary and "logocentric." What has not often been noticed is that the connection—in a revised, perhaps post-metaphysical form—is also a central ingredient in Martin Heidegger's philosophical work. As it seems to me, the topic of estrangement, or "alter-ation" (*Veranderung*, to use a term coined by Michael Theunissen), can actually serve as an Ariadne thread through Heidegger's evolving opus; with progressing years and especially after the *Kehre* (turning), the theme is steadily intensified and radicalized, but without any concession to nomadism. In this chapter, I concentrate on two phases of this evolution: the war years (Heidegger's middle period) and the postwar era (his later period). As I show, Heidegger's thought in the first phase was strongly informed by Friedrich Hölderlin's poetry; during later years, Georg Trakl emerged as an additional guidepost or mentor. In the earlier period, estrangement in Heidegger's work chiefly (though not solely) concerned the relation between German culture and Greece; subsequently, his focus broadened to encompass the future of Western civilization in its relation to the non-West (or the rest of the globe).[2]

---

[2] On *Veranderung*, see Michael Theunissen, *The Other: Studies in the Social Ontology of Husserl, Heidegger, Sartre, and Buber*, trans. Christopher Macann (Cambridge: MIT Press, 1984); also Fred Dallmayr, "Dialogue and Otherness: Theunissen," in *Critical Encounters* (Notre Dame: University of Notre Dame Press, 1987), pp. 209–224. Regarding the periodization of Heidegger's work, I am partially indebted to Otto Pöggeler, *Philosophie und Politik bei Heidegger* (Freiburg-Munich: Alber, 1972).

I

Transgression of self toward otherness is a persistent Heideggerian concern which, without being fully developed at the time, surfaced clearly in his early writings. In *Being and Time* (1927), he presented human *Dasein* not as a self-contained subject or ego but rather as a "being-in-the-world," that is, a being intimately enmeshed in worldliness and hence linked with things and other human beings. The most dramatic opening toward otherness, as outlined in that study, was human "being-toward-death" involving *Dasein's* concrete anticipation of its own nonbeing, an anticipation nullifying all attempts at subjective management. Moreover, self-estrangement through awareness of mortality was closely coupled with appreciation of the difference of fellow beings; for, as Heidegger observed, as an "unsurpassable" possibility, death also renders *Dasein* sensitive to "the existential possibilities" (*Seinkönnen*) of others. Heidegger pursued the erosion of self-enclosure a few years later in *What Is Metaphysics?* whose central theme was nothingness, or nonbeing. Far from portraying *Dasein* as safely ensconced in familiar surroundings, the lecture presented "nothing" (*Nichts*) as the driving force expelling *Dasein* from complacency into the open quest for being. "Projected into nothing," Heidegger stated, "*Dasein* is already beyond the totality of beings"; without this aspect of self-transcendence revealed in its embroilment with nothingness, "*Dasein* could never relate to being, hence could have no self-relationship." In light of these and similar statements, it is difficult to see how Heidegger's early work could fairly be accused—as has occasionally been done—of favoring a metaphysics of identity, that is, a perspective privileging selfhood over otherness, nearness over distance, and native autochthony over estrangement. What accusations of this kind neglect, in my view, is Heidegger's continual insistence (both then and later) on the ontological status of his argument and on the character of *Dasein*—even the most proximate fellow being—as a "creature of distance [*Ferne*]."[3]

---

[3] See Martin Heidegger, *Sein und Zeit*, 11th ed. (Tübingen: Niemeyer, 1967), pp. 260–267 (par. 53); *What Is Metaphysics?* in *Existentialism from Dostoevsky to Sartre*, ed. Walter Kaufmann (New York: Meridian, 1975), p. 251; on man as a "creature of distance," see Heidegger, "Vom Wesen des Grundes" (1929), in *Wegmarken* (Frankfurt-Main: 1967), p. 71. The most vehement attack on Heidegger as a thinker favoring identity and home-bound autochthony was launched by Theodor W. Adorno in *The Jargon of Authenticity*, trans. Knut Tarnowski and Frederic Will (Evanston, Ill.: Northwestern University Press, 1973).

If there is a point to this criticism, it pertains to a certain abstractness of Heidegger's early work, to its aloofness from concrete historical experiences of estrangement. Otherness and distance in that work tend to be treated as constitutive features of *Dasein* as such, not of a distinct *Dasein* lodged in a concrete historical encounter with alien or unfamiliar modes of life. Heidegger modified or abandoned this aloofness in the decade following *Being and Time*, a change (one may surmise) not unrelated to the political events of the decade. Hitler's regime during this period proceeded to elevate a particular kind of *Dasein*, namely, "German being," to a position of absolute political preeminence, while simultaneously seeking to purge native culture of all alien or non-German traces. Although initially in favor of some kind of German resurgence, Heidegger soon perceived the hatefully restrictive character of Nazi ideology, evident in its racial-biological chauvinism and its violent enmity to otherness; repelled by this ideological perversion, he embarked on a search for alternative routes of recovery or reorientation (a search which for him entailed something like "inner emigration").

One of Heidegger's main preoccupations during these years was the endeavor to articulate an alternative conception of "German being," a conception resonating with the longer tradition of German culture and definitely open to the call of nonidentity. The central mentor of this endeavor became Hölderlin, whose poetry was the focus of repeated lecture courses at the University of Freiburg. Provocatively, and seemingly in response to nationalist sentiments, in the winter of 1934 Heidegger offered a course on Hölderlin's "Germania" and "The Rhine"; but the lectures opened with these lines from one of Hölderlin's late fragments: "Forbidden fruit, like the laurel, however, / Is most of all the fatherland. This [fruit] / Everyone should taste last." Moreover, the central tuning pervading the hymns was said to be not nationalist exuberance but rather the mood of mourning, more specifically of "sacred mourning"—about the flight of the gods (and their replacement by mundane, possibly nationalist idols).[4]

Although a counterpoise to nationalist zeal, the lecture course of 1934 did not yet spell out an alternative course of German culture or German being in opposition to chauvinist frenzy. Heidegger took up this task dur-

---

[4] See Heidegger, *Hölderlins Hymnen "Germanien" und "Der Rhein,"* ed. Susanne Ziegler (*Gesamtausgabe*, Vol. 39; Frankfurt-Main: Klostermann, 1980); also Chapter 5 in this volume. In the lecture course, Hölderlin was presented as "poet of the Germans" because his work was able to invent or project an alternative future for "German being."

ing the darkest years of the Hitler era, when German military aggression had plunged Europe and the rest of the world into a global war. In Freiburg in 1941/42, Heidegger offered two consecutive lecture courses again devoted to hymns by Hölderlin, this time "Remembrance" (*Andenken*) and "The Danube" (*Der Ister*). The central theme of both lecture courses was the encounter between native and alien modes of life and the transformative quality of estrangement (seen as a gateway to self-discovery). Commenting on the opening lines of Hölderlin's hymn in which the poet sends distant greetings to southern France, the first lecture course presents "remembrance," or recollection, not as return to a finished past but rather as a meeting ground where past or alien experience reveals itself as also an impending prospect. In Heidegger's words, recollection seems to depart from the present in the direction of what has gone or vanished; but in fact the recollected experience returns to the greeting poet in a vivid countergreeting, one not confined to the given moment. Once we are fully attentive to recollection, he observes, "we discover that the recollected memory in its return does not stop in the present in order to serve merely as a substitute for the past. Rather, the recollected vaults beyond our present and suddenly faces us from the future. From there it approaches as a still unfulfilled promise, as an unexplored treasure." Seen from this vantage, the poet's greetings are a solicitation for an encounter, more specifically for a dialogue (*Gespräch*) between two modes of historical being. Far from aiming at consensus, this dialogue carefully maintains distance between the partners, where distance does not equal rigid separation but rather a "letting be" granting open space for self-discovery and indigenous freedom.[5]

The poet's greetings are sent southward, and indirectly to Greece as the classical South, from where countergreetings reach him while he stays in his homeland. As it happens, at the time of composing his hymn, Hölderlin had just undertaken a journey to southern France, from where he had returned home with new eyes, a new sensibility, for his native context. In a letter mailed to a friend roughly at the time of his journey, Hölderlin had written these lines: "Nothing is more difficult to learn than

[5] Heidegger, *Hölderlins Hymne "Andenken,"* ed. Curd Ochwadt (*Gesamtausgabe*, Vol. 52; Frankfurt-Main: Klostermann, 1982), pp. 54–55, 164–165. In the translation of Michael Hamburger, the opening lines of the hymn read: "The north-easterly blows, / Of winds the dearest to me / Because a fiery spirit / And happy voyage it promises mariners. / But now go, go and greet / The beautiful Garonne / And the gardens of Bordeaux." See Friedrich Hölderlin, *Poems and Fragments*, trans. Hamburger (Ann Arbor: University of Michigan Press, 1967), p. 489.

the free employment of what is indigenous or native [*das Nationelle*]. And as I believe, clarity of presentation is to us [Germans] as originally native or natural as was to the Greeks the fire from heaven." Without in any way reducing the poem to an autobiographical account, Heidegger's interpretation perceives a linkage between the letter and the hymn "Remembrance": in both cases the basic issue is the acquisition and free employment of native endowments, an aim that can be achieved only through estrangement involving the encounter between self and other—here between the "clarity" of Germans and the "heavenly fire" of Greece.

The lecture course elaborates repeatedly and eloquently on the theme of estrangement and its relation to self-discovery. In order to learn or acquire the "free employment" of native endowments, Heidegger observes at one point, it is necessary to enter "into confrontation [*Auseinandersetzung*] with otherness or the alien"; hence the self must go abroad, not in order to "get lost in strangeness" but to "ready itself there for its own tasks." Heidegger is particularly emphatic in denouncing the identification of self or native homeland with an empirical possession or else its elevation to an ideological or chauvinistic doctrine. "The native or indigenous," we read (in a passage implicitly challenging Nazi propaganda),

> cannot be acquired through a compulsive and brutally coercive grasping of one's own being—as if the latter could be fixated like an empirical state of affairs. One's own distinctiveness [*das Eigene*] cannot be proclaimed like a dogma whose dictates are implemented on command. Rather, such distinctiveness is most difficult to find and hence most easy to miss.[6]

Since self and homeland are not ready-made possessions, their acquisition requires a protracted search, a search involving lengthy detours and modes of alienation. Although seemingly proximate or closest at hand, one's own distinctiveness is gained only through distant peregrinations. Search in this case is not a restless or haphazard errancy but rather a quest or inquiry marked by patient and sustained reflection; far removed from ambitions of conquest or rash appropriation, the searching quest exhibits the qualities of reticence, hesitation, and reserve, qualities akin to subdued reverence. Hölderlin's hymn highlights this aspect of reticence and reserve in verses that speak of the spring equinox as a time "when night and day are balanced" and when "over slow footpaths, / Heavy with golden dreams, / Lulling breezes drift." In Heidegger's

---

[6] Heidegger, *Hölderlins Hymne "Andenken,"* pp. 123, 131.

commentary, the slow paths and lulling breezes are not simply "two separate things located in an arbitrarily chosen landscape"; rather, the breezes drift over slow footpaths and crossings, and the latter offer a transit or transition (*Übergang*) in the drifting breezes. As he adds, only a slow and reticent approach can yield access—if at all—to selfhood and one's own distinctiveness, an access completely barred to fabrication or willful control. Heavily laden with "golden dreams," the access route is staked out not by technical blueprints but by prophetic visions and poetic imagination.

In terms of the lecture course, poetic imagination is preeminently marked by patient searching and reflective inquiry, inquiry steeped in remembrance while simultaneously open to impending disclosures. Underscoring the need for imaginative peregrinations, the course also refers to the opening lines in Hölderlin's "Hyperion" and to a draft passage (later discarded) in the hymn "Bread and Wine." In an early version of the Preface to "Hyperion," Hölderlin had noted that "we all traverse an eccentric path and no other road could possibly lead from childhood to full maturity." The passage in "Bread and Wine" had observed that "spirit" or self is "at home not in the beginning, not at the origin; for homeland consumes [or dissipates]"; hence spirit "loves colony [or going abroad] and courageous self-forgetting." Paraphrasing Hölderlin's lines, Heidegger states that "things do not start at the beginning." Spirit or self is not initially "at home" in the homeland, for such coincidence would merely squander resources instead of leading to the "free employment" of endowments; since homeland (*Heimat*) requires self-discovery in the sense of homecoming, "the spirit of home yearns itself for otherness from where alone a return home is possible."[7]

In correlating estrangement or otherness with homecoming, Heidegger distances himself clearly from nomadism or a lifestyle bent on adventure for adventure's sake. He repeatedly emphasizes this contrast—and this in the face of a seeming resemblance or convergence. Hölderlin's hymn at one point talks of the journey of seafarers in terms loosely akin to

---

[7] Ibid., pp. 124, 127–128, 134, 189–190. Countering notions of a fabricated or engineered homecoming, Heidegger insists that "what is truly impending can never be attained by grasping [*Zugriff*]. In the context of genuine history and its transitions, every grasping is a mishap because it destroys the impending in its advent and collapses the possible into a presumed and accidental reality. In a genuine sense, man cannot 'make' history" (p. 127). The lines from "Bread and Wine" (not translated in Hamburger's volume) read "nemlich zu Hauss ist der Geist / Nicht im Anfang, nicht an der Quell. Ihn zehret die Heimat. / Kolonie liebt, und tapfer Vergessen der Geist."

adventure. These seafarers, we read, "Like painters, bring together / The beautiful things of the earth / And do not disdain winged war, and / To live in solitude, for years, beneath the / Defoliate mast, where through the night do not gleam / The city's holidays / Nor music of strings, nor indigenous dancing." These lines vividly depict the travails of a journey on the high seas far from home. In Heidegger's words, the journey under the "defoliate mast" is like a long winter when trees stand bare without leaves and adverse storms embroil the ship in "winged war" with the elements throughout long nights of solitude. As one should note, however, Hölderlin's hymn does not suggest an aimless or hopeless errancy. In gathering the beauty (*das Schöne*) of the earth, the seafarers already intimate a future sharing or conviviality beyond the pale of solitude. Moreover, in a subsequent line, the hymn explicitly foregrounds another feature of seafaring: "But it is the sea / That takes and gives remembrance"—including remembrance of the origin of the journey, of the city's holidays, and of guitar music (*Saitenspiel*) and native dances. In light of these distinct accents, the hymn's sea journey is more than pointless vagrancy or a striving for exotic thrills. As Heidegger observes, the adventurer's lifestyle is geared toward self-indulgence and the restless search for excitement. Hölderlin's seafarers, by contrast, are soberly subdued and pervaded by reticent expectancy; otherness for them is not an exotic stimulus but rather the "first reflective glimpse of self-being." The course at this point singles out for special criticism the figure of the adventurer as it had been extolled by Ernst Jünger in the aftermath of Nietzsche:

> The figure of the adventurer is possible only in the historical space of modernity and modern "subjectivity." Odysseus was not yet an adventurer; and Hölderlin's poetic seafarers no longer fit that mold. Jünger's "adventurous heart" belongs in the domain of the metaphysics of the will to power. But the heart of Hölderlin's companions is different—for it is governed by reserve, in the face of their long unfestive journey.[8]

For Hölderlin's seafarers, the sights and events of the journey are not random happenings but experiences that need to be carefully pondered

---

[8] Ibid., pp. 178–180. The reference in the text is to Ernst Jünger, *Das abenteuerliche Herz*, 2d ed. (Hamburg: Hanseatische Verlagsanstalt, 1938; orig. 1929). In an aside, Heidegger warns of the fascist overtones of adventurism. To the adventurer, he states, reserve and patient caring can only appear as signs of weakness; dedicated to hardness and bold stimulation, the adventurer is likely to "take refuge in some kind of orgy, possibly an orgy of blood." *Hölderlins Hymne "Andenken,"* p. 181.

and patiently endured; the journey for them is a learning process with a transformative character, something that would be impossible in the absence of a self or "self-being" capable of being transformed. For this reason, the travel abroad is at the same time a return to the origin, or source (*Quelle*), although the latter can never be approached directly and requires the detour through estrangement. Hölderlin's hymn contains these lines: "Many a man / Is shy of going to the source; / For wealth begins in / The sea"—a passage that underscores both the reticent secludedness of the source and the enriching qualities of seafaring (where riches include precisely the wealth of the source). In Heidegger's interpretation, "going to the source" is a synonym for homecoming and self-discovery, for the search for one's own distinctiveness—whose "free employment" remains the most difficult task. Relying on some of Hölderlin's letters, Heidegger relates homecoming to the search for "German being" or German culture and seafaring to the exploration of Greek culture in its different spatial-temporal context; as indicated, the central difference resides, respectively, in the clarity of style and presentation and the "fire from heaven."

Precisely because the native endowment of Greek culture was divine spiritual fire, Greek poets and thinkers had to temper and harness this fire by acquiring a clarity of logical presentation that was initially alien to them. Precisely because the native talent of German culture consists in clarity of thought and style, German poets and thinkers have to temper this quality by opening themselves up to divine fiery inspiration that supplements and gives meaning to their talent. In Heidegger's words, native distinctiveness does not mean self-enclosure but is always "related to otherness: fire to presentation and presentation to fire." In the German case, what is needed is that clarity "lets itself be guided by the intrinsic demands of presentation; for clarity can be freely employed only when it measures itself against darkness and thus ripens and matures in the full sense." Again, Hölderlin's hymn offers a cue in these lines: "But someone pass me / The fragrant cup / Full of the dark light"—where darkness is not simply the antithesis of light (or reason).[9]

Seen from the vantage of Hölderlin's hymn, the task and future path of German culture involve a turn to divine spiritual fire, something starkly at odds with progressive rationalization and technological mastery of

---

[9] Heidegger, *Hölderlins Hymne "Andenken,"* pp. 131, 145, 173–175. As Heidegger adds, "The rejection of [modern] 'rationality' must not be equated with the cheap appeal to 'irrationality'; for the latter is only the other side of the coin and equally untenable as the former" (p. 133).

the world. Hölderlin's perspective (fully embraced here by Heidegger) stands particularly opposed to militant nationalism and chauvinistic expansionism—policies which, at the time of the lecture course, Germany was foisting on the world with a vengeance. The homeland Hölderlin's hymn is searching for or distantly intimating is not a factual political entity but rather a hallowed site completely resistant to possessive appropriation; as he had written about the fatherland in his "Germania," "forbidden fruit, like the laurel."

In a dedication attached to his translation of Sophoclean tragedies (dating roughly from the time of "Remembrance"), Hölderlin had expressed his intent to "sing the angels of the sacred fatherland"—a remarkable formulation in several ways. As Heidegger comments, the intent is not to write patriotic songs but to honor poetically the sacred fatherland as a land "steeped in holiness or sacredness"; moreover, the honor is directed not at princes and potentates but at the angels who are guardians of the sacred (*das Heilige*). The latter term, he emphasizes, should not simply be equated with the divine or religious in the sense of an existing or established religion; more broadly, the term is not part of the customary terminology of theology, for "wherever theology arises, the god is already in flight." What is adumbrated here, instead, is a linkage of homeland with a nonpragmatic and nonmanageable wholeness or holiness, a linkage whereby the former can be approached only from the height of the sacred (and not the other way around). This aspect also militates against the reduction of homeland to a concrete political entity or structure:

> What Hölderlin means by fatherland is not exhausted by politics or the political—no matter how broadly the latter is construed. . . . Even if fatherland and the political could be equated, one still has to realize that fatherland is a fruit that can grow only in light and ether, that is, in the element of the highest or the sacred. The latter is the grounding of fatherland and its historical being. But fatherland is highest only to the extent that it originates in the height of the sacred and insofar as this height is discovered as the native home in which, as a shared origin, everyone can at last participate.[10]

The reference to a participation in the end (*zuletzt*) and to a fruit that "everyone should taste last" again points up the elusiveness of the search

---

[10] Ibid., pp. 46–47, 132–135, 140–141.

and the lack of any ready-made access. This lack, in turn, underscores the difference between Hölderlin's (and Heidegger's) notion of sacredness and traditional forms of religious faith. Construed in terms of traditional faith, Heidegger observes, turning to the homeland would mean an attempt to seek refuge in the secure haven of established beliefs, with the goal of guaranteeing personal salvation. Yet, Hölderlin's poetry—and poetry in general—"knows nothing of security and satisfaction; everything remains task." Hölderlin's search for the sacred fatherland involves distant peregrinations and a "long endured need" that presupposes patience and reserve. In terms of the lecture course, such patient reserve was displayed in exemplary fashion by Hölderlin himself—but perhaps not by the poet alone. In a passage that may carry autobiographical connotations, Heidegger states:

> Can we sense the depth of endurance that animates the greetings to that foreign land the poet can no longer inhabit? . . . Can we fathom what it means to remain in the homeland in order to search there for one's own distinctiveness [*das Eigene*]? Do we have the slightest inkling of the patience required for this search in the homeland? But can we also surmise the generosity that must animate this patience so that everyone who seeks the distinctiveness of the fatherland can develop the free employment of one's own endowment in freedom?

What is striking in this passage is the emphasis on generosity (*Grossmut*) and freedom, features that surely were completely alien to fascism and the Germany of the war years. Intensifying the importance of these features, Heidegger stresses the uncontrollable quality of homecoming. To taste the fatherland's fruit last, he notes, means that everyone can undertake the journey and get prepared for self-discovery; the latter preparation, in turn, implies that "no constraint any longer obstructs the free view of the highest" and that "no managerial haste disturbs the forbidden fruit."[11]

As a sacred site, Hölderlin's fatherland is not an empirical terrain and least of all a self-enclosed community. The fruit of protracted search, the home to which homecoming points, is not a fixed abode but a peculiar "in-between" place of transit—a zone located between self and other, between proximity and distance, and also between mortals and immor-

---

[11] Ibid., pp. 134–135, 141–142. In another context, freedom is defined as "open belongingness to being" (p. 41).

tals. As indicated, Hölderlin's hymn speaks of the spring equinox, of the "time in March, / When night and day are balanced." This equinox, Heidegger comments, is a time of transit or transition (*Übergang*), a time when night and day are completely matched and when the "harsh rigidity of winter" is balanced against the "vigorous freshness of summer." Balance or transit in this context signals a reconciliation (*Versöhnung*) of contrasts, not in the sense of a bland amalgamation or leveling of differences but in that of a mutual recognition where each side or partner freely lets the other "be." Transit, we read, "means reconciliation, and reconciliation means that kind of balance [*Ausgleich*] which does not level or erase differences but which accords to each side its equal share, namely, its distinctiveness according to the proper measure of self-being." Hölderlin's hymn in the same context speaks of holidays as corollaries of the equinox or time of transit. In Heidegger's interpretation, holidays at this point are meant as a prelude for a special celebration—the celebration of the "highest balance" or reconciliation, which consists in the meeting of mortals and immortals and which Hölderlin in another hymn ("The Rhine") had called the "bridal feast of humans and gods." As in the case of the spring equinox, this bridal feast, while overcoming mutual separation or isolation, does not produce an indiscriminate merger; rather, both sides "are carried and carry each other reciprocally into their own." The element sustaining or enabling this mutual carrying is again the sacred (*das Heilige*) seen as the bond that "accords to humans and gods respectively their self-being." Sacredness, Heidegger comments, "reigns over humans and over gods alike." Not reducible to fixed entities, gods and humans "need each other; for neither side carries life alone."[12]

Heidegger continued and fleshed out the theme of homecoming through otherness during the following semester in a lecture course devoted to the hymn "The Danube." More specifically than the preceding hymn, "The Danube" is concerned with journeying or seafaring, a concern evident in the focus on the river of that name. The linkage of river and journeying, however, is closer than is suggested by vague analogy. As Heidegger emphasizes, the hymn does not deal with the river Danube as a metaphor or symbol for journeying; instead, the river

---

[12] Ibid., pp. 68–70, 77, 86–88, 92, 97–100. In Heidegger's presentation, the correlation of self and other, mortals and immortals, is an integral feature of ontological "juncture" or "jointedness" (*Seinsfuge*) wherein each being gains the free employment of its own (pp. 100–102). As a sacred event, the bridal feast of humans and gods is neither simply joyous nor sadly mournful; instead, its mood is one of joyous mourning familiar especially from Greek tragedy (pp. 71–72).

"is" (ontologically) itself a journey or peregrination, though not simply an aimless drift. By opening up fertile places for cultivation, the river offers a site for human settlement; at the same time, however, this site is forever "under way" and pointing abroad. In Heidegger's words, the river is both site (*Ortschaft*) and journey or wandering (*Wanderschaft*), in such a way that the site can be reached (*erwandert*) only in the course of the journey. Stated more specifically and more concretely, the stream is "the site of the dwelling of historical human existence on this earth"; and it is also "the journey of the historical homecoming in the location of that site." Differently phrased, the stream means a journey or wandering that incipiently heralds an impending homecoming or the possibility of "being at home" (*Heimischsein*). Homecoming and being at home are not, however, ready-made acquisitions: they are possible only through intense estrangement or exposure to otherness; to this extent, appropriation is closely linked with expropriation, homecoming with the need for exodus:

> Site and journey—emblems of the poetic essence of streams—are related to the impending homecoming into one's own, and this in the special sense that self-discovery and appropriation of one's own are not the easiest and most natural thing but remain the most difficult task—a task that is entrusted to poetic care. . . . Homecoming into one's own implies that, for a long time and perhaps always, man [human existence] is not at home; and this, in turn, implies that man ignores, rejects, and denies—perhaps must deny—the site of home [*das Heimische*]. Homecoming for this reason is a transit through otherness.[13]

To illustrate the sense of journeying through otherness, the lecture course turns back in time to Greek tragedy and particularly to Sophocles' *Antigone*. Focusing initially on the opening line of the first chorus song (*polla ta deina kouden anthropou deinoteron pelei*), Heidegger rejects the customary rendition of *deinon* as "strange" or "enormous"; instead, he proposes to translate the term as "not at home" or "alienated from home" (*unheimisch*) as well as "uncanny" (*unheimlich*), with the uncanniness deriving from a basic estrangement. In rendering *deinon* as *unheimlich*, Heidegger observes, we think in the direction of the uncanny; but the latter we

---

[13] Heidegger, *Hölderlins Hymne "Der Ister,"* ed. Walter Biemel (*Gesamtausgabe*, Vol. 53; Frankfurt-Main: Klostermann, 1984), pp. 36, 39, 51, 60. For perceptive comments on Heidegger's lectures on "The Danube," see Walter Biemel, "Zu Heideggers Deutung der Ister-Hymne," *Heidegger Studies* 3/4 (1987–88): 41–60.

mean in the sense of something that is not "homelike" or "at home" (*heimisch*). It is due only to this estrangement that *deinon* can also acquire the sense of "strange," "frightening," or "terrible." Taken in this vein, "the word of Sophocles that man is the most uncanny creature signifies that man is in a unique sense alienated or not at home and that homecoming hence is his pervasive concern." In Sophocles' tragedy, the opening line of the chorus applies with particular force to Antigone, whose course of action entails complete estrangement from the city. As she herself states in the dialogue with her sister Ismene, Antigone is prepared *pathein to deinon touto*—to suffer the full measure of uncanny estrangement. As Heidegger comments, the phrase *pathein to deinon* indicates that estrangement (*das Unheimische*) is not something "initiated or fabricated" by humans but rather something that makes or transforms humans into "what they are or can be." Although implying suffering, *pathein* denotes not merely passive endurance but the readiness to undergo and shoulder a learning experience. Seen from this vantage, Antigone is not a tragic heroine bent on asserting her individuality or subjectivity, nor is she a religious martyr quietly resigned to passivity; instead, she undergoes estrangement implicit in the human condition, and she does so in a complete and exemplary fashion. Moreover, in pursuing her course, Antigone does not simply go to her doom. Although she is alienated completely from mundane affairs (from the realm of "beings"), Antigone's action honors an abode that is beyond mundane power and ultimately redeems her death (by allowing a *kallos thanein*). In terms of the lecture course, "her dying is a homecoming, but a homecoming in and through estrangement."[14]

As in the preceding lecture course, Heidegger again sharply differentiates journeying through otherness from sheer nomadism or adventurism. In the same chorus song of the tragedy, humans are described as seafaring creatures venturing out into "the tumultuous waves during the southern storms of winter." Yet, Heidegger notes, seafaring here is not a mere errancy from place to place guided by aimless curiosity. As depicted by the chorus, "man is not an adventurer bent on nomadic homelessness; rather, sea, land, and desert are domains man diligently traverses, utilizes, and appropriates to find a home somehow." The adventurer in Heidegger's view may be strange, exotic, or "interesting," but he does

---

[14] Heidegger, *Hölderlins Hymne "Der Ister,"* pp. 87, 127–129. According to Heidegger, *kallos thanein* has nothing to do with "dying in beauty" but denotes instead a rejoining of the "belongingness to being" (p. 129).

not qualify for the term *deinos*. Adventurers are abroad or "not at home" simply in the mode of negation or denial; by contrast, *deinos* signifies uncanny estrangement precisely as a mode of self-being—that mode that does not find access to, or remains excluded from, self-discovery. Genuine estrangement, from this vantage, is intimately related to self-being and being-at-home—whereas the adventurer indiscriminately substitutes the non-home (the lands abroad) for home, thereby losing the sense of either place.

The chorus song addresses the latter dilemma by portraying the adventurer as *pantoporos aporos*, someone who restlessly pursues all kinds of stimulating excitements while being unable to derive any lessons from them. In Heidegger's commentary, *pantoporos aporos* designates a creature bent on experiencing everything but whose exploits fail to yield a genuine learning experience. For someone marked as *deinos*, on the other hand, home and not-home are distinguished but also closely correlated: not-home or estrangement here means a "lack" of home, where lack designates the manner in which homecoming pervades the journey abroad—which is the mode of "present absence" (or of presencing in the mode of absence). Elaborating on this correlation, Heidegger draws some broader philosophical (or ontological) implications:

> Human *Dasein* alone is placed in the midst of beings in such a way that it relates to being as such. Only for such a creature is it possible in the midst of beings to be oblivious or forgetful of being. By virtue of this oblivion *Dasein* in a certain sense is exiled beyond or outside the ground of all beings, that is, outside being.[15]

With specific reference to Antigone, the correlation of homelessness and homecoming, of exile and being, is intimated in the closing verses of the chorus song, which, in a mysterious allusive way, speak of the "hearth" as an abode of (human) being: "Whoever ventures along this way, may he remain a stranger at the hearth, and my thought be shielded from his plans." The question arising here is whether "hearth" denotes a conventional home from which Antigone would be expelled for her transgression; in this case, Heidegger notes, the chorus song would not be a high point of Greek tragedy but a eulogy of mediocrity and placid conformism. What militates against this reading is the depth of the rest of the song, particularly its reference to uncanny estrangement as a con-

[15] Ibid., pp. 89, 91–93.

stitutive feature of human life. In Heidegger's interpretation, hearth (*hestia*) and uncanny estrangement (*deinon*) should be seen as standing in a close relationship, not of mutual exclusion but of reciprocal implication. The chorus song, he states, displays awareness of the *deinon* and of the most uncannily estranged creature; such awareness, however, already points beyond, and adumbrates more than, estrangement and its embodiment (in human *Dasein*). For, if uncanniness consists in being abroad, then "this awareness must already be close to non-home and thus to being-at-home, and must from this proximity derive the law of estrangement." Seen in this light, the closing lines amplify and complement the preceding verses of the chorus song by pointing to the ambivalent character of home and non-home, of homecoming and journey abroad. In terms of the lecture course: "All awareness of the *deinon* as the uncanny is sustained, guided and illuminated by an awareness of the hearth. But if 'hearth' denotes home, and if *deinon* designates what in its highest form remains excluded from the hearth, then *deinon* can mean 'uncanny' only in the sense of estranged or not-being-at-home." Translated into Heideggerian vocabulary, the Sophoclean chorus speaks implicitly of the entwining of presence and absence and, more specifically, of nonbeing (or nothing) and being. Surveying the uncanny in all its possibilities, the chorus points toward "the being of all beings"; wherever uncanny strangeness may venture, it remains "as estrangement everywhere in the context of being."[16]

Antigone's conduct, on this reading, does not actually expel her from the hearth (understood in a broad ontological sense). Although placed beyond the pale of the city and its laws, she is not beyond the pale of a deeper and more genuine abode; although disobedient to the commands of Creon, she remains faithful to the call of being (in its linkage with nonbeing)—a call which, in her own words, "does not date from today or yesterday but from time immemorial, and no one knows wherefrom it arose." According to Heidegger, the closing lines of the chorus speak indeed of expulsion, but not without equivocality; while warning against sheer errancy, they also provide clues for the sense of home (*Heimstatt*), thereby disclosing the constitutive ground of estrangement. Taken in this sense, the lines do not simply expel the stranger but rather render strangeness questionable or ambivalent. The equivocality of the verses

---

[16] Ibid., pp. 120–121, 130–131, 133, 135. As Heidegger adds, "The hearth, as the site of home, is being itself in whose light and splendor, fire and warmth all beings are always already gathered" (p. 143).

relates to the ambiguity of estrangement or homelessness, a condition that can mean either stark oblivion and denial of home or else a journey toward homecoming guided by "remembrance of being and belongingness to the hearth." In terms of the lecture course, Sophocles' tragedy deals basically with the latter kind of estrangement. Although transgressing the city's laws, Antigone is mindful of the immemorial claims of being; although condemned by public "truth," her conduct pays homage to another truth, that of "unconcealment" (*aletheia*). From this vantage, *pathein to deinon touto* in her case means suffering estrangement from beings while in search of the hearth of unconcealment. In Heidegger's words:

> The closing lines of the chorus are of an uncanny equivocality that relates to estrangement itself. . . . The lines point to the latent and still undeveloped venture pervading the tragedy as a whole: the venture to differentiate and take sides between genuine human estrangement and spurious errancy. Antigone is herself this highest venture within the domain of the *deinon*. . . . She is herself the poem of homecoming in and through estrangement.[17]

After this excursus into Greek tragedy, the lecture course returns to "The Danube," underscoring the point that Antigone was not an aimless detour. Both the Sophoclean chorus and Hölderlin's hymn deal basically with estrangement and homecoming, although this affinity does not amount to identity. Heidegger returns at this point to the distinction between German and Greek culture, between clarity of presentation and the "fire from heaven." This distinction points up a difference between the Sophoclean chorus and Hölderlin's hymn; although both address similar issues, the meaning of home and non-home is different in the two cases: "What was native endowment for the Greeks is alien to Germans; and what is native for Germans was alien to the Greeks." According to Heidegger, Hölderlin's hymn, and his work as a whole, is essentially concerned with an impending task: "the historical homecoming of Germans within the context of Western history."

"The Danube" opens with the line "Now come, fire!"—immediately bringing the issue of cultural learning through estrangement to center stage. Imbued with heavenly fire, Greek culture was poised or geared toward the advent and proximity of the gods and the sacred; the difficulty (or alien element) for the Greeks was how to give structure to their

[17] Ibid., pp. 143–146, 151.

visions in order not to be singed or devastated by the intensity of inspiration. By contrast, the native endowment of Germans is precisely the talent for structure, for compact organization, for blueprints and elaborate designs; in fact, they are "carried away" by the zest for "frameworks and disciplines, schemata and taxonomies." This native endowment cannot, however, be fully developed or permit "free employment" until or unless structural grasp is confronted with the "ungraspable" and with the need to live in the face of rupture (or rapture). What Germans lack from this vantage is nothing less than the "fire from heaven," something that can be learned only through distant estrangement and peregrination. In Heidegger's commentary, Hölderlin is the poet of this fiery journey to the southland, a journey from which he is now seeking to return; in the context of German culture, he is "the first to experience and poetically to articulate the German lot of estrangement."[18]

Although now a journey of homecoming, Hölderlin's return does not simply leave Greece or the southland behind; on the contrary, distance and estrangement continue to reverberate in homecoming itself. "The Danube" contains lines indicating that this river "invited Hercules, / Distantly gleaming, down by Olympus, / When he, looking for shadows, / Came up from the sultry isthmus." As Heidegger comments, Hercules dwells as guest from Greece in the homeland of the Danube, carrying with him his native heavenly fire. The hospitality of the river implies a readiness to recognize and honor the stranger and his strangeness, a "letting be" that opens a space between home and abroad. Moreover, as carrier of the heavenly fire, Hercules signals a hallowed space, a meeting place of gods and humans, of immortals and mortals. In the hymn, the Danube is itself presented as a half-god and thus as an element inhabiting the crossroads of a divine–human encounter.

Returning to the theme of homecoming through otherness, the lecture course stresses the dimension of strangeness permeating even the native river celebrated in Hölderlin's hymn. The presence of the guest in the homeland, Heidegger states, means that even and precisely at the "site of home" journeying and wandering (*Wanderschaft*) remain decisive, even though in modified form: the guest from Greece indicates the intertwining of presence and absence or "the presence of the non-home at home." Homecoming and appropriation of one's own, in any event, are

---

[18] Ibid., pp. 153–155, 168–170. For the English version of the hymn, see Hölderlin, *Poems and Fragments*, pp. 492–497.

possible only by means of confrontation and hospitable dialogue with strangeness. This correlation has relevance for the river itself. If homecoming requires departure and journeying abroad, then in seeking its homeland the river must itself travel abroad and return from there to its source. Differently phrased, the river must inhabit its own source in such a manner that it flows back into it from afar. This aspect is indeed recognized in Hölderlin's hymn in these lines: "Yet almost this river seems / To travel backwards and / I think it must come from / The East."[19]

II

The theme of the lecture courses on Hölderlin was not a passing interlude. Although triggered in part by wartime experiences, the issue of homecoming through otherness persisted in Heidegger's later opus, albeit in a somewhat modified sense. Whereas the wartime lectures probed an alternative course of German culture and history, some of the postwar writings explored a broader horizon—that of an alternative future of Western civilization in an emerging global context. In a sense, this issue can be seen as a central, if not the dominant, concern in Heidegger's later work, a concern surfacing under different guises and with varying accents. It is clearly tied in with his perception of the growing preponderance of technology and calculating reason in Western society, that is, with the ascendancy of *Gestell* seen as a metaphysical framework bent on mastery and control. What earlier had been viewed as a peculiar German talent for organization and rigid discipline was now projected, in revised form, onto Western culture in its long-term historical development since antiquity. In a different register, the question of an alternate future resonates with the notion of an "other beginning" (*anderer Anfang*) of Western history, a notion incipiently present in Heidegger's thought since *Being and Time*. The turn from a national German to a more global perspective was accompanied by a readjustment of guiding mentors. Seen initially as the poet of an alternative Germany, Hölderlin was recast to encompass a larger vision; at the same time, his voice was supplemented by those of additional figures ranging from Parmenides and Anaximander to such modern poets as Rilke and Trakl. About a decade

---

[19] Heidegger, *Hölderlins Hymne: "Der Ister,"* pp. 173–178.

after his wartime lectures, Heidegger wrote a longer essay devoted to Trakl's poetic work, an essay that resumed the topic of homecoming through otherness on a new level and with renewed intensity.[20]

The essay's title, "Georg Trakl: A Discussion [*Erörterung*] of His Poetic Work," signals the interpretive aim immediately: to find the locus or site (*Ort*) of Trakl's poetry. Site here is not a geographic place but rather an ontological "gathering" capable of "letting be"—and thus ultimately a home or hearth. In Heidegger's words, "The site, as gathering potency, gathers and sustains everything it embraces—though not in the mode of encapsulating closure, but by permeating everything with its light and thus releasing it into its being." In trying to locate this site, the essay turns initially to one of Trakl's lines, which reads, "Strange is the soul on earth." On the surface, the line seems to convey a thoroughly conventional view, one familiar from traditional metaphysics with its "two worlds" theory. In this view, the soul counts as something imperishable and otherworldly, in contrast to the transitory flux of worldly existence. In Plato's doctrine, the soul belongs to the intelligible or supersensible realm; to the extent that it inhabits the sensible world, it does so as a castaway or displaced stranger desperately yearning to terminate its exile. Curiously, however, the verse is part of a poem titled "Springtime of the Soul," a poem that contains no hint of an immortal soul or supersensible world. Seeking guidance from etymology, Heidegger notes that the German term for "strange" (*fremd*) in its Old High German origins (*fram*) means being under way, or journeying abroad. Thus, strangeness is related to estrangement or distant wandering, but wandering which (again) is not synonymous with errancy or aimless nomadism. Instead, estrangement or journeying abroad implies homecoming toward the proper "site": "Almost unknowingly, the strange follows the call that solicits it on the path into its own." What is this site, and where does the path point? Trakl's verse intimates the answer by speaking of the "earth" (as abode of the strange soul). In this sense, the verse highlights the meaning of "soul" rather than depicting its exile. "The earth," Heidegger states, "is precisely the place which the wandering soul was so far unable to reach. The soul still *seeks* the earth; it does

---

[20] Titled "Georg Trakl: Eine Erörterung seines Gedichtes," the essay was first published in 1953. Under the revised title "Die Sprache im Gedicht" the essay was later incorporated into Heidegger's *Unterwegs zur Sprache* (Pfullingen: Neske, 1959), pp. 35–82. For an English version, titled "Language in the Poem," see Heidegger, *On the Way to Language*, trans. Peter D. Hertz (New York: Harper & Row, 1971; paperback ed. 1982), pp. 159–198.

not flee from it. This fulfills the soul's being: through wandering to seek the earth so that she may poetically build and dwell upon it, and thus may be able to save the earth *as* earth.[21]

Homecoming to the earth, however, is by no means a straight itinerary or a simple return to familiar precincts—because the journey is undertaken by the strange soul or the stranger (*Fremdling*). Homecoming in this case involves the most distant estrangement and, in fact, a journey through "death." In Trakl's poetry, the strange soul is also referred to as something "mortal," "dark," "solitary," "silent," and even as something "pale" and "dead." In one of his poems, the soul of the stranger is called on by a thrush "to go under" (*in den Untergang*), and another poem, "Seven-Song of Death," speaks starkly of "man's decomposed or rotting [*verwest*] form." As Heidegger emphasizes, however, going under and decomposition are still part of the stranger's journey and thus by no means synonymous with a terminal point or catastrophic ending; above all, death here does not mean the simple conclusion of earthly life. "Death," he writes, "denotes here poetically that 'going under' or undergoing into which the strange soul is called"; its death consequently signals "not decay but instead the trespassing or leaving behind of the decomposed figure of man." In terms of the essay, this decomposed figure stands basically for traditional humanity, for what Nietzsche called the "last man." What is the source of this decomposition, the curse engendering its rotting state?

> The curse weighing on decomposing humankind consists in the fact that the latter is struck apart by discord among sexes, tribes, and races [*Zwietracht der Geschlechter*]. In this discord each party abandons itself to the unleashed fury of the disjointed and utter wildness of animality. It is not difference as such but discord which is the curse. In the turmoil of blind wildness, discord carries humankind into irreconcilable division [*Entzweiung*], thereby exiling each party into stark isolation.

The strange soul of the stranger points beyond this divisiveness of decomposition; the stranger is, in fact, "Other to the others," that is, Other to the decomposing humankind. In this manner, the stranger is a guidepost for a new dawn, another beginning. The proper path, we read, is that of a generation "whose difference journeys ahead out of discord

---

[21] Heidegger, "Language in the Poem," pp. 159–163 (in the above and subsequent citations, the translation has been slightly changed for purposes of clarity).

into the gentleness of a simple entwining [*Zwiefalt*], thus following the stranger's footsteps."[22]

Those who follow the stranger's footsteps follow him into his "going under," which is also the waning of the day, the sunset or approaching dusk of evening. The verse about the strangeness of the soul continues with these words: "Spiritually the dusk's / Blueness settles over the tangled forest." References to dusk and blueness are recurrent in Trakl's poetry, often in conjunction with allusions to a spiritual or sacred realm. Thus, one poem speaks of the "sacredness of blue flowers"; another verse offers "And in sacred blueness shining footsteps ring forth." Sunset is also related to the waning of summer and the approach of fall as evening of the year. In the words of the poem "Summer's End," "So quiet has green summer grown, / And through the silvery night there rings / The footstep of the stranger. / Would that a blue deer recalled its path, / The harmony of its spiritual years." As Heidegger comments, the phrase "blue deer" here stands for those humans who are willing to follow the stranger into his going under; illuminated by blue light, the deer is marked not be sheer animality but rather by a "forward-looking remembrance" that keeps track of the stranger's step. Dusk in this context, the essay emphasizes, does not simply mean the disappearance of daylight in the mantle of pitch-black darkness; instead, sunset signals the approach of twilight, more specifically of "dusk's blueness." Moreover, twilight is not restricted to nightfall but also heralds the haziness of dawn, the foreglow of a new day. To this extent, evening's dusk means a setting that is not a terminal endpoint but rather a stepping stone toward that going under "through which the stranger enters into the *beginning* of his journey." The crossroads of dusk and dawn is an in-between zone bathed in blueness, which in turn is the emblem of a sacred turning. In Heidegger's words, blueness (*Bläue*) "gathers the depth of the sacred. The sacred shines or radiates out of blueness while veiling itself in the latter's shelter. The sacred is present in withdrawing; it bestows its own arrival by shielding itself in reserved withdrawal. Light sheltered in darkness is blueness."[23]

Journeying in an in-between zone, the stranger is alienated from ordinary time and ordinary seasons of the year. In Trakl's poetry, he is also called the "departed one"—not in the sense of his simple disappearance but in that of a departure from customary lifeforms in the

---

[22] Ibid., pp. 162, 165, 167–168, 170–171.
[23] Ibid., pp. 164–167, 172.

expectancy of an "other ascent" (*anderer Aufgang*). Returning to the question of the site of Trakl's work, Heidegger at this point circumscribes this site through the term "apartness," or "departedness" (*Abgeschiedenheit*). The paths of apartness lead through estrangement and even through death, where death again does not mean the negation of life. One of Trakl's poems speaks of the burial of the stranger, adding that "in his grave the white magician plays with his snakes." Thus, the departed stranger "*lives* in his grave"—in fact, he lives so peacefully that he is able to play with his snakes, "whose malice has been transformed." In other contexts, the stranger is presented as someone "early departed" or "early deceased," more specifically as the boy Elis who prematurely passed "over the footbridge of bone" and whose forehead "softly bleeds / Ancient legends / And dark augury or the flight of birds."

In Heidegger's commentary, Elis is the figure of the stranger who is called to go under; in his early departure, the boy is able to shelter and preserve the gentle stillness of childhood and even pristine glimpses of age-old visions and "ancient legends." To this extent, far from being simply deceased or spent, the departed stranger harbors a future promise or coming dawn: he "unfolds humankind forward into the beginning of a still untapped potential"; he "guards the stiller childhood for the coming awakening of humankind," beyond the limits of the present "decomposing generation." Seen in this light, the stranger is not so much dead and buried as rather still "unborn," anticipating another mode of life. More precisely, the departed looks ahead "into the blueness of the spiritual night" or evening; his closed eyelids shelter a vision promising a "gentler entwinement" of humankind. In the terms of one of Trakl's verses, "Silent the myrtle blooms over the deceased's white eyelids."[24]

In pointing to a different beginning or an "other ascent," the steps of the departed stranger resonate in "spiritual night" or in the harmony of "spiritual years." To this extent, the locus or site of Trakl's poetry is essentially spiritual, though in a difficult and highly nuanced sense. In Heidegger's commentary, the term "spiritual" (*geistlich*) does not have the connotation of clerical spirituality (in opposition to the worldliness of lay

[24] Ibid., pp. 173–175. Elaborating on the linkage of going under and still "unborn" possibility, Heidegger adds: "The ending—namely, the ending of decomposing mankind—precedes the beginning of the unborn generation. Yet, in its pristine dawn, the beginning has already overtaken the ending. . . . True time is the arrival of what has been; the latter, however, is not what is past but rather the gathering of being which precedes all arrival by sheltering itself, as such gathering, into its more pristine potency" (pp. 176–177).

people) nor does it implicate the metaphysical contrast between spirit and nature or mind and matter. The latter contrast, in particular, is misplaced in this context. Why does Trakl avoid the term "spirited" or "of the spirit" (*geistig*) familiar from German idealism? Heidegger asks, and replies:

> Because spirited or "of the spirit" denotes the opposite of matter. This opposition posits the distinction between two separate realms and, in Platonic-Western language, labels the gulf as one between the supersensible [*noeton*] and the sensible [*aistheton*]. So understood, the realm of the spirited—which in the meantime has become synonymous with the rational, intellectual, and ideological—belongs together with its opposites to the worldview of the decomposing generation. But the dark journey of the "blue soul" parts company with this generation.

In Trakl's poetry, the spiritual indeed derives from spirit (*Geist*), but not in the metaphysical sense; instead, spirit here signifies shining or flaming fire in its ecstatic radiance—what one of his poems calls the "searing flame of the spirit." Spirit as flame can be illuminating, enlightening, or vivifying; but it can also turn into a consuming force that reduces everything to ashes. As Heidegger comments, spirit as fire or flame comprises the possibility of "*both* gentleness and destructiveness." Destructiveness in this context originates in "unbridled license," which consumes itself in its own rebelliousness and thereby actively promotes "evil"; but even evil and its malice remain tied to spirit (as fire): "Evil is spiritual as the blazing terror of blinding delusion which casts everything into broken fragmentation." By contrast, gentle spirit has a mending capacity: "Without dampening the ecstasy of the flame, gentleness holds it gathered in the peace of friendliness."[25]

What accounts for the difference between the two modes of flaming and particularly for the ascendancy of gentleness over destruction? According to the essay, this ascendancy proceeds from the workings of the "soul"—specifically of the soul that is strange or a stranger on earth. Spirit as fire drives the soul to its journey and thus into estrangement and

---

[25] Ibid., pp. 177–179. In his *Of Spirit*, Jacques Derrida comments at length on the changing status of spirit in Heidegger's work, also noting the difference between *geistlich* and *geistig*; although subtle in many ways, however, his observations miss the historical or epochal quality of *geistlich* both in Trakl's poetry and in Heidegger's interpretation. See *Of Spirit: Heidegger and the Question*, trans. Geoffrey Bennington and Rachel Bowlby (Chicago: University of Chicago Press, 1989), esp. pp. 83–98; see also my discussion in Chapter 1 of this volume.

otherness; but in return the strange soul is able to sustain and nourish spirit, by lending it the support of its "patient solitude" and "glow of melancholy." On its distant journey, the soul is called on to undergo the labor of estrangement and departedness, a labor marked intrinsically by pain and suffering (*Schmerz*). In the words of one of Trakl's poems, "O pain, thou flaming vision / Of the great soul." As Heidegger notes, pain here does not have a debilitating or destructive but a transformative and regenerative quality; in painfully undergoing estrangement, the soul's journey is also the gateway to homecoming, to a genuine "letting be" or acceptance of being. Seen from this angle, pain is marked by an inner "turning," a conversion (*Gegenwendigkeit*): although carried along by the fire of spirit, the soul's transformative labor does not lead to self-consuming frenzy but to a radiantly "flaming vision" seasoned by gentleness and patient "mildness." This gentle vision ultimately harbors the "goodness" of life, that is, whatever is good or right in human conduct and relationships. "Painfully good and truthful is what lives," says one of Trakl's verses—a view echoed in this line: "O how righteous are, Elis, all your days." In Heidegger's commentary, "everything that lives is painful," and whatever is good

> is painfully good. Corresponding to the great soul's fundamental trait, everything endowed with soul not only is painfully good but can be genuine or truthful only in this manner. For it is due to the "turning" quality of pain that a living being can provide sheltering disclosure to a co-being in its distinctive otherness, thereby letting it truly be.[26]

As should be emphasized again, pain is not simply torment or a dismal (but perhaps avoidable) fate: linked with the flame of spirit, pain has a cleansing and purifying character. In Trakl's poetry, pain is a consequence of spirit's fire which calls the soul into estrangement and ultimately into apartness or departedness—which turns out also to be a place of healing. "Departedness," Heidegger writes, "works or operates as pure spirit"; it reflects the "quiet flaming of blueness" which, in turn, kindles or arouses a pristine childhood into "a golden new beginning"— as exemplified by Elis's golden vision. Departedness from this angle is

[26] Heidegger, "Language in the Poem," pp. 176, 179–181. As Heidegger adds: "The troubled, hampered, dismal, and diseased, all the distress of decomposition is in fact nothing but the semblance or appearance concealing the one 'truth': the all-pervasiveness of pain. Pain thus is neither obstructive nor useful; rather, it shows the grace or favor [*Gunst*] of the nature of being" (p. 183).

not a place of isolation or abandonment but rather a site of spiritual gathering and reconciliation. Departedness, the essay notes, is "a gathering through which humankind is sheltered once again into its stiller childhood and the latter, in turn, into the early dawn of another beginning." Because of this gathering capacity pervading apartness, the soul's gentleness is able to subdue the spirit of evil and its malice; although it is neither annihilated nor simply denied, evil at this point is "transformed"—and it is in order to undergo and sustain this transformation that the soul must undertake its "great" venture, which is the venture of apartness.

This venture, in the end, is undertaken not so much for its own sake as for the sake of a latent promise, an "unborn" possibility. In the words of one of Trakl's poems, "Today immense pain feeds the searing flame of spirit, / The grandsons yet unborn." The unborn in these lines are called grandsons because they cannot be the sons or immediate descendants of the present decomposing generation. Trakl's poetry not only speaks broadly about estrangement and apartness but intimates a distinct historical panorama: the unfolding story of humankind. In venturing abroad, the soul of the stranger departs from traditional or existing ways of life while opening space for the dawn of an unborn possibility. Located on the site of apartness, Heidegger writes, the language of Trakl's poetry

> adumbrates the homecoming of unborn humankind into the quiet beginning of its stiller nature. The language of this poetry emanates from transition [*Übergang*]. Its path conducts from the descent of decomposition over to the going under into the twilight blueness of the sacred. The poetry originates in the transit or passage across the nocturnal pond of the spiritual night. Its language sings the song of homecoming in apartness, a homecoming which from the lateness of descent returns to the earliness of a quieter, still impending ascent.

One of Trakl's verses is explicit about "the beauty of a homecoming generation."[27]

Reference to a historical panorama, however, would still remain elusive in the absence of additional guideposts linking time and space. The

[27] Ibid., pp. 184–186, 191. Heidegger's essay remonstrates against a purely ahistorical or transtemporal reading of Trakl's poetry: "Trakl's work has been termed 'profoundly unhistorical.' But what is 'history' in this assessment? If the word means no more than 'chronicle,' that is, the rehearsal of past events, then Trakl is indeed unhistorical. His poetry has no need of historical 'objects.' Why not? Because his poetry is historical in the highest sense: it sings of the fortune which casts humankind forward into its still withheld nature, thereby saving or salvaging the latter" (p. 196).

concluding pages of Heidegger's essay are devoted precisely to this linkage. Noting the prominence of twilight (evening blueness) in Trakl's poetry, Heidegger suggests a connection between this twilight and the Occident or Western "evening land" (*Abendland*), a connection that is firmly buttressed by the titles of some of Trakl's poems (such as "Evening Land" and "Occidental Song"). Seen in this light, Heidegger writes, the location inhabited by Trakl's poetry is the site of departedness and, more concretely, the site of the Occident or "evening land." As a place of apartness, he adds, this Occident is "older and this means earlier and more promising than the Platonic-Christian Occident" and indeed than the land "conceived as the European West" or as the locus of Western civilization; for apartness heralds "the beginning of an ascending world-year, not the abyss of decay."

In underscoring the latent promise, Heidegger takes strong exception to the mentality of impending doom and gloom, an outlook rendered fashionable by Oswald Spengler's *Decline of the West* (*Untergang des Abendlandes*). Countering the prophecy of doom, he states, "Sheltered in apartness, the evening land does not go down in decay"; instead, it "remains in wait for its inhabitants as the land of the going under into spiritual night." Hence the land of sunset and going under is at the same time the place of transit "into the beginning of a still concealed dawn." To be sure, transit here implies transformation and change, even radical change. As interpreted by Heidegger, Trakl's poetry indeed envisages a profound transformation of the Occident and not simply its continuance as a place of technological supremacy and mastery of the globe; in the midst of this supremacy, his work holds out the vision of another possibility—the vision of a more peaceful global dwelling, of a "gentler entwinement" of humankind. To this extent, Trakl is the poet of the "still concealed evening land." Poised naturally toward sunset, Trakl's Occident faces its going under not as a threatening dissolution but as an avenue of homecoming, a homecoming into the harmonious blueness of its spiritual years.[28]

---

[28] Ibid., pp. 194, 197. Trakl's poem "Occidental Song" (*Abendländisches Lied*) points to the promise of "*one* generation," emphatically underlining the word "one." As Heidegger comments, this emphatic phrase "contains the keynote in which Trakl's work silently adumbrates the mystery. The unity of the *one* generation arises from the promise which out of departedness—out of its stiller stillness, its 'forest sagas,' its 'measure and rule'— gathers and enfolds along the 'lunar paths of the departed' the discord of peoples into the gentler entwinement of humankind" (p. 195). As he adds, the unity of "one generation" here does not mean the "monotony of dull identity"; rather, the phrase appeals to that potency that "unifies out of the gathering blueness of the spiritual night."

III

The writings reviewed here are unsettling or "estranging" in many ways. As indicated, they project an alternative future first for German culture and later for Western civilization. They are also unsettling, however, for showing a different Heidegger, one whom his detractors are liable to bypass or shun. In the midst of Nazi racialism and chauvinistic aggression, Heidegger's lectures on Hölderlin urged a path of radical German estrangement, a path open to the otherness of Greece and particularly to the sacred fire that kindled Greek spirit. Presented at the height of German military might, the lectures were a manifesto of "inner emigration" from destructive brutality to a more subdued or "spiritual" mode of German being. Later, in the midst of Western global ascendancy, the Trakl essay intimated another kind of exodus, one away from global mastery in the direction of a "gentler entwinement" of humankind, accompanied by a "going under" of the Occident (or *Abendland*) into the twilight of spiritual years. Apart from countering charges of fascist chauvinism, these writings also undermine allegations of a narrow parochialism or provincialism, that is, of a self-enclosed autochthony out of touch with global developments. As the preceding discussion has amply shown, home or homecoming for Heidegger is by no means a native possession but only the farthest horizon of the soul's journey abroad. This journey, one should note, transgresses not only the limits of chauvinism but also the borders of a self-enclosed humanism or anthropocentrism—in the direction of a spiritual in-between zone or sacred meeting ground of humans and gods. To this extent, Heidegger's outlook hardly coincides with shallow pragmatism, that is, with a nonreflective attitude solely concerned with ordinary, everyday affairs.[29]

To be sure, Heidegger's writings may be unsettling in other ways, even for those perhaps willing to accept the notion of an "other" Heidegger. To some, his exodus may seem too radical or uncompromising. Preoccupied with the dictates of political power, experts in global politics are likely to regard his alternative vision as unfeasible, unrealistic, or simply utopian. This estimate, in my view, misjudges both the nature of

---

[29] The rapprochement of Heidegger's thought with pragmatism has been suggested chiefly by Richard Rorty in his "Overcoming the Tradition: Heidegger and Dewey," in *Consequences of Pragmatism (Essays: 1972–1980)* (Minneapolis: University of Minnesota Press, 1982), pp. 37–59. On the charge of provincialism, see Jürgen Habermas, "Urbanisierung der Heideggerschen Provinz," in Hans-Georg Gadamer and Habermas, *Das Erbe Hegels* (Frankfurt-Main: Suhrkamp, 1979), pp. 11–31.

politics and the specific status of Heidegger's vision. Although in a sense ineradicable, power does not simply equal mastery or domination; more important, politics involves not merely the opposition of domination and submission, of rulers and ruled, but also the dimension of human aspirations, hopes, and dreams. The articulation of these aspirations is preeminently the task of poets—individuals who are most unlikely to abuse their insights for manipulative or strategic designs. In Heidegger's writings, alternative paths for the future are not offered as political platforms but ascribed to the poetic works of Hölderlin and Trakl—works that resonate deeply with Heidegger's own "recollective" thinking. Again, this appeal to poets may prove unsettling, not just to political scientists but to literary critics. As it happens, experts on Hölderlin have remonstrated against Heidegger's historical-spiritual reading of the poet, as have Trakl scholars with regard to that poet's status in the postwar essay. No doubt, Heidegger's approach in both instances bears the mark of creative interpretation, with an accent on creative originality. In the case of Hölderlin, the lecture courses deemphasize or blend out the poet's democratic-anarchistic leanings, and the Trakl essay may slight some metaphysical components. None of this would have been disturbing to Heidegger himself, who readily acknowledged the multivocality of any poetic work. As he writes in the postwar essay, Trakl's poetry speaks "out of equivocal ambiguity," which is not synonymous with "vague equivocation"; instead, its words arise out of a unifying gathering which, in strict terms, "remains always unsayable."[30]

Numerous other aspects in these works of Heidegger seem unsettling, startling, or at least intriguing—and deserve brief mention. In view of my own chosen habitat, I myself find repeated references to "Americanism" in the Hölderlin lectures somewhat disturbing. In the lectures of winter 1941, the corrosion of language and the rise of "culture industry"

---

[30] Heidegger, "Language in the Poem," p. 192. For an alternative reading of Hölderlin's poetry, see, for example, Theodor W. Adorno, "Parataxis: On Hölderlin's Late Poetry," in *Notes to Literature*, ed. Rolf Tiedemann, trans. Shierry Weber Nicholsen (New York: Columbia University Press, 1992), 2:109–149; and Peter Szondi, *Hölderlin-Studien: Mit einem Traktat über philologische Erkenntins* (Frankfurt-Main: Suhrkamp, 1979). Much of the discussion revolves around Heidegger's reading and application of Hölderlin's letter to Böhlendorf of 1801; see also Andrzej Warminski, *Readings in Interpretation: Hölderlin, Hegel, Heidegger* (Minnesota: University of Minnesota Press, 1987). Hölderlin's hymn "Remembrance" (*Andenken*) has been given an alternative (idealist) reading by Dieter Henrich—though one which, in my view, is not incompatible with Heidegger's approach; see Henrich, *Der Gang des Andenkens: Beobachtungen und Gedanken zu Hölderlins Gedicht* (Stuttgart: Klett-Cotta, 1986).

are ascribed broadly to Americanism or the ongoing Americanization of Western societies; in the lectures of the following summer, America appears as a stand-in for the cult of quantitative "bigness," a cult buttressed by a fascination with technology and the complete absence of "historical sense" (*Geschichtslosigkeit*).[31] Although few would deny the sway of technocratic and consumerist tendencies, these hardly form the sum total of American culture; above all, "ahistoricism" is a curious charge when applied to a country fond of continuously rehearsing revolutionary and civil war traditions. The impression can hardly be avoided that "America" here figures as a summary label of disapproval, and not as the name for a concrete historical configuration endowed with its own intrinsic tensions and cultural dilemmas.

The impression of summary labeling also applies to some Western thinkers repeatedly invoked in the lectures, foremost among them Nietzsche—which is surprising in view of Heidegger's intense involvement with Nietzschean thought in previous years. The lectures on "Remembrance" portray Nietzsche's work not as a critical debunking but as the final outgrowth and culmination of Western metaphysics bent on technological mastery. Embryonically present in Plato's rationalism, Heidegger writes, modern technology "gains its ultimate justification in a perspective couched deliberately as the reversal of Platonism: in Nietzsche's metaphysics of the will to power." The same lectures erect a sharp contrast between Nietzsche and Hölderlin, restricting the former to ambitions of anthropocentric mastery while heralding Hölderlin as the "precursor of the overcoming of metaphysics." The lectures on "The Danube" depict Nietzsche's view of art as part and parcel of modern (metaphysical) aesthetics, an aesthetics geared toward subjective fulfillment and power enhancement; in the same context, Sophocles' concept of the uncanny (*deinon*) is carefully distinguished from modern power politics, and especially from Nietzsche's notion of the "blond beast" or "beast of prey." In some measure, no doubt, passages of this kind can be ascribed to the agonies and afflictions of the war years (when Nietzschean doctrines were ruthlessly exploited by Nazi propaganda).[32]

An intriguing and important theme touched on in these writings is

---

[31] Heidegger, *Hölderlins Hymne "Andenken,"* pp. 10, 27, 134; *Hölderlins Hymne "Der Ister,"* pp. 68, 86, 179.

[32] *Hölderlins Hymne "Der Ister,"* pp. 44, 109, 112; *Hölderlins Hymne "Andenken,"* pp. 78, 91, 143, 152. The latter course contains these sharp lines: "'Nietzsche and Hölderlin'—an abyss separates the two. In a profoundly different manner, the two chart the proximate and most distant future of Germany and the Occident [*Abendland*]" (p. 78).

Heidegger's relation to Hegel's philosophy and particularly to Hegelian dialectics. At a first glance, homecoming through otherness bears an undeniable affinity with Hegel's conception of alienation and dialectical sublation (*Aufhebung*). Heidegger's lectures on Hölderlin repeatedly allude to this affinity, while also underscoring basic differences. In discussing the transit or transition (*Übergang*) between home and abroad, and between mortals and immortals, the lectures on "Remembrance" alert one to the similarity with Hegelian sublation and reconciliation. In talking about this mediating zone, we read, "we move into the proximity of Hegel's metaphysics"; for "the phrase 'everything is transition' could be taken as the foundational core of that metaphysics." Yet, despite this proximity—a closeness buttressed by ties of friendship dating from the Tübingen years—Heidegger sharply sets off Hegel's idealist philosophy against the sense animating Hölderlin's hymn. The same phrase "everything is transition," Heidegger insists, has a "radically different meaning" for Hegel and Hölderlin, a difference anchored not in "two opposing metaphysical positions" but in the fact that Hölderlin "exists from metaphysics" (to which Hegel remains bound). The precise character of the difference is not elaborated in the lectures, although clues are by no means lacking. The lectures on "Remembrance" attribute the distinction, in part, to the "formal" character of Hegel's dialectics and, more specifically, to his neglect of the "domain of transience" and its ontological status. The lectures on "The Danube" allude briefly to Heidegger's discussion of Hegel's concept of experience, that is, to his commentary on the Introduction to Hegel's *Phenomenology of Spirit* (a commentary dating roughly from the same period). In that discussion, Heidegger took issue with the construal of absolute spirit as apodictic knowledge or complete transparency, placing the accent instead on the interplay of concealment and revealment, an interplay which, without canceling absoluteness, showed the latter as concretely inhabiting the "domain of transience," or finite, human being-in-the-world.[33]

It is stated elusively, but the relation of Hölderlin and Hegel has deeper significance for the broad theme of homecoming through otherness. Although intensely concerned with otherness, Hegel's philosophy ultimately sublated estrangement in the crowning phase of metaphysics, and thus in the triumphant ascendancy of Western systems of thought

---

[33] *Hölderlins Hymne "Andenken,"* pp. 98–99; *Hölderlins Hymne "Der Ister,"* p. 170, n. 4. See also Heidegger, *Hegel's Concept of Experience*, trans. J. Glenn Gray and Fred D. Wieck (New York: Harper & Row, 1970).

around the globe. By exiting from this metaphysics, Hölderlin, by contrast, paved the way for an alternative future—pointing in the end toward that "gentler entwinement" of humankind envisaged in Trakl's poetry. Seen from this angle, the difference between Hölderlin and Trakl—and between the two phases sketched in these pages—begins to blur, making room for a long-range concordance. This concordance is not just a matter of conjecture; it finds support in Hölderlin's work. The hymn "Remembrance" contains these lines: "But where are the friends? Where Bellarmine / And his companions? . . . / But now to India / These men have gone." Likewise, "The Danube" signals the return from abroad in the opening stanza: "We, however, sing from the Indus, / Having arrived from afar." Indus and India refer to the "morning-land" as silent counterpart of the Occident, as the Other of the evening-land.

Thematized prominently in the Trakl essay, the correlation or rather entwinement of Orient and Occident was a recurrent concern in Heidegger's later work. Reflecting on the future of the West in the aftermath of the war, Heidegger pondered the possibility of an alternative to global mastery, wondering whether the real evening-land is "perhaps only coming or dawning." A decade later, in an essay addressed to Ernst Jünger, he opposed to planetary dominion the alternative path of re-collective thinking and living, a path that might allow genuine human "building and dwelling" on a global scale. Persistently, these writings challenged Western thought to move abroad—not toward aimless nomadism but in search of the twilight of its own evening (which would be its home). Homecoming in this sense means not nostalgic return but openness to an untapped promise—the promise of fresh encounters in the calm of spiritual years. In the words of Hölderlin's elegy "Homecoming" (*Heimkunft*),

> Silence often behooves us: lacking are holy names;
> Hearts may beat high, while lips are wary of speech?
> Yet a lyre to each hour lends the right mode,
> And, perhaps, delights heavenly ones who draw near.[34]

---

[34] Hölderlin, *Poems and Fragments*, pp. 261, 491, 493. For Heidegger's commentary on the elegy, see his "Heimkunft/An die Verwandten," in *Erläuterungen zu Hölderlins Dichtung*, ed. Friedrich-Wilhelm von Herrmann (*Gesamtausgabe*, Vol. 4; Frankfurt-Main: Klostermann, 1981), pp. 9–31; see also Heidegger, "The Anaximander Fragment," in *Early Greek Thinking*, trans. David F. Krell and Frank A. Capuzzi (New York: Harper & Row, 1975), pp. 17, 57, and *The Question of Being*, trans. William Kluback and Jean T. Wilde (New Haven, Conn.: College and University Press, 1958), p. 107.

CHAPTER SEVEN

Heidegger as "Friend of the World"

Among philosophers in our century, no one is deemed more cryptic or enigmatic than Martin Heidegger. Wedded to logical analysis, many Anglo-American thinkers shun his work because of its presumed obscurity and lack of coherence. Although favored by some of his devotees, this image of Heidegger is in my view vastly overdrawn. Many of his writings, though philosophically challenging, are couched in a deceptively simple style almost completely free of philosophical jargon. In many instances, what obstructs access for English-speaking readers is the quality of existing translations, whose stilted literalness often suggests the musings of a ponderous and pedantically esoteric mind. In the German original, stylistic denseness or complexity tends to be confined mostly to Heidegger's early writings, including *Being and Time;* with advancing years, however, his language becomes increasingly mellow and easy flowing, at points approximating the unaffected simplicity of one of his favorite novelists, Adalbert Stifter. Not infrequently the accusation of obscurity is coupled with the charge of solipsism, of the withdrawal of the thinker into the shell of personal inwardness and self-identity. In the reading of some of his detractors, Heidegger was unable to transgress the traditional limits of subjectivity; in the terminology of *Being and Time,* authentic *Dasein* is claimed to be synonymous with a private fortress immune from the inroads of world and other human beings. Given this retreat into privacy, the argument goes, Heidegger was lured into the abyss of a private language—a cul-de-sac that in large measure accounts for his incoherence.[1]

[1] This line of argument has been advanced particularly by Frankfurt School theorists; see, for example, Theodor W. Adorno, *The Jargon of Authenticity,* trans. Knut Tarnowski

Like the claim of obscurity, I find the charge of solipsism misguided and, in fact, entirely mistaken. One of the central features of *Being and Time* (and one of its crucial departures from traditional philosophy) is its accent on the "worldliness" of *Dasein*, that is, on human existence seen as intrinsically permeated by world (or as a "being-in-the-world"). World in this context embraces not only the array of objects and utensils but also, and prominently, fellow beings, thematized under the label "co-being" (*Mitsein* or *Mitdasein*). Given the worldliness of existence, co-being here means not a serial juxtaposition but rather a constitutive juncture or correlation; as I propose to show in this chapter, Heidegger's thought makes a significant contribution to the topic of fellowship and indeed to the understanding of friendship, where friendship denotes not a fusional merger or consensus but a mutuality predicated on the acknowledgment of differences.

In *Being and Time*, human dialogue was presented not merely as spoken interaction but as a reciprocal mode of listening attentive to otherness. Listening, Heidegger wrote, involves the "existential openness of *Dasein* as co-being for the Other," particularly for the "voice of the friend that every *Dasein* carries with it." Some fifteen years later, in a lecture course on Hölderlin, Heidegger termed genuine dialogue the "midpoint [*Wesensmitte*] of the friendship of friends." In listening to each other, the partners of such dialogue recognize each other in their difference or distinctness, a distinctness that involves not separation but a mode of mutual "letting be" and "setting free" which allows human "truth" to emerge; the emblem of such truth, again, is friendship.[2] For present purposes, I concentrate on an essay composed another fifteen years later—the essay titled "Hebel—the House-Friend" (*Hebel—der Hausfreund*). The essay

---

and Frederic Will (Evanston, Ill.: Northwestern University Press, 1973); Jürgen Habermas, *The Philosophical Discourse of Modernity: Twelve Lectures*, trans. Frederick Lawrence (Cambridge: MIT Press, 1987), pp. 138–152.

[2] Martin Heidegger, *Sein und Zeit*, 11th ed. (Tübingen: Niemeyer, 1967), p. 163 (par. 34); for the English translation, see *Being and Time*, trans. John Macquarrie and Edward Robinson (New York: Harper & Row, 1962), p. 206; see also *Hölderlins Hymne "Andenken,"* ed. Curd Ochwadt (*Gesamtausgabe*, Vol. 52; Frankfurt-Main: Klostermann, 1982), pp. 164–165. Reflecting on these lines in Hölderlin's hymn, "But where are the friends? Where Bellarmine / And his companions?" Heidegger observes, "The question regarding the friends is the question concerning the nature of future friendship. In the ambience of this friendship, the poet is himself also a friend" (p. 169). I am indebted to Krzysztof Ziarek for alerting me to this passage in the lecture course. For a general discussion of co-being in Heidegger's work, see Fred Dallmayr, *Twilight of Subjectivity* (Amherst: University of Massachusetts Press, 1981), pp. 64–71.

was written in memory of the Swabian poet Johann Peter Hebel, the author of the "Alemannian Poems" (1803) and especially of the "Treasure Chest" (*Schatzkästlein*, 1811). In his essay, Heidegger comments on the significance of Hebel's role as (self-described) "Rhenish house-friend." Moving beyond the immediate occasion, however, he also alerted us to the importance of friendship in our own time, and especially to the need for a house-friend of the world.

I

Before turning to the issue of genuine fellowship, Heidegger's essay offers a brief introduction to the life and work of Hebel, who lived from 1760 to 1826. Although born in Basel, his actual homeland was the so-called Wiesental, a valley stretching from the upper bend of the Rhine deep into the Black Forest. As it happens, the fortunes of Hebel's life kept him mostly away from this valley. Educated first in Karlsruhe and later in Erlangen (where he studied theology), Hebel spent the longer part of his mature life as a school principal in the former city. Yet, geographic distance or dislocation did not jeopardize an inner proximity. In Heidegger's words, the gentle lure of his homeland "kept him steadily in its spell." It was out of attachment to and longing for his valley that he composed the "Alemannian Poems," which were written in the dialect peculiar to his native region. The use of dialect in his poems and many other writings seems to mark Hebel as a local or parochial figures segregated from the "high culture" with its universal traffic of ideas. But this judgment—favored by urban intellectuals—misconstrues the nature of poetry and language. As Heidegger observes:

> Given its dialect form, the opinion might arise that Hebel's poetry belongs to a narrowly confined world. Moreover, many claim that dialect is simply a mistreatment or corruption of the written or standard language. This opinion, however, is mistaken. Dialect is the mysterious source of every historically grown language; this source nurtures everything sedimented in the spirit of language.

Seen in this light, dialect is not an isolated backwater but rather the nourishing stream sustaining standardized language, thereby preventing the latter's ossification. The same correlation governs the circulation of high and low culture, and of universal and vernacular or folk literature.

Fully attentive to this correlation, Hebel's dialect transcended its particular locality: "Hebel is no mere folk or dialect poet; rather, he is a world-wide poet" (or one open to global horizons).[3]

The correlation of high and low culture, however, does not fully capture the distinctive quality of Hebel's work. According to Heidegger, this quality emerges only once attention is focused on his status as "house-friend." Among other things, Hebel is known for authoring or editing a yearly almanac that bore the title "Calendar of the Rhenish House-Friend." In this almanac, Hebel assembled all kinds of stories and pieces of information that might be relevant to the ordinary lives of people throughout the year. In announcing his calendar, the poet expressed the hope that it might become a "welcome and beneficial publication or appearance [*Erscheinung*]" in his native region and in all of Germany. Concentrating on the term "appearance," Heidegger comments that the almanac was meant to be a luminous event, capable of "steadily illuminating the everyday affairs" of people. Moreover, it was to be a "welcome" publication in the sense of being freely accepted instead of being foisted on the people by the government or state. Finally, its "beneficial" character was to derive from its effort of accompanying readers in their daily activities and of participating supportively in their joys and woes. In this announcement, the friendly disposition of the Rhenish house-friend was already clearly indicated, a disposition that was then concretely implemented and demonstrated in the annual "appearance" of the almanac.

Hebel's friendliness was not, however, restricted to the days and years of his almanac; it radiated far beyond the historical confines of his life. One reason for this broad luminosity was the "Treasure Chest," a volume in which Hebel collected some of the best stories and insights of his almanacs while simultaneously suffusing them with the spirit of his "Alemannian Poems." In Heidegger's account, the spirit of Hebel's poetry was sublated (*aufgehoben*) in his "Treasure Chest" in the triple sense in which Hegel used that term. For Hegel, to sublate meant first of all to "lift up" for focused attention; next, it denoted preservation or retention; finally and most important, it signified elevation or ennoblement and hence transformation or transfiguration. In this sense, the publication of 1811 was an ennobling transfiguration of Hebel's entire work; more broadly, it offered a treasure chest of friendliness and of German literature. "Ennobling" in this context, Heidegger adds, should not be taken to suggest elitism or a turning away from everyday affairs; on the con-

---

[3] Heidegger, *Hebel—der Hausfreund*, 5th ed. (Pfullingen: Neske, 1985), pp. 6–8.

trary: "Ennobling transformation here happens through intensified or elevated language; but elevation points toward simplicity. To elevate language into simplicity means: to transform everything into the mild splendor of the calmly resounding word. This ennobled wording marks Hebel's poetry."[4]

Yet, the character of the Rhenish house-friend needs further specification. In what sense is he a friend and what sort of house does he befriend? In good measure, clues to the answers can be obtained from Heideggerian philosophy, from his early formulation of human "being-in-the-world" to his later views on "building and dwelling" and on the "four-fold" entwinement of the regions of the world. In our present time, Heidegger notes, the term "house" frequently stands for nothing more than an assortment of rooms or for an external container of human existence. Such a spatial container, however, is not properly a house. In a genuine sense, a building becomes a house only through human "dwelling"; in the same way, construction of a house qualifies as genuine "building" only to the extent that it allows dwelling to happen in its different modalities and forms. Properly construed, Heidegger writes, dwelling is the insertion of humans in the various dimensions of being; it designates the "manner in which humans undertake their journey [*Wanderung*] on the earth under the sky from birth until death." Dwelling from this angle is by no means stationary or locally confined; rather, it involves a continuous journeying or wandering—a wandering in and through the entwinement of regions, namely, the "in-between" zone between earth and sky, between mortals and immortals, between happiness and sorrow. In a shorthand formula, this in-between zone can be termed "world," which implies that the house in which humans dwell is ultimately the world itself. Individual buildings, villages, and cities, by comparison, are simply localities in which the multiple dimensions of the world's in-between zone intersect or are gathered; these localities allow human dwelling to happen in the proximity of the earth and of concrete neighbors and under the vast expanse of the sky. Applying these considerations to Hebel's almanacs and "Treasure Chest," one might say that the house befriended by the Rhenish house-friend is the world; differently phrased, the house-friend's friendliness is turned caringly "toward the whole and far-flung dwelling of humans" in the world.[5]

---

[4] Ibid., pp. 8–12.
[5] Ibid., pp. 12–14. See also in this context Heidegger, "Building Dwelling Thinking," in *Poetry, Language, Thought*, trans. Albert Hofstadter (New York: Harper & Row, 1971), pp. 145–161.

Heidegger's commentary on this point is not mere philosophizing exegesis; it finds ample support in Hebel's work. The "Treasure Chest" opens with a section titled "General Reflections on the Edifice of the World [*Weltgebäude*]." In this section, Hebel introduces in sequence the main inhabitants of that edifice: first the earth, then the sun, next the moon, and finally the planets and shooting stars. It is in the presentation of the moon that the character of the house-friend as "friend of the world" is elucidated. Responding to the question of the moon's function in the sky, Hebel observes: "So much is certain: with its gentle light—which is a reflex of the sunlight—the moon illuminates our nights, and watches as boys and girls embrace. The moon is thus the genuine house-friend and the first calendar-maker of our earth, and the supreme night watchman while others are asleep." In these lines, the moon appears as house-friend of the world: its soft and gentle light transfuses or transfigures human nights; its mellow glow differs from the flaming heat of the sun, from which its light nonetheless derives. In these respects, the moon's role matches that of the poetic house-friend Hebel: just as the moon transmits borrowed light, the poet first receives his word from elsewhere (from his muse) and then conveys it to his readers. Like the moon, the poetic house-friend is a night watchman who solicitously guards the peace and tranquillity of fellow humans, that is, their proper dwelling on earth. Akin to the first calendar maker in the sky, the poet's almanacs are meant to accompany the journey of humans through their days and years. In Hebel's words, the house-friend watches or looks on as boys and girls embrace—and does so not in an obtrusive or inquisitive way but with supportive largesse. As Heidegger comments, the house-friend makes sure "that lovers are granted that gentle lunar light which is neither merely earthly not heavenly but both in intimate entwinement"; thus, the house-friend's attitude emits a "reticent-reserved, but vigilant radiance" that envelops all things in "soft, almost imperceptible light."[6]

Hebel's "Treasure Chest" delineates the character of the house-friend in many other places. One particularly telling passage reads as follows: "Diligently the Rhenish house-friend wanders up and down the Rhine river and glances into many a window—but is not being noticed; he sits in many a restaurant—but without being recognized; he walks with many a solid man for a stretch of the way—but without showing his identity." These lines highlight the present-absent quality of the house-friend. The latter is not merely a detached spectator neutrally observing

---

[6] Heidegger, *Hebel—der Hausfreund*, pp. 14–17. In the above and the next several paragraphs, Hebel citations are taken from Heidegger's essay.

human behavior like a scientist or botanist; instead, the house-friend is a concerned participant in human lives, but a reflective participant who is and is not part of everyday affairs. As a reflective partner, the house-friend ponders human conduct but does not pontificate or impose his views on others. In terms of another passage, "The house-friend thinks by himself, but does not always speak his mind"; even when he does speak out, he is careful not to be drawn into the frenzied "word battles" (*Wortkriege*) that tend to mar or vitiate human interactions. His words prefer the mellow tone of reticence and reserve, while shunning militant aggressiveness. As Heidegger points out, "In the mode of reticence—hovering between saying and not saying—the friendliness of the house-friend reaches and touches the reader"; although attentive to human dwelling, the house-friend enters and participates in the house of the world—but "like a guest who remains alien." According to Heidegger, this mode of reticent presence (or present absence) is a general hallmark of poetry as such: "The poet gathers the world into a saying whose word emits that gentle-reticent glow wherein the world appears as if seen for the first time."[7]

Hebel's "Treasure Chest," written in a poetic mode, is not intended simply to impart knowledge or factual information to readers; still, it is not devoid of educational purpose. According to its opening pages, the "Treasure Chest" wishes to induce readers to think more seriously about the structure of the "world edifice," particularly about the processes and laws of the natural universe; in pondering these processes, readers are exhorted to pay heed to the "scientists and astronomers" of modern times, above all to the "upright Copernicus." To this extent, Hebel's book pays tribute to scientific advances of his age, to the spirit of Enlightenment (broadly conceived) that was beginning to affect the Rhineland and even Hebel's native valley. Yet, while paying such tribute, the book resists any kind of trendiness or simple surrender to notions of scientific progress; instead, the endeavor of the Rhenish house-friend is to familiarize readers with current knowledge without uprooting or alienating them from nature or the "world edifice" as it is experienced in everyday life. In this sense, the "Treasure Chest" builds a bridge between tradition and modernity, between science (or the scientific view of nature) and prescientific experience in the life-world. As Heidegger elaborates this point:

> The house-friend shows nature *also* in its scientific calculability; but he does not lose himself in this perspective. The house-friend draws attention to

[7] Ibid., pp. 17–19.

calculable nature; at the same time, however, he retrieves and reintegrates this scientific conception into the *naturalness (Natürlichkeit]* of nature. This naturalness of nature is essentially and historically much older than nature seen as object of modern natural science.

In ancient Greek thought, the naturalness of nature is called *physis*, a term that captures the appearance and disappearance of every being in its presence and absence. In Hebel's work, this naturalness is manifested in the rising and setting of the sun, the moon, and the stars, an alternation that allows and guards human dwelling on earth. Although invoking the Copernican conception of the sun, Hebel's poetry also speaks of the sun in prescientific language, calling it a "fabulous woman" (*tolle Frau*) from whom everything wants to receive "light and warmth" and who stead- fastly remains "benevolent and friendly."[8]

As Heidegger admits, however, Hebel's mediating bridge is no longer entirely viable or sufficient in our age of advanced scientific and tech- nological development. From this level of complexity no straight path can lead back to the relative simplicity of Hebel's time. With the disman- tling of earlier bridges, Heidegger notes, our age is faced with a profound dilemma, the dilemma of a yawning abyss between knowledge and experience, between scientific technology and life-world. This steadily deepening gulf is what drives our age "we know not where." The basic core of the dilemma resides in the fact that "technologically controllable nature" and "natural nature as found in customary, historically grown modes of human dwelling" confront each other "like two hostile domains that depart from each other with constantly accelerating speed." In this situation of confrontation or disjunction, a tendency prevails in advanced societies to erect "calculable nature" into the dominant and only correct view of the world and accordingly to transform all human thinking into a form of quantitative calculation. By contrast, the naturalness of nature tends to be degraded into a mere phantasm, an empty flight of fancy that no longer appeals even to poets. An age marked by such disjunction is a desolate or destitute period: what is lacking is not only Hebel's mediating bridge but also, and above all, the presence of a house-friend who can genuinely be a friend of the world. According to Heidegger, such a friend would have to be able to enhance and mediate both domains—and in fact all possible domains—of our time. In his words:

[8] Ibid., pp. 20–22. See also in this context Manfred Riedel, "Naturhermeneutik und Ethik im Denken Heideggers," *Heidegger Studies* 5 (1989): 153–172, and *Hören auf die Sprache* (Frankfurt-Main: Suhrkamp, 1990), pp. 230–299.

Today we drift aimlessly through a world in which the house-friend is missing—a friend who would be equally attentive and empathetic to the technologically constructed world edifice *and* to the world seen as house for a more original dwelling. What is lacking is a house-friend who would be able to reintegrate the calculability of technological nature into the open mystery of a newly experienced naturalness of nature.[9]

Although it highlights a deep need of our time, Heidegger's essay does not spell out how and by whom this need might be fulfilled. Returning to its chosen topic, however, the essay alerts us to helpful clues and direction signals to be gleaned from Hebel's work. What above all provides guidance in Hebel's poetry is his genuine friendliness, his willingness to make room for both enlightened knowledge and ordinary experience and thus for a gently clear-sighted form of human dwelling on earth. Hebel's mediating capacity is manifested in his nuanced and sensitive approach to language, an approach reconciling high and low culture, standardized language and local dialect; his "Treasure Chest" in particular stands as a high point of cultural mediation and reconciliation. As Heidegger observes, the secret of the "Treasure Chest" resides in the fact that Hebel was able to "integrate the idiom of his Alemannian dialect into 'high' German language"; in this manner, the poet allows standard language "to resonate with the pure echo of the dialect's richness." This echo would be stifled or obstructed if "high" language were completely standardized, and especially if it were streamlined into a mere technological medium of information exchange. Such streamlining would undermine not only the rich multivocality of natural language but also the deeper truth of human living and dwelling—a truth Hebel once expressed in these words: "Whether we wish to admit it or not, we are plants that arise from their roots in the earth in order to blossom and bear fruit in the sky." Like Hebel's entire work, this phrase pinpoints the entwinement of regions which allows human dwelling to happen and whose juncture constitutes the house of the world. Hebel's poetry combines the earthly quality of dialect with the transparency of standard language, thus moving "between the depth of perfect sensuality and the height of spirited boldness." In moving and journeying in this in-between zone, Hebel's work exemplifies the meaning of friendship, thereby clearing a path for a future generation that wishes to befriend the world.[10]

---

[9] Heidegger, *Hebel—der Hausfreund*, pp. 23–24.
[10] Ibid., pp. 25–29.

II

To the English-speaking reader, Heidegger's comments may seem intriguing but perhaps unpersuasive to those unfamiliar with Hebel's work (which remains untranslated). The character of this work is, however, well represented by the "Treasure Chest"—a collection of stories, usually ending with a moral lesson (*haec fabula docet*). One of the opening stories is titled "Memorabilia from the Orient" (where Orient stands for the Ottoman Empire). The story deals with a rich and highly placed man in Turkey who is approached by a beggar asking for alms. An inveterate miser, the rich man not only refuses the beggar's request but pushes him away with insults and bodily blows; to chase him still farther away, he finally throws a stone at him. Embittered, the poor beggar goes away, but he puts the stone into his pocket for safe keeping. A few years later, the rich man, because of some misdeeds, falls from power and position; as part of his punishment, he is carried through town riding backward on a mule. Among the bystanders watching the procession is the beggar, who recognizes his assailant. Remembering the insult, he takes the stone from his pocket and is just about to throw it at the disgraced rider—when he suddenly thinks better of it, drops the stone, and goes away. Hebel draws several lessons from this story. The first concerns the fickleness of human fortune, where prosperity and misery can alternate without warning. This fickleness should caution against arrogance and rudeness in good times toward poor and less fortunate people, for "things can be entirely different at nightfall from what they were at dawn." Next, the story warns against carrying a stone in one's pocket and a grudge or thoughts of revenge in one's heart. Generally speaking, thoughts of revenge are always misguided: to practice revenge against the rich and powerful is dangerous and foolhardy; but to pursue it against someone whose luck has run out (and this was the beggar's first thought) is ignominious and inhuman. Regarding the old and time-honored motto that it is right to do good to one's friends and evil to one's enemies, the Rhenish house-friend offers a countermaxim: it is right "to do good to one's friends and to treat enemies so that they become friends."[11]

Another story illustrating the same point, but in a more caustic and sardonic vein, is titled "The Cheap Meal." Two restaurant owners are bitter enemies and ready to inflict every possible harm on each other. One day a guest enters one of the two restaurants, sits down, and

[11] Johann Peter Hebel, *Werke* (Munich: Hanser, 1954), pp. 9–10.

demands to be served a good meal "for his money." After emptying a bowl of soup, he proceeds to order some meat and vegetables "for his money"—and also a good glass of wine on the same terms. After having feasted extensively, when it is time to pay the bill, the guest takes a small coin from his pocket and offers it to the owner saying, "Here is my money." Stunned, the owner remonstrates that this meagre amount does not come near to covering the bill—only to be told by the guest that he ordered a good meal "for his money" and no more. Finding himself cheated, the owner quickly considers how he can draw some benefit from his loss—and remembers his enemy and competitor. Turning to the guest, he tells him to forget about the bill, keep quiet about the incident, and go to the other restaurant to obtain another cheap meal in the same way. Already passing through the doorway, the guest stops briefly to announce that he had just come from the other restaurant, whose owner had given him the same instruction. The lesson Hebel derives from the story fits the old adage that "whoever seeks to inflict ill on another is likely to suffer the same ill himself." In this case, the guest as outsider or third person was able to benefit from the mutual ill will of the two owners. As Hebel adds, however, in addition to being the beneficiary the guest could turn out to be the benefactor of the two opponents—provided that they are willing to learn from their experience. In his words: "The clever customer could have earned for himself the gratitude of the two owners if they had drawn a lesson from their loss and had become reconciled with each other. For peace nurtures and sustains while discord debilitates and destroys [*Frieden ernährt, aber Unfrieden verzehrt*]."[12]

The peace and friendliness praised in the "Treasure Chest" is not restricted to close personal relations but cuts across distinctions of religion, ethnicity, and status. Regarding status and wealth, two stories may briefly illustrate the drift of Hebel's thought. One shows the arrogance of public officialdom and its pointlessness. One day a poor man is running hurriedly through the streets of the city; in his hurry, he nearly bumps into a high city official who is walking along the street. Greatly annoyed, the official asks the poor man about the purpose of his hurry—he responds by saying that he cannot tell. Still more annoyed, the official insists on hearing the motive for the haste and the destination of the fast pace, only to be assured by the man that he does not know himself. Feeling slighted, the official summons a nearby policeman and threatens to put the poor man in jail. At this point, the man remonstrates, saying:

12 Ibid., pp. 13–15.

"Now you see that I have spoken the truth. For how could I know a moment ago that I was going to jail, and how do I know even now that this is my destination?" Sensing the wisdom of this response, the official lets the man go, reproaching himself silently for his haughty behavior.

Another story, "Kannitverstan," comments on disparities of wealth. A poor German artisan visits the city of Amsterdam and is greatly impressed by its wealth and splendor. Walking through the streets, he notices a palatial house with ornaments, high windows, and six chimneys on the roof. Astonished, the artisan asks a passer-by the name of the owner of the building. Unfamiliar with the German language, the passer-by quickly says "Kannitverstan" ("I cannot understand") and moves on. Taking this to be the name of the owner, the visitor marvels at the wealth of Mr. Kannitverstan, which differs so drastically from his own indigence. His amazement is increased when he comes to the harbor with its many ships filled to the brim with precious cargo. Pointing to one of the biggest ships, he again asks for the name of the owner—and receives the same reply, "Kannitverstan." Overwhelmed by these dazzling riches, he is just about to sink into an abyss of self-pity when a large funeral procession comes around the corner, with a black carriage drawn by four horses and followed by a huge throng of people. Curious, he approaches a member of the procession and inquires after the name of the deceased—again to be told "Kannitverstan." Now, the whole fragility of human fortune strikes the artisan like a thunderbolt, showing him in quick succession the height of human glory and its demise. This lesson he carries away from his visit. In later years, Hebel reports, when he reflected on disparities of wealth he would "remember Mr. Kannitverstan in Amsterdam—his palatial house, his rich ship, and his narrow grave."[13]

Hebel's stories also transcend divergences of ethnic and religious background. Several stories are about the "Orient," particularly about people of the Muslim faith—and always in a friendly, respectful tone. One story, "The Wise Sultan," deals with the Great Sultan of Turkey and his prudent behavior in his own religious context. Once on a Friday, when he is on the way to the mosque, the sultan is approached by a beggar who addresses him reverently saying, "Almighty sultan, do you believe in the words of the prophet?" Hearing the expected response, "Yes, indeed, I believe in the prophet's words," the beggar continues: "Well, according to the prophet's Koran, all Muslims are brothers. Hence, brother, please share your inheritance with me." Smiling at the boldness of the ap-

[13] Ibid., pp. 18–19, 48–51.

proach, the sultan gives the beggar alms and tries to proceed on his way—but is held back by the beggar, who complains about the relative insignificance of the alms in comparison with the sultan's wealth. Pondering the situation, the sultan replies: "Dear brother, be content and don't tell anyone how much I have given you; because the House of Islam is large, and if all brothers desired an equal part, your share would be even less, and you should have to repay them." A similar spirit pervades stories about Jews—who, in Hebel's time, were still living mostly in ghettoes. One such story highlights the wisdom and insight of the philosopher Moses Mendelsohn, who, in order to earn a living, worked for some time as accountant for a merchant of limited intelligence. As Hebel recounts, Mendelsohn was "a very pious and wise man who was highly respected and beloved among the most prestigious and learned men of his time." One day a friend visits the philosopher as he is laboring over a difficult accounting problem. "Dear Moses," he says, "is it not a pity and indefensible that an intelligent man like you should have to work in the employ of a man who is intellectually your inferior? Do you not have more brains in your little finger than he does in his whole body?" Far from becoming conceited by this flattering remark, Mendelsohn puts his pen behind his ear, looks calmly at his friend, and says: "I think providence has quite well arranged things. For as things stand, my employer can use my services and I can gain a livelihood. But if I were the employer and he my accountant, I would not be able to use him."[14]

Hebel's gentle spirit radiates from all his writings. One of his later stories, "The Walk to the Lake" (1820), combines in a most appealing way the different dimensions of experience—what Heidegger calls the regions of the world—while simultaneously contrasting and reconciling human faculties: philosophical reasoning is juxtaposed to religious faith and both, in turn, are counterbalanced by the promptings of the heart (what Pascal called *raison du coeur*). The story involves a group of friends, men and women, who one fine summer evening stroll to a restaurant at the lake. On the way there, they encounter a cripple whose deformed

[14] Ibid., pp. 65–66, 92–93. The "Treasure Chest" also contains a story about the prophet Muhammad and the wisdom displayed in his going to the mountain when the mountain did not wish to come to him—the lesson being: do what needs to be done without waiting for miracles (pp. 256–257). Several stories attack the practice of Jew-baiting, which was then quite prevalent. In one story, someone is trying to bait a Jew by saying, "Do you know that, in France, Jews in the future have to ride on asses?" To which the Jew replies, "If this is so, then we better *both* stay right here—even though you are not Jewish" (p. 29). Another story shows how a Jew is able to overcome the hostility of some boys who like to taunt and insult him through prudent and persistent acts of kindness (pp. 179–180).

body startles and shocks them. The pastor, it seems, is inclined to leave the disfigurement to inscrutable providence, but the medical doctor in the group proceeds to offer a rational, philosophical explanation by resorting to the laws of probability. According to the doctor, all kinds of human forms or shapes are possible and equally probable in the course of history; the cripple is one such possibility. Moving beyond this particular encounter, the doctor next holds forth on the broad range of possibilities encompassed by humankind. One such possibility, he concedes to a questioner, would be "the worst of all": a universal scourge or monster, a global thunderstorm "disruptive of all thrones and altars and putting the world in flames." But there is also the possibility of "the best of all": of a human combining in his person all the wisdom and love of past rulers and lawgivers "from King Solomon to Emperor Franz I" and devoid of all hatred and ill will; under the auspices of this person, all the dreams and prophecies of humankind would be fulfilled and swords would be turned into ploughshares. Since this person is a rational possibility, he has to appear sometime in history—even if the worst of humans should come first and attempt to destroy the world. For, the doctor reasons, the worst is only the warrant of the best, since no pendulum swings steadily to one extreme; moreover, "the sustaining and saving powers in general always outweigh the destructive ones." If, as it seems now, the best of humans appears late in time, then this is something worth waiting for, and "the morning light will dawn for humankind in the evening." Hearing this, the pastor thinks that the doctor's argument contains religion—although perhaps a peculiar one. All through the discussion, however, a young law student has been attentive to the "beautiful Adeline," who walks beside him: he finds in her beauty concrete assurance of the doctor's hopes for the best. When asked finally by a woman in the group whether the young couple has seen the sun setting over the lake, the girl answers honestly "No"—while the boy thinks "not setting but rising" (*nicht unter, aber auf*).[15]

III

Hebel's work is permeated with good will and fellow feeling, but he is not naive. Living in an era marked by revolutionary upheavals and

[15] Ibid., pp. 287–294. For a revised critical edition of the story, see Hebel, *Der Statthalter von Schopfheim: Der Spaziergang an den See*, ed. Adrian Braunbehrens and Peter Pfaff (Karlsruhe: Müller, 1988), pp. 29–37.

almost constant warfare, the poet was well acquainted with enmity and the conflictual character of many human relations. One story in his "Treasure Chest" silhouettes kindness precisely against the backdrop of rudeness, and good will against the foil of ill will. Asked how he acquired his kindness and good manners, the protagonist of the story responds: by living among rude and unkind people, who taught him how *not* to behave. In his essay on Hebel, Heidegger celebrates the same gentle virtues that were dear to the poet, though again not naively. Friendliness in Heidegger's portrayal does not equal meek conformism or an absence of diversity and contestation. Pointing to the initial announcement of the yearly almanac, he notes that Hebel aspired for his calendar to be the best and "victorious in any competition." While offering his calendar to people as a house-friend, the poet thus was by no means averse to friendly competition. In Heidegger's words, Hebel was not reluctant to admit that "everything genuine created by humans is the gift of victory in a noble contest," and this goes "even for a calendar."[16]

Still, friendly competition is not the same as radical conflict or a life-and-death struggle. The mellowness of *Hebel—the House-Friend* is quite a distance removed from Nietzschean agonal strife, which Heidegger himself had endorsed in some of his earlier writings (when he spoke, for instance, of the rift between earth and world or between juncture and disjuncture). Now, in supporting a gentler compatibility, Heidegger exposes himself to accusations that have been leveled periodically, throughout history, against models of social cohesion and fellowship—that is, accusations of simplemindedness or else obfuscation. As is well known, the orderly structure of Plato's *Republic* has been attacked as an emblem of authoritarian conformism (if not of totalitarian repression). Likewise, the Hegelian notion of the state with its twin pillars of *Sittlichkeit* and constitutional balance has been taken to task for ignoring the class conflict latent in bourgeois society, and hence for serving as an apology for ruling elites. Moving outside the confines of Western culture, one can find similar charges addressed at Confucianism, whose central concept of fellow feeling (*jen*) is meant to underscore and foster human sociability—but was often exploited by Chinese rulers for the sake of political repression. As an antidote to such repressiveness, defenders of emancipatory politics are likely to appeal to thinkers whose work foregrounds confrontation over consensus. Among ancient writers, Thucydides is liable to be the preferred author; in the modern age, Machiavelli with his praise of conflictual politics is bound to serve as favorite mentor,

[16] Heidegger, *Hebel—der Hausfreund*, pp. 9–10; see also Hebel, *Werke*, p. 10.

at least for the period of early modernity until he is eclipsed by Marx. Read in conjunction, these thinkers seem to downgrade sociability and to erect conflict or aggressiveness into the sole political virtue.

Although useful as a broad benchmark, the distinction between fellowship and conflict should probably not be overdrawn. First of all, consensual thinkers (or those labeled as such) are not nearly as confining as they are alleged to be. In the case of Plato, social order was predicated on the crucial premise of justice or fairness, a requirement that presumably ruled out arbitrary oppression. In the parallel Chinese example, sociability or fellow feeling was frequently held to be incompatible with unjust and one-sided domination, a point Mencius developed in the direction of a popular "right of resistance" against oppressive rulers. Without explicating such a right, Hegel's philosophy was emphatic about the need of social justice as an underpinning of public *Sittlichkeit;* moreover, conflict was built into the core of the Hegelian "struggle for recognition," though without vitiating the possibility of reconciliation. On the other hand, conflictual thinkers are not always as hard-nosed as many believe, Marx being a case in point. A student of Hegel, Marx considered class struggle not as interminable but rather as a stepping stone to a future classless society—thus privileging in the long run human sociability and harmony. Taking some cues from Marx, one might ask opponents of consensus how far they are willing to push their commitment to discord and "radical" struggle (a struggle sometimes loosely associated with Nietzschean teachings). Where does one draw the line between useful discord and destructive violence, and how can one ensure that favoring the former does not inevitably entail privileging the latter? These questions, I submit, are not idle queries in a century devastated by two world wars and continuously rent by bloody conflicts between diverse ethnic, religious, and national groupings. Does an age like ours not demonstrate the superiority of the path of nonviolence, if necessary the path of nonviolent resistance?

To demarcate the latter path from violent destruction, however, nonviolent struggle itself must be animated from the beginning by some respect for opponents and hence by a form of fellow feeling or sympathy. In the midst of concrete struggle, resistance must make room and constantly hold open the vision of reconciliation, thus always keeping in reserve the palm of peace. This vision, in turn, cannot simply be taken for granted. Although perhaps not alien to human nature, fellowship and peaceableness also need to be cultivated and nourished, which brings into view the permanent importance of the teachers of fellowship, from

Confucius to the Rhenish house-friend. In his later writings, Heidegger clearly seeks to emulate these teachings, thereby offering himself as a kind of philosophical house-friend of the world. Heidegger's essay on Hebel uncovers the different dimensions of the world which today need befriending; but his brief allusions perhaps bear further elaboration. In Heidegger's presentation, Hebel's work is able to bridge and reconcile enlightened reasoning and experiential life-world; as shown in "The Walk to the Lake," his thought is ample enough to encompass reason, faith, and the promptings of the heart. According to Heidegger, the basic dilemma of our time is the division between reason and experience, between science and ordinary understanding; hence the house-friend's sympathy toady must extend to science and technology as well as to the life-world, to "calculable" nature as well as to nature's primordial "naturalness." Among other things, this view should help undermine the image of Heidegger as an enemy of modernity and (worse) as an enemy of science. Modern science and technology were to him not so much avoidable mistakes as a kind of "world destiny" that we (modern societies) have to shoulder, undergo, and perhaps move through. The issue was not how to eliminate technology but rather how to prevent our impulse to control nature from stifling and smothering "natural" nature seen as our sustaining and nourishing habitat.[17]

Transposed to the arena of global politics, the division between science and life-world translates into the division between "developed" and "developing" (or Third World) countries—which, with some exceptions, is the distinction between Western and non-Western societies. In this relationship, the house-friend is most glaringly lacking today. With steadily accelerating pace, the entire world is coming under the grip of the process of modernization, or Westernization—which to a large extent means the transformation of traditional societies under the aegis of Western science and technology as well as Western forms of economic production. Seemingly relentless and irresistible, this process inflicts heavy trauma and dislocation on developing countries and non-Western modes of life, dislocations that are the breeding ground of intense antagonism and enmity. Faced with the challenge of Western technological and economic power (not to speak of military threats), non-Western societies

[17] On the issue of technology, see, for example, Michael E. Zimmerman, *Heidegger's Confrontation with Modernity: Technology, Politics, and Art* (Bloomington: Indiana University Press, 1990); and Hans Seigfried, "Heideggers Technikkritik," in *Lebenswelt und Wissenschaft*, ed. Carl F. Gethman (Bonn: Bouvier, 1991), pp. 209–242.

are prone to retreat into the shell of time-honored customs and traditions, a retreat sometimes giving way to belligerent fundamentalism. In a sense, this response matches the challenge by way of reversal: the abstract universalism of Western science is replaced by a narrowly ethnic or religious parochialism. Pursued as a defensive strategy, such parochialism is liable to fail: given the dynamics of global development, parochial retreat ensures "backwardness," thereby unwittingly contributing and paying homage to unchecked Western supremacy. Realizing this outcome, developing societies sometimes opt for rapid modernization with a vengeance; yet, in seeking to emulate and check Western power, this policy is liable to erode or undermine indigenous traditions and beliefs— which is another form of submission. In this situation, a global house-friend is desperately needed: someone who is able to mediate between Western modernity and native traditions, between scientific nature and calculating reason, on the one hand, and the naturalness of historically grown life-worlds, on the other.

The role of such a house-friend is not to unify or amalgamate cultures in an indiscriminate blend. Being a stranger or journeyman, the house-friend does not come equipped with the fire of a unifying vision or program but rather emits a borrowed "lunar" light that envelops all things in its soft glow while allowing them to be different. In this sense, the house-friend keeps his distance while respecting and preserving the distance of all beings from each other. In Hebel's words, the house-friend "glances into many a window, without being noticed," and "sits in many a restaurant, without being recognized." While being a steady and reliable companion, the house-friend remains a guest in everyone's house, reticently shying away from any kind of obstructive intrusion; companionship or fellowship in this case signals not a merger but rather a reserved presence or a present absence. To this extent, the house-friend is not completely alien to non-Western thought. In the words of the Japanese poet Daito Kokushi:

> To be apart from one another for millions of eons
> and not to be distant for a single moment,
> To be together all day long
> and not together for a single instant.

These words, in turn, echo the lines of the Chinese poem: "Though apart ten thousand miles / We see the crescent moon over Ch'ang-an." Keeping himself in the background or in reserve, the house-friend is also reticent in his speech. Although he reflectively ponders things and thinks his part, he does not always speak out; even when speaking out, he does so without fuss or pretense. It is in this reserved and unpretentious manner that Hebel offered his "Alemannian Poems" to his readers, as a bouquet of simple flowers gathered in his valley:

> A small gift. Yet, as well as it is possible
> The valley's muse has smilingly and gently
> Wound them into this garland;
> And may its worth be measured solely
> By the purity of friendship offering it to you.[18]

[18] Hebel, *Alemannische Gedichte*, ed. Wilhelm Zentner (Stuttgart: Reclam, 1960), p. 11. The Japanese and Chinese verses are cited in Keiji Nishitani, *Nishida Kitaro*, trans. Yamamoto Seisaku and James W. Heisig (Berkeley: University of California Press, 1991), pp. 32, 38. In the above paragraph, I use "he" to avoid the more cumbersome "he/she"— although I intend the latter meaning.

CHAPTER EIGHT

Heidegger and Zen Buddhism:
A Salute to Keiji Nishitani

From the pine tree
learn of the pine tree.
—Bashō

For Western readers, Martin Heidegger seems both close and exceedingly distant; his thought appears in some ways homegrown and quite familiar, and in other ways alien and strangely unfamiliar. Critics of his work sometimes attack it as narrowly parochial or provincial, because of its presumed rootedness in a local habitat (the Black Forest region); yet critics (sometimes the same ones) also object to its aloofness, unintelligibility, and penchant for mysticism—charges which (more than personal bias) reflect a sense of cultural rupture.

Heidegger himself would hardly have been surprised by this conflicting reception. In his "Vom Wesen des Grundes" he described human *Dasein* as a creature of "distance" or farness, a distance that alone can nurture a true closeness to things and fellow beings. Likewise, in his comments on Friedrich Hölderlin he portrayed "homecoming" not as a retreat into a native habitat but as a journey homeward through the most distant peregrinations. These considerations apply to his own philosophical journey, particularly to his much-discussed "overcoming" of Western metaphysics—which was by no means a simple elimination. Without encouraging a cultural leap, Heidegger's overcoming led him into distant and alien terrain, and ultimately in the direction of Eastern culture and thought—a culture Kitaro Nishida, the founder of the so-called Kyoto School, has circumscribed as "the urge to see the form of the formless, and hear the sound of the soundless."[1] Attentiveness to this far-off sound, I believe, is at the heart of Heidegger's distance and seeming aloofness. More than any other Western thinker in the twentieth century, Heidegger is culturally decentered, lodged at the crossroads of East and West, and thus at the site of a possible or impending global dialogue.

In this chapter I explore one facet of this dialogue, namely, the relationship between Heidegger and Zen Buddhism as the latter is articulated by Keiji Nishitani. The choice of this facet is not accidental. A leading representative of the Kyoto School and a former pupil of Nishida, Nishitani has also been a close student of Heidegger's work and frequently refers in his publications to the latter's teachings. For his own part, Heidegger was not unfamiliar with the Kyoto School, having become acquainted with its activities through visits by Count Shuzo Kuki, a contemporary of Nishitani and like him an associate of Nishida. References to the same Count Kuki, one may note, are interspersed throughout the "Dialogue on Language" contained in *Unterwegs zur Sprache*.[2]

Given the extensive lifework of Keiji Nishitani, my discussion here must be selective and circumscribed—in a manner that does not, I hope, truncate the richness of his insights. For English-speaking readers, the major publication available in translation is *Religion and Nothingness*, a study which, I believe, ably reflects the core of Nishitani's Buddhist

[1] Kitaro Nishida, *A Study of Good*, trans. V. H. Viglielmo (Tokyo: Japanese Government Printing Bureau, 1960), p. 191. See also Martin Heidegger, "Vom Wesen des Grundes," in *Wegmarken* (Frankfurt-Main: Klostermann, 1967), p. 71, and "Heimkunft/An die Verwandten," in *Erläuterungen zu Hölderlins Dichtung*, ed. Friedrich-Wilhelm von Herrmann (*Gesamtausgabe*, Vol. 4; Frankfurt-Main: Klostermann, 1981), pp. 29–30.

[2] See Heidegger, "Aus einem Gespräch von der Sprache (Zwischen einem Japaner und einem Fragenden)," in *Unterwegs zur Sprache* (Pfullingen: Neske, 1959), pp. 83–155; for an English version, see "A Dialogue on Language (between a Japanese and an Inquirer)," in *On the Way to Language*, trans. Peter D. Hertz (New York: Harper & Row, 1982), pp. 1–54. On Nishitani and the Kyoto School, see the Foreword by Winston L. King and the Translator's Introduction in Keiji Nishitani, *Religion and Nothingness*, trans. Jan Van Bragt (Berkeley: University of California Press, 1982), pp. vii–xlv. See also Frederick Franck, ed., *The Buddha Eye: An Anthology of the Kyoto School* (New York: Crossroads, 1982); and Hans Waldenfels, *Absolute Nothingness: Foundations for a Buddhist–Christian Dialogue*, trans. James W. Heisig (New York: Paulist Press, 1980). On the relation of the Kyoto School and Nishitani to Heidegger, see Yasuo Yuasa, "The Encounter of Modern Japanese Philosophy with Heidegger," and Nishitani, "Reflections on Two Addresses by Martin Heidegger," in *Heidegger and Asian Thought*, ed. Graham Parkes (Honolulu: University of Hawaii Press, 1987), pp. 155–174 and 145–154. See also Hartmut Buchner, ed., *Japan und Heidegger: Gedenkschrift der Stadt Messkirch zum 100. Geburtstag Martin Heideggers* (Sigmaringen: Jan Thorbecke, 1989).

outlook and which I have chosen therefore as my guiding text. Again, my ambition is not to present a comprehensive review; instead, I focus on two crucial themes that permeate the entire study: the themes of nothingness or emptiness and of "thinghood" seen as a "gathering" of being. In both cases, I explore affinities and differences between Nishitani's and Heidegger's accounts, in the hope of fostering and perhaps deepening dialogue between the respective philosophical orientations.

I

As is well known, nothingness, or emptiness, stands at the center of all forms of Buddhist thought, including Zen Buddhism; it is this aspect which, to Western minds, frequently suggests an attitude of complete withdrawal or world denial. Yet, as one should note, nothingness here does not simply mean negativity or denial; far from denoting a vacuum, the term designates the inner core of reality, or the other side of being—which carries life-affirming and sustaining implications. It is in this sense that the term figures in the title of Nishitani's *Religion and Nothingness*. As he states in the opening chapter, nothingness, or nihility, comes to the fore whenever the routine course of our life is disrupted by calamities or inner doubt: "When we become a question to ourselves and when the problem of why we exist arises, this means that nihility has emerged from the ground of existence and that our very existence has turned into a question mark." Once this happens, the taken-for-granted meaning of our life and world is suddenly shattered and we realize that we have been hovering over an abyss all along. From the vantage of ordinary meaning, what surfaces now is the meaninglessness that lies in wait at the bottom of everyday, routine engagements and activities; in Zen Buddhist terms, a nagging sense of nihility brings the "restless, forward-advancing pace of life" to a halt and instead "turns the light to what is directly underfoot." Both religiously and philosophically, this experience of disruption, this stepping back to see what is underfoot, may be described as a turning, a conversion. In Nishitani's words:

> This fundamental conversion in life is occasioned by the opening up of the horizon of nihility at the ground of life. It is nothing less than a conversion from the self-centered (or man-centered) mode of being, which always asks

what *use* things have for us (or for man), to an attitude that asks for what *purpose* we ourselves (or man) exist.[3]

According to Nishitani, the turn to nothingness as emptiness is slow and arduous and occurs over several successive steps. The first step of human awareness is the standpoint of sense perception and rational analysis, a standpoint familiar to Western readers from the traditions of empiricism and rationalism. For Nishitani, these traditions are predicated on the separation or juxtaposition of consciousness and world, that is, on the subject-object division pervading particularly modern Western thought. To confront the world in this manner, he writes, means "to look at things *without* from a field *within* the self"; it means assuming "a position vis-à-vis things from which self and things remain fundamentally separated from one another," a position he variously calls the "field of consciousness" or "field of reason."

This position was epitomized and made canonical in the thought of Descartes with his categorial distinction between *res cogitans* (consciousness) and *res extensa* (extended matter). On the one hand, he notes, Descartes established the *ego cogito* as "a reality that is beyond all doubt"; on the other hand, things in the natural world "came to appear as bearing no living connection with the internal ego" and thus resembled "the cold and lifeless world of death." As Nishitani adds, this division and the treatment of the world as lifeless mechanism came to furnish the foundation for natural science and for modern scientific technology; for, from the vantage of the *cogito*, the world of nature was bound to look "like so much raw material" available for human control and exploitation. Although modern natural science seeks to uncover the objective and invariant laws of nature, these laws are not independent of the *cogito* and its designs to enhance its self-preservation. "The significance of man operating in accord with the laws of nature, as well as of the laws of nature becoming manifest through and as the work of man," we read, is most thoroughly visible in "a technology dependent on machinery." It is in this domain in which knowledge and purposive activity work in closest unity, that "the fog lifts" from modern science: "Machines and mechanical technology are man's ultimate embodiment and appropriation of the laws of nature."[4]

[3] Nishitani, *Religion and Nothingness*, pp. 4–5.
[4] Ibid., pp. 9–11, 81–82.

In Nishitani's view, Descartes's doubt was only partially radical, because it accepted as given or left unexplored the status and meaning of the *cogito* and its relation to the world. Once this acceptance is canceled, once the *cogito* is no longer seen as a substance (or *res*), the path is open to a deeper radicalism, to the level of a nonsubstantive subjectivity positing the world and itself out of its own nothingness. In his words, this path leads to "the ground of the subjectivity of the *cogito*" on a plane where "the orientation of the subject to its ground is more radical and thoroughgoing than it is with the *cogito*." According to *Religion and Nothingness*, this path has been opened up chiefly by modern existentialism with its focus on alienated existence and the abyss of self-constitution. "This way of thinking about the *cogito*," we read, "is 'existential' thinking." Radical reflection of this kind penetrates deeper than "the self-evidence of self-consciousness clinging to itself"; rather, it yields an awareness that "can only emerge in the reality of an *Existenz* that oversteps the limits of being."

In existentialist terminology, this overstepping or transgressing is the hallmark of "ecstasy," or the "ek-static" (self-transcending) quality of existence—a quality that radically subjectifies nothingness. From this deeper vantage, Nishitani observes, nothingness is "shifted to the side of the subject itself, and the freedom or autonomy of the subject is said to be a function of existence (*Existenz*) stepping over itself into the midst of nihility." Nishitani calls the domain opened up by existential questioning the "field of nihility," a field closely connected with the modern (Western) problem of nihilism. "Only when the self breaks through the field of consciousness, the field of *beings*," he writes, "and stands on the ground of nihility is it able to achieve a subjectivity that can in no way be objectified." At this point, "nihility appears as the ground of everything that exists"; as a corollary, consciousness with its separation of inside and outside is "surpassed subjectively," so that nihility also "opens up the ground of the *within* and the *without*."[5]

As portrayed in Nishitani's study, the leading representatives of subjective existentialism are Friedrich Nietzsche and Jean-Paul Sartre, with Nietzsche being the more radical of the two. Both thinkers, Nishitani notes, show similar tendencies: "In each of them atheism is bound up with existentialism," which means that atheism or nothingness has been "subjectivized" and nihility has become "the field of the so-called *ekstasis* of self-existence." Yet, between the two, he adds, Nietzsche's position is

[5] Ibid., pp. 14–17, 67.

"far more comprehensive and penetrating" than Sartre's, due to the latter's identification of existentialism with a subjective humanism. Sartre, we are told, describes existence as a human "project," namely, the project of continually going beyond the self, of continually "overstepping" oneself. Thus, he recognizes a mode of transcendence or self-transcendence with the "form of *ekstasis*, a standing-outside-of-oneself." This *ekstasis*, however, remains grounded in human subjectivity, which reconnects Sartre's thought with the Cartesian ego (despite a shift from theism to atheism).

Sartre shares with Descartes the belief in the ego or *cogito* as basic warrant of cognitive truth. Thus, whatever transcendence Sartre's position may allow for "remains glued to the ego." Although he considers nothingness to be "the ground of the subject," he nonetheless presents it "like a wall at the bottom of the ego or like a springboard underfoot of the *cogito*," thus turning it into a principle that shuts the ego "up within itself." By contrast, Nietzsche much more resolutely sought to transgress the ego. As shown in his mature works, Nishitani observes, Nietzsche attempted "to posit a new way of being human beyond the frame of the 'human,' to forge a new form of the human from the 'far side,' beyond the limits of man-centered existence, from 'beyond good and evil,'" This direction was clearly evident in his image of the overman seen as the embodiment of the doctrine that "man is something that shall be overcome." Consequently, he adds, it was chiefly and centrally in Nietzsche's work that atheism achieved "its truly radical subjectivization" and that nihility acquired "a transcendent quality by becoming the field of the ecstasy of self-being."[6]

Yet, no matter how radicalized, subjectivity and subjectivization for Nishitani do not constitute the endpoint of relentless doubt. What still needs to happen, he points out, is a radical questioning of subjectivity itself and of its ecstatic nihility; only through such questioning is it possible to reach the level of "absolute emptiness," or *śūnyatā*, which is at the heart of Buddhist thought. Buddhism, he writes, goes beyond these

---

[6] Ibid., pp. 31, 33, 55–56. With reference to Sartre, Nishitani further elaborates: "We may well appreciate his intentions, but . . . so long as we maintain the standpoint of self-consciousness, the tendency to take ourselves as objects remains, no matter how much we stress subjectivity. Moreover, even though Sartre's theory appears to preserve the dignity of man in his subjective autonomy and freedom, the real dignity of man seems to me to belong only to one who has been 'reborn,' only in the 'new man' that emerges in us when we are born by dying, when we break through nihility" (pp. 32–33). The citation in the text is to Friedrich Nietzsche, *Thus Spoke Zarathustra*, trans. Walter Kaufmann (New York: Viking Press, 1966), p. 12.

previous existential positions in speaking of "the emptiness of the nihilizing view," by which it means "that 'absolute emptiness' in which nihilizing emptiness would itself be emptied." From the vantage of this emptiness, both the field of consciousness with its separation of inside and outside and the nihility grounded in ecstatic self-being can for the first time "be overstepped," or left behind, in favor of a sphere that is "the true no-ground [*Ungrund*]."

Buddhism thematizes as gateway to this no-ground the experience of the "Great Doubt," in which the distinction between doubter and doubted drops away and the self *becomes* doubt itself. In the tradition of Zen, this passage is known as "the doubt of *samādhi* [concentration]"; it, in turn, is closely linked with the "Great Death" and the achievement of the non-ego (*anātman*). In Western philosophical and religious thought, this passage was most perceptively envisaged by Meister Eckhart with his distinction between God and godhead and his equation of the latter with "absolute nothingness," which is also seen as the matrix or field of "our absolute death-*sive*-life." The nothingness of godhead envisaged by Eckhart, Nishitani comments, "must be said to be still more profound than the nihility that contemporary existentialism has put in the place of God"; in existentialist terms, nihility appears "as the ground of self-being and renders it ecstatic, but this ecstasy is not yet the absolute negation of being and thus does not open up to absolute nothingness." This reservation applies even to Nietzsche's work. His later thought, it is true, distinctly adumbrates the standpoint of "an absolute negation-*sive*-affirmation." Yet, his "absolute affirmation or *Ja-sagen*" finds expression in confusing formulas like "life" or "will to power," which brings into view the difference between life affirmation as a power "forcing its way through nihility to gush forth" and life as "absolute death-*sive*-life."[7]

The problem is how to formulate and render intelligible emptiness as absolute death-*sive*-life or negation-*sive*-affirmation. A central chapter in Nishitani's study, "Nihility and *Śūnyatā*," is devoted to this question. As he observes, *śūnyatā* is "another thing altogether from the nihility of

---

[7] Nishitani, *Religion and Nothingness*, pp. 18, 21, 34, 59, 63, 65–66. The difference, he adds, can also be expressed as one "between a nihility proclaiming that 'God is dead' and an absolute nothingness reaching a point beyond even 'God'"; accordingly, one might perhaps say "that the nihility of Nietzsche's nihilism should be called a standpoint of *relative absolute nothingness*" (p. 66). In an intriguing side glance, Nishitani mentions emptiness in connection with the Christian notions of *kenosis* and *ekkenosis* (self-emptying): "What is *ekkenosis* for the Son is *kenosis* for the Father. In the East, this would be called *anātman*, or non-ego" (p. 59).

nihilism." As epitomized in Western existentialism, nothingness as nihility is still seen as a reference point of subjectivity or as something to
which existence relates; differently put, it functions as representational
correlate of existence. By contrast, nothingness in the sense of *śūnyatā*
means emptiness of a kind that "empties itself even of the standpoint that
represents it as some 'thing' that is emptiness" or to which existence
merely relates.

Basically, Buddhist *śūnyatā* does not denote nihilism or nihility in the
sense of a simple negation of, or antithesis to, being; instead, it intimates
the nothingness *of* being or the emptiness harbored by being itself. In
Nishitani's words, "True emptiness is not to be posited as something
outside of and other than 'being'; rather, it is to be realized as something
united to and self-identical with being," a point captured in the phrase
"being-*sive*-nothingness." This view has deep roots in the tradition of
Mahāyāna Buddhism with its opposition to the subject-object split and
all forms conceptual bifurcation: "In the context of Mahāyāna thought,
the primary principle of which is to transcend all duality emerging from
logical analysis, the phrase 'being-*sive*-nothingness' requires that one take
up the stance of the '*sive*' and from there view being as being and
nothingness as nothingness." From the vantage of the *sive*, attachment
both to (ontic) being and to nothingness as nihility is overturned or
canceled. In this sense, *śūnyatā* represents "the endpoint of an orientation
to negation" by operating a double negation. In terms of the study,
śūnyatā might be called "an absolute negativity" inasmuch as it is a
standpoint "that has negated and thereby transcended nihility, which
was itself a transcendence-through-negation of all being." Along the
same lines, emptiness can also be termed "an abyss for the abyss of
nihility."[8]

As Nishitani elaborates, Buddhist *śūnyatā* coincides neither with existentialist nihilism nor with Western-style atheism construed as denial of a
personal God. Drawing again on Meister Eckhart's distinction between
God and godhead, he sees the latter notion as transgressing the customary division of theism and atheism. Eckhart, he writes, "refers to the
'essence' of God that is free of all form—the complete 'image-free' (*bildlos*)
godhead—as 'nothingness,' and considers the soul to return to itself and
acquire absolute freedom only when it becomes totally one with the
'nothingness' of godhead. This is not mere theism, but neither, of course,
is it mere atheism." The critique of a personalized divinity in favor of

---

[8] Ibid., pp. 95–98.

emptiness finds a parallel in the transition from subjectivity or the ego to a selfhood moored in nonbeing or nothingness. On the level of everyday life—the level of sense perception and reason—existence construes itself as a self or person, and moreover as a self seemingly at one with itself. At this point, selfhood or personality designates "a self-enclosed confinement or self-entangled unity," one "shackled to its own narcissism. It is a grasping *of* the self *by* the self, a confinement of the self by the self that spells attachment *to* the self."

As previously indicated, existentialism opens up the "abyss of nihility," but only by radicalizing subjectivity into a mode of ecstatic self-constitution. Moving beyond this point, *śūnyatā* as emptiness involves a radical "disentanglement" from self-attachment or subjectivity and a transgression of the latter in favor of the non-ego. "In a word," Nishitani writes, *śūnyatā* is "the field of what Buddhist teaching calls *emancipation*, or what Eckhart refers to as *Abgeschiedenheit* (detachment)." The same field might also be called selfhood in a new, nonsubjectivist sense: "True emptiness is nothing less than what reaches awareness in all of us as our own absolute *self-nature*." This paradox was well expressed in Dōgen's statement: "To learn the Buddha way is to learn one's self; to learn one's self is to forget one's self."[9]

In the context of his discussion of *śūnyatā* Nishitani also comments on Heidegger's work, in a manner I find dubious or at least puzzling. As he correctly remarks, since his early writings Heidegger effected a close connection of being and nothingness: "In Heidegger's terms, the being of beings discloses itself in the nullifying of nothingness (*das Nichts nichtet*)." He also sensibly and persuasively differentiates this conception from Sartre's mode of existentialism: "Insofar as Sartre locates subjectivity at the standpoint of the Cartesian ego, his nothingness is not even the 'death' of which Heidegger speaks, the mode of being of this ego is not a 'being unto death.'" Despite these perceptive remarks, the study in the end ties Heidegger to existentialist nihility or nihilism, that is, to a view that still treats nothingness as negativity and as something outside existence. In Heidegger's work, we read, nothingness is still being viewed "from the bias of self-existence as the groundlessness (*Grundlosigkeit*) of existence lying at the ground of self-existence" and thus as something "lying outside of the 'existence' of the self." This view, Nishitani asserts, is evident in Heidegger's talk of self-existence as "held suspended in

⁹ Ibid., pp. 99, 103, 105–107. The reference is to Dōgen's *Shōbōgenzō genjōkōan*, trans. W. Wadell and A. Masao, in *Eastern Buddhist* (n.s.) 5 (1972): 134.

nothingness"—despite the "fundamental difference of his standpoint from other brands of contemporary existentialism or nihilism." As he grants, the notion of a suspension in nothingness marks "a great step forward" in the conception of self-existence as "existence-in-ecstasy." Nonetheless, the step falls short of reaching *śūnyatā*: "In Heidegger's case, traces of the representation of nothingness as some 'thing' that is nothingness still remain."[10]

These comments can hardly be reconciled with Heidegger's texts. From his early period, I believe, his writings sought to extricate themselves, by and large successfully, from the equation of nothingness with negativity or a realm outside being and existence. As articulated in *Being and Time*, the notion of "being-unto-death" designated, not a terminal point or a sphere beyond life, but an intrinsic possibility and defining character of human existence itself. As Heidegger wrote at the time, "As the end of *Dasein* or existence, death is *Dasein's* innermost possibility"— where possibility does not mean a theoretical or practical option *Dasein* might or might not choose but rather an inner latency steadily permeating life from the beginning. "Poised toward this possibility," he added, "*Dasein* discovers its innermost potentiality of being in which the very being of *Dasein* is at stake." As one may also recall, *Being and Time* contains a strong critique of the modern reliance on subjectivity and the *cogito*, a critique in many ways resembling Nishitani's.

Taking a broad historical view, Heidegger's remarks spanned the tradition of modern thought from Descartes to Kant to Husserl (and the beginning of existentialism). Although acknowledging the power of Cartesian doubt, Heidegger challenged as dubious the basic Cartesian starting point: the ego as a thinking substance. "With the principle '*cogito sum*,'" he wrote, "Descartes claimed that he was putting philosophy on a new and secure footing; but what he left undetermined in this 'radical' departure was the mode of being of the *res cogitans* or—more precisely— the ontological meaning of the '*sum*.'" A similar halfheartedness, in his view, was operative in Kantian philosophy, despite its comparative refinement of critical reflection. Although exposing previous misconceptions and confusions, Kant neglected to undertake a prior ontological analysis of the subjectivity of the subject; although demonstrating the "untenability of the ontic thesis regarding a psychic substance," he refrained from offering an ontological interpretation of selfhood. In attenuated form, the same defect was still evident in Husserl's treatment

---

[10] Nishitani, *Religion and Nothingness*, pp. 33, 96, 98, 109.

of subjectivity and in Max Scheler's (quasi-existentialist) notion of personality. Irrespective of the differences between Husserl and Scheler, Heidegger observed, they concur at least negatively in this respect: "They no longer raise the question of the 'being of a person.'"[11]

Antisubjectivism (as a gateway to nonbeing) remained a persistent theme in Heidegger's evolving opus. Although in *Being and Time* nothingness was still viewed mainly from the vantage of *Dasein*—which may be the basis for Nishitani's objections—the issue was steadily radicalized in subsequent writings, in a manner pointing toward the field of *śūnyatā*. A crucial marker along this road was the essay *What Is Metaphysics?* written shortly after the publication of *Being and Time*. Metaphysics in that essay is contrasted to the outlook of modern science (deriving from Descartes) with its focus on the *res extensa* as an empirically given domain—and its consequent neglect of nothingness. "Nothingness," Heidegger there observes, "is absolutely rejected by science and abandoned as null and void"; thus, "science wishes to know nothing of nothing(ness)." In terms of the essay, nothingness is not simply a synonym for negation or negativity. Instead of being a derivative of negation or the semantic "not," Heidegger insists that nothingness is "more original than the 'not' and negation."

From the vantage of *Dasein*, nothingness is encountered in the state of dread (*Angst*), which is not mere anxiety or nervousness but rather a basic openness to nonbeing. At this point the essay develops the notions of the "nihilating" quality of nothingness (*das Nichts nichtet*) and of the suspension or "suspendedness" (*Hineingehaltenheit*) of *Dasein* in nonbeing, a suspension denoting *Dasein's* exposure not to an alien domain outside being but to its own intrinsic abyss. "Nothingness," Heidegger states, "is neither an object nor anything that 'is' at all; it occurs neither by itself nor 'apart from' beings, as a sort of adjunct. Nothingness is that which makes the disclosure of being(s) as such possible for our human existence." Sharpening this point further, he adds: "Nothingness does not merely designate the conceptual opposite of beings but is an integral part of their essence. It is in the being of beings that the nihilation of nothingness [*das Nichten des Nichts*] occurs."[12]

[11] Martin Heidegger, *Sein und Zeit*, 11th ed. (Tübingen: Niemeyer, 1967), pp. 24, 47, 250, 258–259, 263 (pars. 6, 9, 50, 52–53); trans. John Maquarrie and Edward Robinson as *Being and Time* (London: SCM Press, 1962), pp. 45–46, 73, 303, 307–308, 366–367.

[12] Heidegger, *What Is Metaphysics?* in *Existentialism from Dostoevsky to Sartre*, ed. Walter Kaufmann (New York: Meridian, 1975), pp. 244–46, 248–251 (translation slightly changed for purposes of clarity).

A further, still more important marker on the same road is the *Beiträge zur Philosophie*, written about a decade after *Being and Time*. As Heidegger notes in the *Beiträge*, traditional Western thought has tended to treat nothingness simply as negativity or a vacuum, a view that readily gives rise either to a "pessimistic nihilism" or to a "heroic" counterposture (centered on will to power). Transgression of this traditional outlook requires an overcoming of this kind of nihilism. "Nothingness," he writes, "is neither negative nor is it a goal or endpoint; rather, it is the innermost trembling [*Erzitterung*] of being itself and thus more real than any [ontic] being." Seen from this vantage, nothingness denotes neither a representational or conceptual entity nor a propositional denial but instead a nihilating potency participating obliquely in the ongoing happening or disclosure of being: "Nonbeing happens [*west*] and being happens or occurs; nonbeing occurs through nonhappening or nondisclosure [*Unwesen*], whereas being occurs as nihilating agency." The relationship of being and nothingness is thus one of mutual implication and intertwining; it is not predicated on antithesis or reciprocal exclusion. As Heidegger queried, "What if being itself happened through self-withdrawal and thus in the mode of refusal? Would such a refusal be simply nothing or rather the highest gift? And is it due to this nihilating refusal of being itself that 'nothingness' acquires that enabling potency on which all doing or creating depends?" In articulating the relation of being and nothingness, *Beiträge* approximates the *sive* postulated by Nishitani as characteristic of the field of *śūnyatā* (and surfacing in such expressions as "life-*sive*-death," "negation-*sive*-affirmation"). In Heidegger's sense, *sive* means neither a radical disjuncture nor a smooth blending but rather a chasm or discordant mutuality: "And finally, regarding the Yes and No— where do both originate together with their distinction and contrast? Differently phrased, who founded the difference between affirmation and negation, and the 'And' relating affirmation and negation?"[13]

In light of these and similar textual passages, Nishitani's critical objections can scarcely be sustained. Heidegger's thought, one may say, departs not only from scientific objectivism but also from existentialist nihilism (as defined in *Religion and Nothingness*) with its separation of subjectivity and nonbeing. More important, Nishitani's own presentation seems to depend strongly on something like Heidegger's notions of

---

[13] Heidegger, *Beiträge zur Philosophie (Vom Ereignis)*, ed. Friedrich-Wilhelm von Herrmann (*Gesamtausgabe*, Vol. 65; Frankfurt-Main: Klostermann, 1989), pp. 246–247, 266–267.

ontological difference and of the discordant juncture of being and noth-ingness. In the absence of these notions, I fear, Nishitani's portrayal of *śūnyatā* often appears strained or confusing and even perilously close to metaphysical bifurcations (of inside and outside, within and without). As previously indicated, genuine emptiness is said to be "united to and self-identical with being." At the same time, however, *śūnyatā* is also depicted as an "absolute transcendence of being" in that it "absolutely denies and distances itself from any standpoint shackled in any way whatsoever to being." In this sense, Nishitani asserts, emptiness can "well be described as 'outside' of and absolutely 'other' than the standpoint shackled to being—provided we avoid the misconception that emptiness is some 'thing' distinct from being and subsisting 'outside' of it." The complexity of these comments, or their status at the verge of traditional metaphysics, is compounded by these additional observations: "In spite of its transcen-dence of the standpoint shackled to being, or rather because of it, empti-ness can only appear as a self-identity with being, in a relationship of *sive* by which both being and emptiness are seen as copresent from the start and structurally inseparable from one another."[14] Attention to Hei-degger's writings, I believe, can rescue these statements from opacity or contradiction, thereby enhancing the persuasiveness of Nishitani's work—just as the latter can serve to elucidate Heidegger's exploration of being-*sive*-nothingness as an ontological happening (or *Ereignis*).

II

According to Nishitani, the field of *śūnyatā* is not only the abode of a selfhood stripped of subjectivity or egocentrism but also the place where things acquire their proper mode of being. Seen as genuine emptiness, he writes, *śūnyatā* is "the point at which each and every entity that is said to exist becomes manifest: namely, as what it is in itself, in the form of its true suchness." Here, things no longer are mere representations of thought; rather, they show themselves as what they are "on their home-ground" or, in Buddhist terms, in their "unattainable" mode of being. On the field of sense perception and consciousness, as indicated above, things are simply objective entities standing in opposition to a self-conscious ego. Differently phrased, objects are simply representations or

---

[14] Nishitani, *Religion and Nothingness*, p. 97.

something that has been represented as objective targets by and for consciousness.

Once this level is broken through or abandoned, making room for nihility to emerge, things lose their representational status and are swallowed up in the vortex of ecstatic subjectivity and self-grounding; while escaping the clutches of objectifying consciousness, they remain tied to the dilemmas of self-constitution. Only emptiness, or *śūnyatā*, grants to things full emancipation. In Nishitani's words:

> Prior to the appearance that things take on the field of consciousness, where they are objectivized as external realities, and prior to the more original appearance things assume on the field of nihility, where they are nullified, all things are on the field of emptiness in their truly elemental and original appearance. In emptiness things come to rest on their own home-ground.

Access to this ground is no longer provided through consciousness or representation but through a more elemental mode of shared habitation, one in which "hills, rivers, the earth, plants and trees, tiles and stones, all of these are the self's original part" (or part of selfhood). In contrast to rational cognition, this access might be called a "knowing of non-knowing."[15]

This mode of knowing has remained largely alien to Western thought. In traditional Western philosophy, things or beings in general have typically been conceptualized in terms of categories like "substance" or "subject" (*subjectum*). Although initially the underpinnings of the notion of substance remained unexplored, Nishitani observes, Kant's "Copernican revolution" showed clearly its dependence on consciousness and subjective representations. "The circumstances," he writes, "underlying the formation of the concept of substance cry out for the standpoint of a 'subject' resistant to all objective comprehension; no doubt Kant marks a milestone in the awareness of such a subject." Yet, resort to the subject, in turn, was fraught with a basic quandary; for, infected with the Cartesian doubt, the subject also comes to doubt itself and ultimately engulfs both subjectivity and the world in a comprehensive and relentless mode of doubting—which signals the way toward *śūnyatā*.

"Traditional ontology," we read, "was incapable of descending to the

---

[15] Ibid., pp. 106–110. The citation is from Musō Kokushi's *Muchū mondō* ("Questions and Answers in a Dream").

kind of field where questioner and questioned are both transformed into a single great question mark so that nothing is present save one great question"—the field which, in Buddhist terms, may be described as the "self-presentation of the Great Doubt." Questioning or doubting at this point is no longer equivalent to nihility or an existentialist nihilism, which merely negates the reality of things; rather, questioning and negation of this nihility allow things and beings properly to be: "If in nihility everything that exists reveals its original form as a question mark at one with the subject itself, then the standpoint of nihility itself needs in turn to be transcended." The field of emptiness now comes into view, a plane where things appear on their home-ground beyond the categories of substance and subject. But what is their mode of appearance?[16]

To elucidate this mode of appearance, Nishitani discusses the example of fire. From a traditional cognitive perspective, the issue turns on the substance, or "whatness," of fire, which is said to reside in its power and activity of combustion. Once the gaze is raised beyond particular instances to the essential substance of fire, we arrive at the "form" of fire in a Platonic sense: "Fire here displays itself, and displays itself to us; this is its *eidos*. Only on such an eidetic field can we distinguish fire from anything else and recognize its unique properties of combustion." Moving beyond the strictly Platonic conception, Aristotle correlated essential being or *eidos* with actual being and hence conceived the substance of something as consisting of both form and matter and their dynamic interrelation. In the case of fire, its ideal essence or potential for combustion becomes real and manifest through emergence of the potential in actual combustible matter (like firewood). Both Platonic essentialism and Aristotelian teleology, however, remained focused on the question of whatness, leaving the mode of being itself opaque; both perspectives attempted "to pursue the fact *that* something is (its actual being) through the medium of *what* it is (its essential being)."

Switching the focus radically, Nishitani invokes the ancient Eastern saying that "fire does not burn fire," a saying paralleled in phrases like "water does not wash water" and "the eye does not see the eye." As he points out, this saying does not refer to an objective substance or essential form but rather to the selfhood or suchness of fire on its own home-ground—that is, to "the self-identity of fire to fire itself." The fact that fire does not burn itself does not cancel its capacity to burn firewood;

---

[16] Nishitani, *Religion and Nothingness*, pp. 110–112.

thus, the suchness or selfhood of fire transcends the dualism of essence and actuality, form and matter: "That a fire has been kindled and is burning brightly means that the fire does not burn itself, that it insists on being itself and existing as what it is. In this fact of fire's not burning itself, therefore, the essential being and actual being of fire are one." Due to its simultaneous burning and not burning, the selfness of fire also transcends the bifurcation of action and passivity, doing and suffering: "As something that burns firewood, fire does not burn itself; as something that does not burn itself, it burns firewood." This burning while not burning might be called an "action of non-action."[17]

Once attention is focused on the self-being of fire (or of water or other things), selfness no longer denotes an objective substance or self-contained (ontic) nature. Just as knowing is pervaded by non-knowing and action by non-action, so selfness is dispersed in *śūnyatā*. If we suppose, Nishitani writes, that the essential "self-nature" of fire consists in its power and work of combustion, "then the selfness of fire resides at the point of its so-called *non*-self-nature." In contrast to the notion of substance that comprehends the selfness of fire in its "fire-nature" (and thus ontically), "the true selfness of fire is its non-fire-nature" and thus lies in "non-combustion."

According to Nishitani, combustion without the attendant quality of non-combustion is spurious and unintelligible, which is the chief defect marring empiricism and rationalism. From Nishitani's vantage, combustion "has its ground in non-combustion: because of non-combustion, combustion is combustion." The same might be said of water: its wetness or washing capacity derives from the fact that water does *not* wet or wash itself. Generally speaking, the selfhood or nature of things and human beings emerges not *intentione recta* as a positive substance but only from the vantage of a complete self-emptying or conversion: self-nature is such as it is "only as the self-nature of *non*-self-nature." Again, the accent on "non" should not be taken in the sense of negation or nihility. On the contrary, having passed through nihilation, things and existence in the field of *śūnyatā* reemerge in their pristine being and concrete reality, although subtly transformed. In Nishitani's words, "On the field of emptiness all things appear again as substances, each possessed of its own individual self-nature, though of course not in the same sense that each possessed on the field of reason" (or consciousness). On the

[17] Ibid., pp. 113–116.

plane of emptiness, "substantiality is an absolutely non-substantial substantiality."[18]

This nonsubstantial substantiality, or being, of things has long been the topic of Eastern, especially Japanese, poetry. The haiku poet Bashō pointed to the state of things on their home-ground when he wrote, "From the pine tree learn of the pine tree, and from the bamboo of the bamboo." As Nishitani comments, Bashō invites us here to "betake ourselves to the dimension where things become manifest in their suchness, to attune ourselves to the selfness of the pine tree and the selfness of the bamboo." He also suggests that "poetic truth and true poetry" seem to emerge most fully when things appear on the field of *śūnyatā*.

When standing or moving on its home-ground, a thing may be said to settle or gather itself together in its being; for this reason, the ancient term *samādhi* (settling, gathering, or concentrating) seems appropriate to designate this mode of selfness. In Nishitani's words, the term *samādhi* has traditionally been used to denote the attitude in which "a man gathers his own mind together and focuses it on a central point," leaving behind ordinary self-consciousness. Although the word first refers to a mental state, he observes, it may also apply to "the mode of being of a thing in itself [or in its selfness] when it has settled into its own position. In that sense, we might call such a mode of being 'samādhi-being.'" In settling into its selfness, a thing may also be said to move into its own center or midpoint, a point where it is no longer something else. Again invoking traditional terminology, the study speaks here of "the middle" of things, thereby indicating not a vague form of mediation but a center of gravity: "The center represents the point at which the being of things is constituted in unison with emptiness, the point at which things establish themselves, affirm themselves, and assume a 'position.' And there, settled in their position, things are in their *samādhi*-being."[19]

Settling into the center, however, is by no means the same as self-centeredness or egocentric isolation—mainly because selfness coincides with emptiness on the field of *śūnyatā*. Moreover, in settling and gathering itself, a thing does not exclude other things or beings that likewise gather themselves in *samādhi*-being—all of which happens on the plane of emptiness. As Nishitani observes, focusing on *śūnyatā* means "reverting to the point where things themselves are all gathered into one." Yet, oneness here should not be misconstrued in the sense of a simple unity or

---

[18] Ibid., pp. 117–118, 124–125.
[19] Ibid., pp. 128–131.

uniformity. In traditional Western philosophy, things or beings tend to be integrated or streamlined into a uniform metaphysical system, but one that shuns nothingness, or "the nihility opening up at its ground." In such a total system excluding nothingness, the study notes, "the idea that 'all beings are One' leads to the positing of a oneness seen as mere non-differentiation."

This kind of holism is rudely shattered by the rise of nihility. At this juncture, integral unity breaks down entirely, making room instead for multiplicity and differentiation, to such a degree that "all things appear isolated from one another by an abyss." Under the impulse of nihility, we read, all things "scatter apart from one another endlessly"; each being retreats into a self-enclosure or solitariness "absolutely shut up within itself." Negating and transcending this isolation in turn, śūnyatā opens up the possibility of renewed coexistence, but in a mode that recognizes and is predicated on radical multiplicity. In Nishitani's account, śūnyatā is a matrix in which the centers of all beings intersect, where each thing in fact is the center of all things or beings and where each accordingly holds all others in being, in place. What this means, he writes, is that "the center is everywhere"; each thing "in its own selfness shows the mode of being of the center of all things" and becomes in effect their "absolute center." In lieu of a unified system, we find here a dispersed centering, a centered dispersal; the phrase "All are One," he adds, can only mean "a gathering of things together, each of which is by itself the All, each of which is an absolute center." This dispersed oneness may also be termed "world," as the place where each thing by itself and all things jointly are gathered together.[20]

As center of the world, each thing gathers or assembles all things on its home-ground, allowing them to participate in its being and drawing on their continued support; in this sense, each thing is unique and sovereign in itself—but by no means in a mode of isolation. For, while assembling others on its home-ground, each thing also stands in a relation of servant or service to all other things, supporting them in turn as world centers. Borrowing from Christian theology, Nishitani calls this complex relationship "circuminsession" or "circuminsessional interpenetration." As he points out, the selfness or centered autonomy of each thing involves the "subordination *of* all other things" to its center; but given the centered autonomy of other things, subordination here also means service or "subordination *to* all other things" in the sense that each thing, in full

---

[20] Ibid., pp. 140, 143–147.

autonomy, allows all others to be what they are. This means, Nishitani comments, that "a system of circuminsession has to be seen here, according to which, on the field of *śūnyatā*, all things are in a process of becoming master and servant to one another."

Such reciprocity is possible only because of emptiness or self-emptying whereby "each thing is itself in not being itself, and is not itself in being itself." That a thing is not itself, Nishitani adds, implies that, although remaining itself or at its center, it is also in the home-ground of everything else; figuratively speaking, "its roots reach across into the ground of all other things and help to hold them up and keep them standing." At the same time, that a thing is itself involves that all other things, though still themselves, are "in the home-ground of that thing" and that, precisely when a thing is on its own home-ground, "everything else is there too" as the roots of every other being "spread across into its home-ground." This linkage of selfness or autonomy and openness to otherness or difference is at the heart of the standpoint of *śūnyatā*, a vantage from which the being of all things is disclosed as essentially circuminsessional. Circuminsession, moreover, is only dispersed centering, or gathering that does not yield uniformity. This gathering is evident in the pine tree and the bamboo invoked by Bashō, and in all other beings: "Even the very tiniest thing, to the extent that it 'is,' displays in its act of being the whole web of circuminsessional interpenetration that links all things together. In its being, we might say, the world 'worlds.' "[21]

Nishitani's account, as summarized here, is powerful and captivating as a restatement of the deepest intentions of Zen Buddhism; for Western readers, it also serves to shed new light on, or lend support to, many of Heidegger's later teachings. On the whole, those teachings have tended to be neglected or undervalued in contemporary Western philosophy; for many interpreters (even well-meaning ones), notions like the "fourfold," "nonobjective thinghood" and the "worlding of the world" have re-

---

[21] Ibid., pp. 147–150. As he adds a bit later: "Through this circuminsessional interpenetration, all things are gathered together, and as such render possible an order of being, a 'world,' and consequently enable the existence of things as well. . . . All things 'are' in the home-ground of any given thing and make it to 'be' what it is. With that thing as the absolute center, all things assemble at its home-ground. This assembly is the force that makes the thing in question be, the force of the thing's own ability to be. In that sense, we also said that when a thing *is*, the world *worlds*" (p. 159). In this context, see also Nishitani, "The I-Thou Relation in Zen Buddhism," in *The Buddha Eye*, ed. Franck, pp. 47–60.

mained whimsical speculations or else empty puns and wordplays. Even intimations of these notions in Heidegger's earlier writings, I believe, have not been taken seriously enough in contemporary philosophy, including social philosophy. Thus, in the case of *Being and Time*, little has been made of such conceptions as "emancipatory care" or a "letting be" based on mutual freedom—formulations which distantly foreshadow the later "fourfold" and carry a distinct affinity with Nishitani's idea of circuminsession.

The affinity is more fully evident in Heidegger's thought on thinghood, a topic that underwent continual reassessment in his writings. In his early work, things were treated predominantly as objects or utensils, that is, as beings "present-at-hand" or "present-to-hand"—which seemed to feature the role of *Dasein* unduly. This outlook was radically reformulated in his later work. For present purposes, I concentrate on Heidegger's postwar essay "The Thing" (*Das Ding*), which succinctly and lucidly delineates his thinking in this field.

According to Heidegger, things tend to be distant from our understanding irrespective of physical proximity. Western thought, he notes, has so far "paid as little heed to the thinghood of things as to proximity as nearness [*Nähe*]." In conformity with traditional metaphysics, things are primarily viewed as representational objects, that is, as targets presented to and represented in consciousness—a conception that still reverberated in *Being and Time*. Correcting the notion of beings-at-hand, the essay resolutely departs from the metaphysical tradition. "Neither does the thinghood of a thing," we read, "consist in its being a represented object nor can it at all be defined in terms of the objectivity [*Gegenständlichkeit*] of an object." Objectivity in the latter sense is the guidepost of modern science in its endeavor to gain an explanatory grasp of nature and the world. As Heidegger observes, however, science—notwithstanding its advances—cannot yield access to things in their thinghood, that is, outside the range of reification.

Despite its rigor and seemingly unlimited scope, things elude science's grasp, leaving as targets of scientific inquiry only "what *its* kind of representation has admitted beforehand as possible objects of research." In sidestepping the domain of thinghood, moreover, modern science actively conceals that domain from view by denying the reality of nonobjectified things and thus, in a way, nullifying their existence. In both its aims and effects, Heidegger states, scientific inquiry transforms thinghood into a "nonentity or nullity" by not granting to things their "yardstick of reality." To this extent, the destructive potential of the atom bomb is only the consistent result of the nihilating thrust implicit in modern science's approach to the world:

> Although compelling in its own sphere (that of objects), scientific reason had already annihilated things as things long before the atom bomb exploded. The latter's explosion was only the crudest of all crude confirmations of the long-since-accomplished nihilation of things: confirmation that the thing as thing remains null and void, that the thinghood of things remains concealed, forgotten.[22]

While distancing itself from objectification, Heidegger's essay also challenges the focus on production, that is, the reduction of things to fabricated utensils (or beings-to-hand). Deviating again from earlier categorial distinctions, Heidegger minimizes the difference between representation and fabrication at least in its relevance to the domain of thinghood. When we take a thing as a fabricated product, he writes, we still treat it as an object and thus objectify its mode of being. To be sure, the thing at this point is no longer viewed as a mere representational object; but in return it is now an object "which a process of production sets up before and over against us [*gegenüber und entgegen*]." In this manner, the objectness of the object, as something that stands over against a subject, is actually reinforced, thus completely obstructing access to thinghood.

Taking the example of a jug, the essay opposes fabrication to mode of being: "The jug is not a vessel because it was fabricated; rather, the jug had to be made because it is this kind of vessel." In much of traditional philosophy, fabrication is linked with a metaphysical essentialism or idealism, whereby the essence of an object serves as blueprint for its production. Attacking this tradition with the same example, Heidegger observes that the essence of an object (construed as *eidos* or idea) "characterizes the jug solely in the respect in which the vessel stands over against the maker as something to be made or produced." Yet, the mode of being or thinghood of the jug—"what the jug is as this jug-thing"—can never be learned, let alone properly thought, from the vantage of the *eidos*. "This is why Plato," he adds, "who construed the presence of present phenomena from the vantage of *eidos*, had no more understanding of the nature of thinghood than did Aristotle and all subsequent thinkers."

---

[22] Heidegger, "The Thing," in *Poetry, Language, Thought*, trans. Albert Hofstadter (New York: Harper & Row, 1971), pp. 166–167, 170 (in the above and subsequent citations I have slightly altered the translation for purposes of clarity).

Instead, leaving his imprint on a long line of philosophers, Plato experienced "everything present as an object of production," by treating the *eidos* as model of concrete phenomena. But, whether under the auspices of representation or fabrication, objectifying thought cannot clear a path to the thinghood of things.[23]

According to Heidegger, such a path is opened by focusing on a thing's mode of being—for instance, on the jug's mode of being a vessel. The mode of being a vessel, however, is constituted by the jug's ability to contain a content like water or wine. But wherein does the containing capacity reside? From the vantage of objectifying thought, this capacity resides in the solid structure of the jug, in its sides and its bottom—a conception Heidegger rejects as still alien to the jug's thinghood. When we fill the jug with water or wine, we read, we pour the liquid "between" the sides and "over" the bottom, that is, between and over structural features which, while impermeable, do not account for the jug's holding quality. Moving beyond objective structures, Heidegger leaps briskly from presence to absence—and thus basically into the field of *śūnyatā*.

What happens when we fill the jug, he writes, is that the pouring "flows into the empty jug." Thus, the emptiness of the jug is actually what does the holding: "The emptiness, this void or nothingness of the jug, is what the jug *is* [or its mode of being] as the holding vessel." Seen in this light, the fabrication of a thing is only ancillary or an accessory to its mode of being, which in a way shapes its own producer. Given that the jug's holding quality resides in its emptiness or void, "the potter who forms the sides and bottom on his wheel does not actually make the jug as vessel; he only shapes the clay." Still more strictly phrased, the potter shapes or assists in the emergence of emptiness; it is "for, in, and out of emptiness" that he molds the clay into the vessel form. In this manner, the process of fabrication is nearly reversed; for it is the jug's emptiness or void "that shapes or conditions every step in the process of making the vessel." The same consideration also jeopardizes objectness, or the status of representational objectivity: "The thinghood of the vessel does not lie at all in its material substance but in the emptiness that holds."[24]

As Heidegger elaborates, the holding quality of the vessel's emptiness can be seen as a gathering capacity, a capacity that operates on several levels or in different modalities. First of all, holding can mean accepting what is poured in as well as keeping the accepted liquid. In this sense,

[23] Ibid., pp. 167–169.
[24] Ibid., p. 169.

emptiness holds in a twofold manner—by taking and retaining. The unity or shared objective of the two modes resides in the outpouring of the liquid, an objective for which "the jug is fitted as a jug." In Heidegger's words, the twofold manner of holding "rests on the outpouring"; in the latter, the void's holding quality "achieves its authentic mode of being." In German, the outpouring of a liquid is *schenken*, which carries the double sense of pouring and giving (or donating). Accordingly, the nature of the holding emptiness can be said to be "gathered in the *schenken*" (in the sense of both pouring and giving); differently phrased, *schenken*—as constitutive feature of the jug's mode of being—"gathers in itself the twofold manner of holding, in the direction of the outpouring [of liquid]." Heidegger now continues his creative or suggestive use of the German language, in a manner resisting easy translation. As he notes, a gathering of mountains (*Berge*) in German is called *Gebirge*. In a similar fashion, the gathering of the twofold mode of holding into outpouring and of the entire process into *schenken* can be called a *Geschenk* (or poured gift). In this sense, the thinghood of the jug resides in the poured gift accomplished by the vessel.[25]

Gathering in Heidegger's sense, however, is not restricted to particular thinghood or the level of the jug's self-being. Beyond or rather by virtue of its unique self-being, the jug is able to gather on its ground all other modes of being, without assimilating them into its particularity. This aspect emerges once attention is shifted to the character of the poured gift and its potential beneficiaries. In terms of the essay, the poured gift may be water or wine, liquids that reflect the intimate collaboration of earth and sky. Water, Heidegger writes, may derive from a mountain spring. This spring, however, dwells in the rock, and in the rock "dwells the dark slumber of the earth which receives rain and dew from the sky." Thus, the water of the spring exhibits the intertwining of earth and sky. The same holds true in the case of wine, that gift of the vineyard in which "the earth's nourishment and the sky's sun are bequeathed to one another." Seen from this vantage, the thinghood of the jug—assembled in its poured gift (*Geschenk*)—allows earth and sky to dwell together.

The scope of gathering expands in light of the gift's beneficiaries. Water or wine is usually meant for human consumption, that is, as a drink for the benefit of mortal humans. On this level, the pouring of liquid "quenches their thirst, refreshes their leisure, and enlivens their

25 Ibid., pp. 171–172.

conviviality." On occasion, however, the outpoured gift may be specially consecrated in the context of a ritual sacrifice, as a libation destined for the immortal gods. In this instance, the pouring is a festive giving and the drink is elevated to the status of a consecrated feast. Thus, in the case of ordinary liquid, the jug's self-being assembles mortals on its ground, just as in the case of libation it attracts immortals into its abode. The full scope of the gathering is highlighted: "In the poured gift of the jug earth and sky, mortals and immortals dwell together *all at once*." The four, in fact, are intimately correlated: preceding all (ontic) entities, they are "enfolded into a single fourfold [*Geviert*]."[26]

Relying on this insight, Heidegger uses the remainder of the essay to further explore and clarify the character of the "fourfold" and its peculiar type of gathering. As he emphasizes, dwelling together here does not mean a merely external juxtaposition or purely static constellation. Rather, dwelling together is an ongoing happening (*Ereignis*), one that allows each of the four to be on their own while simultaneously linking them. Even thinghood itself is a happening, one that gathers (in conformity with the Old German term *thing*). Coining one of his better known (or notorious) phrases, Heidegger observes that "the thing things" (*das Ding dingt*), where "thinging" means gathering; the thing gathers by "allowing the fourfold to happen" but also by assembling the fourfold on the ground of every particular thing's self-being. As he adds, the four are neither identical nor strictly external to each other; instead, they are mutually implicated in each other, in a manner approximating Nishitani's circuminsession.

Pointing in the latter direction, Heidegger speaks of reciprocal mirroring: "Each of the four mirrors in its own way the being of the others; in doing so, each mirrors itself back into its own within the gathered fourfold"—without thereby retreating into a separate identity. Moreover, mirroring is not the copying of an external image or object; rather, clarifying, or "clearing," the status of each partner, mirroring "appropriates the mode of being of the four into their simple gathering" (where appropriation also denotes expropriation). According to the essay, the mirroring interplay of the fourfold—earth and sky, mortals and immortals—can be called "world." Just as in the case of thinghood, world has to be seen in a transitive sense as a happening. World, Heidegger writes, is or has its being in "worlding," a happening that cannot be derived from or explained by other factors or premises. The fourfold, he concludes,

[26] Ibid., pp. 172–173.

happens as or through the "worlding of the world"; in turn, this world-ing—manifesting the "mirror play" of the four—allows thinghood to emerge or to happen, that is, the "thinging of things."[27]

III

Let us return to Nishitani and Zen Buddhism. The affinities between Heidegger's essay and Nishitani's account of *samādhi*-being are evident; equally noticeable, however, are some divergences of accent and detail. As before, I first mention some ambiguities or points of unevenness which, in my view, weaken Nishitani's account. A major unevenness has to do with the relation between selfhood, more specifically human self-hood, and world—or between human existence and circuminsession (as the interplay of the fourfold). After elucidating the status of world and selfhood on the field of *śūnyatā*, Nishitani curiously proceeds to drive a wedge between these two aspects. "The self," he writes assertively, "has its home-ground at a point disengaged from the world and things and, at bottom, that is where it comes to rest. One might call this 'transcendence' in a sense similar to that found in contemporary existential philosophy."

Accentuating the division, Nishitani proceeds to separate selfhood not only from world and things but also from temporality. "The self," we read, "is, at every moment of time, ecstatically outside of time." To stand ecstatically outside time and outside the "cycle of birth and death" implies, in turn, the capacity of the self "to precede the world and things, to be their master. This, at bottom, is the sort of thing we 'are' in our home-ground, in our selfness." Occasionally, Nishitani's stress on ec-static separation acquires overtones of a Sartrean or Fichtean capacity of self-constitution. "This pure selfness," he states, "appears at the point that the self is an absolutely protensive position (in the sense that the being of the self is the self's positing of itself)"; being unable to rely on either world or time signifies the self's "absolute freedom." As it hap-pens, statements of this kind are counteracted quickly by reaffirmations of circuminsession and of the field of *śūnyatā* as the meeting ground of all

---

[27] Ibid., pp. 173–174, 179–180. As one should note, the emphasis on thinghood does not involve any kind of "reification" (a danger already obviated by the rejection of objectifica-tion). The essay is careful to stress the intimate connection or proximity (*Nähe*) of humans and things: "When and how do things emerge as things? They do not emerge *as a result* of human machinations; but neither do they appear *without* the vigilance of mortals. The first step toward such vigilance is the step back from merely representational or explanatory thinking toward an attentive or commemorative thinking [*andenkendes Denken*]" (p. 181).

beings—as expressed in Muso Kokushi's phrase, "Hills and rivers, the earth, plants and trees, tiles and stones, all of these are the self's own original part."[28]

Another point of divergence needs to be mentioned. In Heidegger's essay, thinghood and world denote a meeting place of earth and sky, mortals and immortals (or immortal gods). From a Zen Buddhist perspective, as elaborated by Nishitani, there does not seem to be room for immortal gods, and perhaps not even for humans seen as mortals; *śūnyatā* and the Great Doubt seem radically to obliterate these kinds of beings. But perhaps the distinction here is deceptive. As Nishitani repeatedly points out, nihilation on the field of *śūnyatā* does not create a vacuum but rather allows things and beings to emerge in their suchness or selfness. Thus, commenting on Kokushi's phrase (cited above), he writes: "Hills and rivers are here hills and rivers in *not* being hills and rivers, just as the self is the self in *not* being the self. And yet it is only here that hills and rivers are real hills and rivers in their suchness, only here that the self is the real self in its suchness." Although these comments seem to apply chiefly to hills and rivers and a general selfhood, there is no reason (in my view) why their scope cannot be expanded to include mortals and even immortals or divinities.

The latter point is admittedly contentious. What surfaces here behind subtle philosophical formulas is, among other things, the long-standing tension between Buddhism and Hinduism, mainly between the former's nontheism and the latter's polytheism or pantheism. Given the non-negative or non-nihilistic character of *śūnyatā*, the tension between gods (or God) and no gods seems to be not irremediable, in the sense that one conception permanently shades over into, or makes room for, the other. As Nishitani recognizes, this insight is not unfamiliar to Christian theology. Referring to Meister Eckhart's statement "I flee from God for the sake of God," he observes: "Fleeing God for God's sake seems to mean that the here-and-now *Dasein* of man can bear witness *essentially* to God only through man's truly finding himself in the nothingness of the godhead."[29]

The reconciliation of Buddhism and its parent Hinduism is, of course,

---

[28] Nishitani, *Religion and Nothingness*, pp. 152, 156, 159–160, 164. Nishitani, it is true, seeks to mollify the issue by correlating the self's status "outside of time" with its standing "bottomlessly within time" (p. 160), and also by reinterpreting circuminsession: "Even though we speak of hills and rivers as the self's original part, hills and rivers are here hills and rivers in *not* being hills and rivers, just as the self is the self in *not* being the self" (p. 166).

[29] Ibid., pp. 64, 166.

not the primary concern of these pages. The central motive animating the present chapter has been my hope of contributing to the dialogue between diverse cultural traditions, here the traditions of Western philosophy and of East Asian thought. Such a dialogue is possible only if traditions are willing to emerge from their historical isolation and to expose themselves to the agonies of questioning and renewed self-reflection. In the present instance, both protagonists of the imagined dialogue have made exemplary strides in the direction of an innovative rearticulation of time-honored premises and styles of argumentation. Reared in the tradition of Zen Buddhism, Nishitani has been a diligent student of the history of Western philosophy, from Plato to the present; exposure to this literature has prompted him to not merely imitate the Western idiom but to rethink and reformulate traditional Buddhist insights in the light of an expanded and more diversified cultural frame of reference. For his part, Heidegger engaged in a lifelong effort to reassess and "deconstruct" Western metaphysical assumptions, an effort that led him in some respects into the proximity of Eastern thought (a proximity far removed from a simple convergence). To be sure, the encounter sketched here is only one facet of a much larger cross-cultural involvement whose contours and tasks can only dimly be gauged. One of the genuinely lasting contributions of Heidegger's work is to have pointed the way toward such an engagement; it is for others to follow his lead. What lies in store for those pursuing this task is not only a better understanding of other cultures but the prospect of reinvigorated self-understanding (through otherness). The balance between self-understanding and understanding of others is the finely calibrated juncture (*Fuge*) of peace.

Index

Library of Congress Cataloging-in-Publication Data

Dallmayr, Fred R. (Fred Reinhard), 1928–
    The other Heidegger / Fred Dallmayr.
        p.   cm. — (Contestations)
    Includes bibliographical references and index.
    ISBN 0-8014-2909-9 (alk. paper)
    1. Heidegger, Martin, 1889–1976.   I. Title.   II. Series.
B3279.H49D26   1993
193—dc20   93-13757